1st Workshop on Computational Approaches to Code Switching 2014

Held at the Conference on Empirical Methods in Natural Language Processing (EMNLP 2014)

Doha, Qatar
25 October 2014

ISBN: 978-1-63439-481-9

Printed from e-media with permission by:

Curran Associates, Inc.
57 Morehouse Lane
Red Hook, NY 12571

Some format issues inherent in the e-media version may also appear in this print version.

Printed by Curran Associates, Inc. (2014)

Association for Computational Linguistics
209 N. Eighth Street
Stroudsburg, Pennsylvania 18360

Phone: 1-570-476-8006
Fax: 1-570-476-0860

acl@aclweb.org

Additional copies of this publication are available from:

Curran Associates, Inc.
57 Morehouse Lane
Red Hook, NY 12571 USA
Phone: 845-758-0400
Fax: 845-758-2634
Email: curran@proceedings.com
Web: www.proceedings.com

Introduction

Code-switching (CS) is the phenomenon by which multilingual speakers switch back and forth between their common languages in written or spoken communication. CS is pervasive in informal text communications such as news groups, tweets, blogs, and other social media of multilingual communities. Such genres are increasingly being studied as rich sources of social, commercial and political information. Apart from the informal genre challenge associated with such data within a single language processing scenario, the CS phenomenon adds another significant layer of complexity to the processing of the data. Efficiently and robustly processing CS data presents a new frontier for our NLP algorithms on all levels. The goal of this workshop is to bring together researchers interested in exploring these new frontiers, discussing state of the art research in CS, and identifying the next steps in this fascinating research area.

The workshop program includes exciting papers discussing new approaches for CS data and the development of linguistic resources needed to process and study CS. We received a total of 17 regular workshop submissions of which we accepted eight for publication (47% acceptance rate), five of them as workshop talks and three as posters. The accepted workshop submissions cover a wide variety of language combinations from languages such as English, Hindi, Bengali, Turkish, Dutch, German, Italian, Romansh, Mandarin, Dialectical Arabic and Modern Standard Arabic. Although most papers focus on some kind of social media data, there is also work on more formal genres, such as that from the Canadian Hansard.

Another component of the workshop is the First Shared Task on Language Identification of CS Data. The shared task focused on social media and included four language pairs: Mandarin-English, Modern Standard Arabic-Dialectal Arabic, Nepali-English, and Spanish-English. We received a total of 42 system runs from seven different teams. Each team submitted a shared task paper describing their system. All shared task systems will be presented during the workshop poster session and a subset of them will also present a talk.

We would like to thank all authors who submitted their contributions to this workshop and all shared task participants for taking on the challenge of language identification in code switched data. We also thank the program committee members for their help in providing meaningful reviews. Lastly, we thank the EMNLP 2014 organizers for the opportunity to put together this workshop.

See you all in Qatar, see ypu al in Qatar at EMNLP 2014!
Workshop co-chairs,

Mona Diab
Julia Hirschberg
Pascale Fung
Thamar Solorio

Workshop Co-Chairs:

Mona Diab, George Washington University
Julia Hirschberg, Columbia University
Pascale Fung, Hong Kong University of Science and Technology
Thamar Solorio, University of Houston

Program Committee:

Steven Abney, University of Michigan
Laura Alonso i Alemany, Universidad Nacional de Córdoba
Elabbas Benmamoun, University of Illinois at Urbana-Champaign
Steven Bethard, University of Alabama at Birmingham
Rakesh Bhatt, University of Illinois at Urbana-Champaign
Agnes Bolonyia, NC State University
Barbara Bullock, University of Texas at Austin
Amitava Das, University of North Texas
Suzanne Dikker, New York University
Björn Gambäck, Norwegian Universities of Science and Technology
Nizar Habash, Columbia University
Aravind Joshi, University of Pennsylvania
Ben King, University of Michigan
Constantine Lignos, University of Pennsylvania
Yang Liu, University of Texas at Dallas
Suraj Maharjan, University of Alabama at Birmingham
Mitchell P. Marcus, University of Pennsylvania
Cecilia Montes-Alcala, Georgia Institute of Technology
Raymond Mooney, University of Texas at Austin
Borja Navarro Colorado, Universidad de Alicante
Owen Rambow, Columbia University
Yves Scherrer, Université de Genève
Chilin Shih, University of Illinois at Urbana-Champaign
Jacqueline Toribio, University of Texas at Austin
Rabih Zbib, BBN Technologies

Table of Contents

Workshop Program

Saturday, October 25, 2014

Session 1: Workshop talks

09:00–09:10 *Welcome Remarks*
The organizers

09:10–09:30 *Foreign Words and the Automatic Processing of Arabic Social Media Text Written in Roman Script*
Ramy Eskander, Mohamed Al-Badrashiny, Nizar Habash and Owen Rambow

09:30–09:50 *Code Mixing: A Challenge for Language Identification in the Language of Social Media*
Utsab Barman, Amitava Das, Joachim Wagner and Jennifer Foster

09:50–10:10 *Detecting Code-Switching in a Multilingual Alpine Heritage Corpus*
Martin Volk and Simon Clematide

10:10–10:30 *Exploration of the Impact of Maximum Entropy in Recurrent Neural Network Language Models for Code-Switching Speech*
Ngoc Thang Vu and Tanja Schultz

10:30–11:00 ***Coffee Break***

Session 2: Workshop Talks and Shared Task Systems

11:00–11:20 *Predicting Code-switching in Multilingual Communication for Immigrant Communities*
Evangelos Papalexakis, Dong Nguyen and A. Seza Doğruöz

11:20–11:40 *Twitter Users #CodeSwitch Hashtags! #MoltoImportante #wow*
David Jurgens, Stefan Dimitrov and Derek Ruths

11:40–11:50 *Overview for the First Shared Task on Language Identification in Code-Switched Data*
Thamar Solorio, Elizabeth Blair, Suraj Maharjan, Steven Bethard, Mona Diab, Mahmoud Ghoneim, Abdelati Hawwari, Fahad AlGhamdi, Julia Hirschberg, Alison Chang and Pascale Fung

11:50–12:10 *Word-level Language Identification using CRF: Code-switching Shared Task Report of MSR India System*
Gokul Chittaranjan, Yogarshi Vyas, Kalika Bali and Monojit Choudhury

Saturday, October 25, 2014 (continued)

12:10–12:30 *The CMU Submission for the Shared Task on Language Identification in Code-Switched Data*
Chu-Cheng Lin, Waleed Ammar, Lori Levin and Chris Dyer

12:30–14:00 ***Lunch break***

Session 3: Shared Task and Next Steps

14:00–14:20 *Language Identification in Code-Switching Scenario*
Naman Jain and Riyaz Ahmad Bhat

14:20–14:40 *AIDA: Identifying Code Switching in Informal Arabic Text*
Heba Elfardy, Mohamed Al-Badrashiny and Mona Diab

14:40–15:00 *The IUCL+ System: Word-Level Language Identification via Extended Markov Models*
Levi King, Eric Baucom, Timur Gilmanov, Sandra Kübler, Dan Whyatt, Wolfgang Maier and Paul Rodrigues

15:00–15:30 *Panel Discussion: Next Steps in CS Research*
Group Discussion

15:30–16:00 ***Coffee Break (Posters set up time)***

Session 4: Poster Session

16:00–17:30 *Workshop and Shared Task Posters*
Multiple presenters

Mixed Language and Code-Switching in the Canadian Hansard
Marine Carpuat

"I am borrowing ya mixing ?" An Analysis of English-Hindi Code Mixing in Facebook
Kalika Bali, Jatin Sharma, Monojit Choudhury and Yogarshi Vyas

DCU-UVT: Word-Level Language Classification with Code-Mixed Data
Utsab Barman, Joachim Wagner, Grzegorz Chrupała and Jennifer Foster

Foreign Words and the Automatic Processing of Arabic Social Media Text Written in Roman Script

Ramy Eskander, Mohamed Al-Badrashiny[†], Nizar Habash[‡] and Owen Rambow
Center for Computational Learning Systems, Columbia University
{reskander,rambow}@ccls.columbia.edu
[†]Department of Computer Science, The George Washington University
[†]badrashiny@gwu.edu
[‡]Computer Science Department, New York University Abu Dhabi
[‡]nizar.habash@nyu.edu

Abstract

Arabic on social media has all the properties of any language on social media that make it tough for natural language processing, plus some specific problems. These include diglossia, the use of an alternative alphabet (Roman), and code switching with foreign languages. In this paper, we present a system which can process Arabic written in Roman alphabet ("Arabizi"). It identifies whether each word is a foreign word or one of another four categories (Arabic, name, punctuation, sound), and transliterates Arabic words and names into the Arabic alphabet. We obtain an overall system performance of 83.8% on an unseen test set.

1 Introduction

Written language used in social media shows differences from that in other written genres: the vocabulary is informal (and sometimes the syntax is as well); there are intentional deviations from standard orthography (such as repeated letters for emphasis); there are typos; writers use non-standard abbreviations; non-linguistic sounds are written (*haha*); punctuation is used creatively; non-linguistic signs such as emoticons often compensate for the absence of a broader communication channel in written communication (which excludes, for example, prosody or visual feedback); and, most importantly for this paper, there frequently is code switching. These facts pose a well-known problem for natural language processing of social media texts, which has become an area of interest as applications such as sentiment analysis, information extraction, and machine translation turn to this genre.

This situation is exacerbated in the case of Arabic social media. There are three principal reasons. First, the Arabic language is a collection of varieties: Modern Standard Arabic (MSA), which is used in formal settings, and different forms of Dialectal Arabic (DA), which are commonly used informally. This situation is referred to as "diglossia". MSA has a standard orthography, while the dialects do not. What is used in Arabic social media is typically DA. This means that there is no standard orthography to begin with, resulting in an even broader variation in orthographic forms found. Diglossia is seen in other linguistic communities as well, including German-speaking Switzerland, in the Czech Republic, or to a somewhat lesser extent among French speakers. Second, while both MSA and DA are commonly written in the Arabic script, DA is sometimes written in the Roman script. Arabic written in Roman is often called "Arabizi". It is common in other linguistic communities as well to write informal communication in the Roman alphabet rather than in the native writing system, for example, among South Asians. And third, educated speakers of Arabic are often bilingual or near-bilingual speakers of another language as well (such as English or French), and will code switch between DA and the foreign language in the same utterance (and sometimes MSA as well). As is well known, code switching is common in many linguistic communities, for example among South Asians.

In this paper, we investigate the issue of processing Arabizi input with code switching. There are two tasks: identification of tokens that are not DA or MSA (and should not be transliterated into Arabic script for downstream processing), and then the transliteration into Arabic script of the parts identified as DA or MSA. In this paper, we

Proceedings of The First Workshop on Computational Approaches to Code Switching, pages 1–12,
October 25, 2014, Doha, Qatar.

use as a black box an existing component that we developed to transliterate from Arabizi to Arabic script (Al-Badrashiny et al., 2014). This paper concentrates on the task of identifying which tokens should be transliterated. A recent release of annotated data by the Linguistic Data Consortium (LDC, 2014c; Bies et al., 2014) has enabled novel research on this topic. The corpus provides each token with a tag, as well as a transliteration if appropriate. The tags identify foreign words, as well as Arabic words, names, punctuation, and sounds. Only Arabic words and names are transliterated. (Note that code switching is not distinguished from borrowing.) Emoticons, which may be isolated or part of an input token, are also identified, and converted into a conventional symbol (#). This paper presents taggers for the tags, and an end-to-end system which takes Arabizi input and produces a complex output which consists of a tag for each input token and a transliteration of Arabic words and names into the Arabic script. To our knowledge, this is the first system that handles the complete task as defined by the LDC data. This paper focuses on the task of identifying foreign words (as well as the other tags), on creating a single system, and on evaluating the system as a whole.

This paper makes three main contributions. First, we clearly define the computational problem of dealing with social media Arabizi, and propose a new formulation of the evaluation metric for the LDC corpus. Second, we present novel modules for the detection of foreign words as well as of emoticons, sounds, punctuation marks, and names in Arabizi. Third, we compose a single system from the various components, and evaluate the complete system.

This paper is structured as follows. We start by presenting related work (Section 2), and then we present relevant linguistic facts and explain how the data is annotated (Section 3). After summarizing our system architecture (Section 4) and experimental setup (Section 5), we present our systems for tagging in Sections 6, 7 and 8. The evaluation results are presented in Section 9.

2 Related Work

While natural language processing for English in social media has attracted considerable attention recently (Clark and Araki, 2011; Gimpel et al., 2011; Gouws et al., 2011; Ritter et al., 2011; Derczynski et al., 2013), there has not been much work on Arabic yet. We give a brief summary of relevant work on Arabic.

Darwish et al. (2012) discuss NLP problems in retrieving Arabic microblogs (tweets). They discuss many of the same issues we do, notably the problems arising from the use of DA such as the lack of a standard orthography. However, they do not deal with DA written in the Roman alphabet (though they do discuss non-Arabic characters).

There is some work on code switching between Modern Standard Arabic (MSA) and dialectal Arabic (DA). Zaidan and Callison-Burch (2011) are interested in this problem at the inter-sentence level. They crawl a large dataset of MSA-DA news commentaries. They use Amazon Mechanical Turk to annotate the dataset at the sentence level. Then they use a language modeling approach to predict the class (MSA or DA) for an unseen sentence. There is other work on dialect identification, such as AIDA (Elfardy et al., 2013; Elfardy et al., 2014). In AIDA, some statistical and morphological analyses are applied to capture code switching between MSA and DA within the same sentence. Each word in the sentence is tagged to be either DA or MSA based on the context. The tagging process mainly depends on the language modeling (LM) approach, but if a word is unknown in the LM, then its tag is assigned through MADAMIRA, a morphological disambiguator Pasha et al. (2014).

Lui et al. (2014) proposed a system that does language identification in multilingual documents, using a generative mixture model that is based on supervised topic modeling algorithms. This is similar to our work in terms of identifying code switching. However, our system deals with Arabizi, a non-standard orthography with high variability, making the identification task much harder.

Concerning specifically NLP for Arabizi, Darwish (2013) (published in an updated version as (Darwish, 2014)) is similar to our work in that he identifies English in Arabizi text and he also transliterates Arabic text from Arabizi to Arabic script. We compare our transliteration method to his in Al-Badrashiny et al. (2014). For identification of non-Arabic words in Arabizi, Darwish (2013) uses word and sequence-level features with CRF modeling; while we use SVMs and decision trees. Darwish (2013) identifies three tags: Arabic, foreign and others (such as email addresses and URLs). In contrast, we identify a bigger set: Arabic, foreign, names, sounds, punctuation and emoticons. Furthermore, Darwish (2013) uses around 5K words for training his taggers and 3.5K words for testing; this is considerably smaller than our training and test sets of 113K and 32K words, respectively.

Chalabi and Gerges (2012) presented a hybrid approach for Arabizi transliteration. Their work does not address the detection of English words, punctuation, emoticons, and so on. They also do not handle English when mixed with Arabizi.

Voss et al. (2014) deal with exactly the problem of classifying tokens in Arabizi as Arabic or not. More specifically, they deal with Moroccan Arabic, and with both French and English, meaning they do a three-way classification. There are many differences between our work and theirs: they have noisy training data, and they have a much more balanced test set. They also only deal with foreignness, and do not address the other tags we deal with, nor do they actually discuss transliteration itself.

3 Linguistic Facts and Data Annotation

3.1 Arabizi

Arabizi refers to Arabic written using the Roman script (Darwish, 2013; Voss et al., 2014). Arabizi orthography is spontaneous and has no standard references, although there are numerous commonly used conventions making specific usage of the so-called Arabic numerals and punctuation in addition to Roman script letters. Arabizi is commonly used by Arabic speakers to write mostly in dialectal Arabic in social media, SMS and chat applications.

Arabizi orthography decisions mainly depend on a phoneme-to-grapheme mapping between the Arabic pronunciation and the Roman script. This is largely based on the phoneme-to-grapheme mapping used in English (in Middle Eastern Arab countries) or French (in Western North African Arab countries). Since there is no standard orthography for Arabizi, it is *not* a simple transliteration of Arabic. For example, in Arabizi, words omit vowels far less frequently than is done when writers follow standard Arabic orthography. Furthermore, there are several cases of many-to-many mappings between Arabic phonemes and Roman script letters: for example, the letter "t" is used to represent the sound of the Arabic letters ت *t*[1] and ط *T* (which itself can be also be represented using the digit "6").

Text written in Arabizi also tends to have a large number of foreign words, that are either borrowings such as *telephone*, or code switching, such as *love you!*. Note that Arabizi often uses the source language orthography for borrowings (especially recent borrowings), even if the Arabic pronunciation is somewhat modified. As a result, distinguishing borrowings from code switching is, as is usually the case, hard. And, as in any language used in social media and chat, Arabizi may also include abbreviations, such as *isa* which means إن شاء الله *Ăn šA' Allh* 'God willing' and *lol* 'laugh out loud'.

The rows marked with **Arabizi** in Figure 1 demonstrate some of the salient features of Arabizi. The constructed example in the figure is of an SMS conversation in Egyptian Arabic.

3.2 Data Annotation

The data set we use in this paper was created by the Linguistic Data Consortium (Bies et al., 2014; LDC, 2014a; LDC, 2014b; LDC, 2014c). We summarize below the annotation decisions. The system we present in this paper aims at predicting exactly this annotation automatically. The input text is initially segregated into Arabic script and Arabizi. Arabic script text is not modified in any way. Arabizi text undergoes two sets of annotation decisions: Arabizi word tagging and Arabizi-to-Arabic transliteration. All of the Arabizi annotations are initially done using an automatic process (Al-Badrashiny et al., 2014) and then followed by manual correction and validation.

Arabizi Word Tagging Each Arabizi word receives one of the following five tags:

- *Foreign* All words from languages other than Arabic are tagged as *Foreign* if they would be kept in the same orthographic form when translated into their source language (which in our corpus is almost always English). Thus, non-Arabic words that include Arabic affixes are not tagged as *Foreign*. The definition of "foreign" thus means that uninflected borrowings spelled as in the source language orthography are tagged as "foreign", while borrowings that are spelled differently, as well as borrowing that have been inflected

[1] Arabic transliteration is presented in the Habash-Soudi-Buckwalter scheme (Habash et al., 2007): (in alphabetical order) *AbtθjHxdðrzsšSDTĎςγfqklmnhwy* and the additional symbols: ' ء, Â أ, Ă إ, Ā آ, ŵ ؤ, ŷ ئ, ħ ة, ý ى.

(1)

Arabizi	Youmna	i	need	to	know	anti	gaya	wala	la2	?
Tag	*Name*	*Foreign*	*Foreign*	*Foreign*	*Foreign*	*Arabic*	*Arabic*	*Arabic*	*Arabic*	*Punct*
Arabic	يمنى	اي	نيد	تو	نو	انتي	جاية	ولا	لأ	؟
	ymný	*Ay*	*nyd*	*tw*	*nw*	*Anty*	*jAy¯h*	*wlA*	*lÂ*	*?*
English	Youmna	I	need	to	know	you	coming	or	not	?

(2)

Arabizi	Mmmm	ok	ana	7aseb	el	sho3'l	now	w	ageelk	isa	:-)
Tag	*Sound*	*Foreign*	*Arabic*	*Arabic*	*Arabic*	*Arabic*	*Foreign*	*Arabic*	*Arabic*	*Arabic*	*Arabic*
Arabic	ممم	اوكيه	انا	حاسيب	ال[+]	شغل	ناو	و[+]	اجي[-]لك	ان[-]شاء[-]الله	#
	mmm	*Awkyh*	*AnA*	*HAsyb*	*Al[+]*	*šgl*	*nAw*	*w[+]*	*Ajy[-]lk*	*An[-]šA'[-]Allh*	*#*
English	mmm	OK	I	will-leave	the	work	now	and	I-come-to-you	God-willing	:-)

(3)

Arabizi	qishta!:D
Tag	*Arabic*
Arabic	قشطة![-]#
	qšT¯h![-]#
English	cream!:D (slang for *cool!*)

Figure 1: A short constructed SMS conversation written in Arabizi together with annotation of word tags and transliteration into Arabic script. A Romanized transliteration of the Arabic script and English glosses are provided for clarity. The cells with gray background are the parts of the output that we evaluate.

following Arabic morphology, are not tagged as "foreign" (even if the stem is spelled as in the source language, such as *Almobile*). The Arabic transliterations of these words are not manually corrected.

- *Punct* Punctuation marks are a set of conventional signs that are used to aid interpretation by indicating division of text into sentences and clauses, etc. Examples of punctuation marks are the semicolon **;**, the exclamation mark **!** and the right brace }. Emoticons are not considered punctuation and are handled as part of the transliteration task discussed below.
- *Sound* Sounds are a list of interjections that have no grammatical meaning, but mimic non-linguistic sounds that humans make, and that often signify emotions. Examples of sounds are *hahaha* (laughing), *hmm* (wondering) and *eww* (being disgusted). It is common to stretch sounds out to make them stronger, i.e., to express more intense emotions. For example, *hmm* could be stretched out into *hmmmmm* to express a stronger feeling of wondering. The Arabic transliterations of these words are not manually corrected.
- *Name* Proper names are tagged as such and later manually corrected.
- *Arabic* All other words are tagged as *Arabic* and are later manually corrected.

See the rows marked with **Tag** in Figure 1 for examples of these different tags. It is important to point out that the annotation of this data was intended to serve a project focusing on machine translation from dialectal Arabic into English. This goal influenced some of the annotation decisions and was part of the reason for this selection of word tags.

Arabizi-to-Arabic Transliteration The second annotation task is about converting Arabizi to an Arabic-script-based orthography. Since, dialectal Arabic including Egyptian Arabic has no standard orthography in Arabic script, the annotation uses a conventionalized orthography for Dialectal Arabic called CODA (Habash et al., 2012a; Eskander et al., 2013; Zribi et al., 2014). Every word has a single orthographic representation in CODA.

In the corpus we use, only words tagged as *Arabic* or *Name* are manually checked and corrected. The transliteration respects the white-space boundaries of the original Arabizi words. In cases where an Arabizi word represents a prefix or suffix that should be joined in CODA to the next or previous word, a [+] symbol is added to mark this decision. Similarly, for Arabizi words that should be split into multiple CODA words, the CODA words are written with added [-] symbol delimiting the word boundaries.

The Arabic transliteration task also includes handling emoticons. Emoticons are digital icons or sequences of keyboard symbols serving to represent facial expressions or to convey the writer's emotions. Examples of emoticons are :d, :-(, O.O and ♡ used to represent laughing, sadness, being surprised and positive emotion, respectively. All emoticons, whether free-standing or attached to a word, are replaced by a single hash symbol (#). Free-standing emoticons are tagged as *Arabic*. Attached emoticons are not tagged separately; the word they are attached to is tagged according to the usual rules. See Figure 1 for examples of these different decisions.

Since words tagged as *Foreign*, *Punct*, or *Sound* are not manually transliterated in the corpus, in our performance evaluation we combine the decisions of tags and transliteration. For foreign words, punctuation and sounds, we only consider the tags for accuracy computations; in contrast, for names and Arabic words, we consider both the tag and transliteration.

4 System Architecture

Figure 2 represent the overall architecture of our system. We distinguish below between existing components that we use and novel extensions that we contribute in this paper.

4.1 Existing Arabization System

For the core component of Arabizi-to-Arabic transliteration, we use a previously published system (Al-Badrashiny et al., 2014), which converts Arabizi into Arabic text following CODA conventions (see Section 3). The existing system uses a finite state transducer trained on 8,500 Arabizi-to-Arabic transliteration pairs at the character level to obtain a large number of possible transliterations for the input Arabizi words. The generated list is then filtered using a dialectal Arabic morphological analyzer. Finally, the best choice for each input word is selected using a language model. We use this component as a black box except that we retrain it using additional training data. In Figure 2, this component is represented using a central black box.

4.2 Novel Extension

In this paper, we add **Word Type Tagging** as a new set of modules. We tag the Arabizi words into five categories as discussed above: Arabic, Foreign, Names, Sounds, and Punctuation. Figure 2 illustrates the full proposed system. First, we process the Arabizi input to do punctuation and sound tagging, along with emoticon detection. Then we run the transliteration system to produce the corresponding Arabic transliteration. The Arabizi input and Arabic output are then used together to do name tagging and foreign word tagging. The *Arabic* tag is assigned to all untagged words, i.e., words not tagged as Foreign, Names, Sounds, or Punctuation. The outputs from all steps are then combined to produce the final Arabic transliteration along with the tag.

5 Experimental Setup

5.1 Data Sets

We define the following sets of data:

- *Train-S*: A small size dataset that is used to train all taggers in all experiments to determine the best performing setup (feature engineering).
- *Train-L*: A larger size dataset that is used to train the best performing setup.
- *Dev*: The development set that is used to measure the system performance in all experiments
- *Test*: A blind set that is used to test the best system (LDC, 2014a).

The training and development sets are extracted from (LDC, 2014b). Table 1 represents the tags distribution in each dataset. Almost one of every five words is not Arabic text and around one of every 10 words is foreign.

5.2 Arabizi-to-Arabic Transliteration Accuracy

For the Arabizi-to-Arabic transliteration system, we report on using the two training data sets with two modifications. First, we include the 8,500 word pairs from Al-Badrashiny et al. (2014), namely 2,200 Arabizi-to-Arabic script pairs from the training data used by Darwish (2013) (manually revised to be CODA-compliant) and about 6,300 pairs of proper names in Arabic and English from the Buckwalter Arabic Morphological Analyzer (Buckwalter, 2004). (Since these pairs are not tagged, we do not use them to train the taggers.) Second, we exclude all the foreign tagged words from training the transliteration system since they were not manually corrected.

Table 2 shows the overall transliteration accuracy of Arabic words and names only, using different training data sets and evaluating on *Dev* (as determined by the gold standard). The accuracy when using the original Arabizi-to-Arabic transliteration system from Al-Badrashiny et al. (2014) gives an accuracy of 68.6%. Retraining it on *Train-S* improves the accuracy to 76.9%. The accuracy goes up further to 79.5% when using the

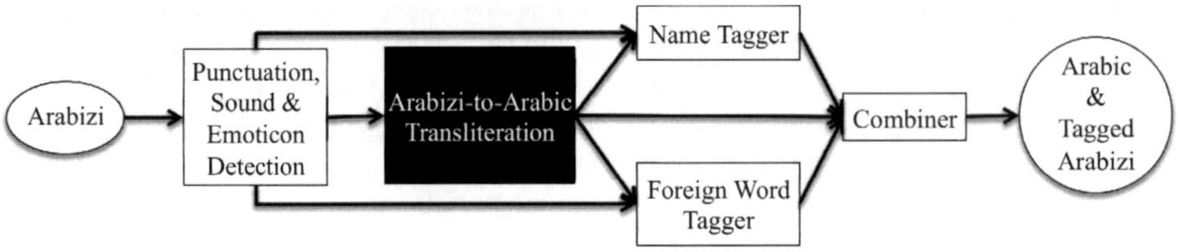

Figure 2: The architecture of our complete Arabizi processing system. The "Punctuation, Sound and Emoticon Detection" component does labeling that is read by the "Name" and "Foreign Word" taggers, While the actual Aribizi-to-Arabic transliteration system is used as a black box.

Data	# Words	Arabic	Foreign	Name	Sound	Punct	Emoticon
Train-S	21,950	80.5%	12.1%	2.8%	1.7%	1.3%	1.6%
Train-L	113,490	82.3%	9.8%	2.4%	1.8%	1.1%	2.6%
Dev	5,061	76.3%	16.2%	2.9%	1.8%	1.2%	1.5%
Test	31,717	86.1%	6.0%	2.7%	1.6%	0.9%	2.8%

Table 1: Dataset Statistics

Data	Translit. Acc.
Al-Badrashiny et al. (2014)	68.6%
Train-S	76.9%
Train-L	79.5%

Table 2: Transliteration accuracy of Arabic words and names when using different training sets and evaluating on *Dev*

bigger training set *Train-L*. The overall transliteration accuracy of Arabic words and names on *Test* using the bigger training set *Train-L* is 83.6%.

6 Tagging Punctuation, Emoticons and Sounds

6.1 Approach

We start the tagging process by detecting three types of closed classes: punctuation, sounds and emoticons. Simple regular expressions perform very well at detecting their occurrence in text. The regular expressions are applied to the Arabizi input, word by word, after lower-casing, since both emoticons and sounds could contain either small or capital letters.

Since emoticons can be composed of just concatenated punctuation marks, their detection is required before punctuation is tagged. Once detected, emoticons are replaced by #. Then punctuation marks are detected. If a *non-emoticon* word is only composed of punctuation marks, then it gets tagged as *Punct*. Sounds are targeted next. A word gets tagged as *Sound* if it matches the sound detection expression, after stripping out any attached punctuation marks and/or emoticons.

6.2 Results

Table 6 in Section 9 shows the accuracy, recall, precision and F-score for the classification of the *Punct* and *Sound* tags and detection of emoticons. Since emoticons can be part of another word, and in that case do not receive a specific tag (as specified in the annotation guidelines by the LDC), emoticon evaluation is concerned with the number of detected emoticons within an Arabizi word, as opposed to a binary tagging decision. In other words, emoticon identification is counted as correct ("positive") if the number of detected emoticons in a word is correct in the test token. The *Punct* and *Sound* tags represent standard binary classification tasks and are evaluated in the usual way.

7 Tagging Names

7.1 Approach

We consider the following set of binary features for learning a model of name tagging. The features are used either separately or combined using a modeling classifier implemented with decision trees.

- **Capitalization** A word is considered a name if the first letter in Arabizi is capitalized.

- **MADAMIRA** MADAMIRA is a system for morphological analysis and disambiguation of Arabic (Pasha et al., 2014). We run MADAMIRA on the Arabic output after running the Arabizi-to-Arabic transliteration. If the selected part-of-speech (POS) of a word is proper noun *(NOUN_PROP)*, then the word is tagged as *Name*.
- **CALIMA** CALIMA is a morphological analyzer for Egyptian Arabic (Habash et al., 2012b). If the Arabic transliteration of a given Arabizi word has a possible proper noun analysis in CALIMA, then the word is tagged as *Name*.
- **Maximum Likelihood Estimate (MLE)** An Arabizi word gets assigned the *Name* tag if *Name* is the most associated tag for that word in the training set.
- **Tharwa** Tharwa is a large scale Egyptian Arabic-MSA-English lexicon that includes POS tag information (Diab et al., 2014). If an Arabizi word appears in Tharwa as an English gloss with a proper noun POS, then it is tagged as *Name*.
- **Name Language Model** We use a list of 280K unique lower-cased English words associated with their probability of appearing capitalized (Habash, 2009). When using this feature, any probability that is not equal to one is rounded to zero.

All the features above are modeled after case-lowering the Arabizi input, and removing speech effects. Any attached punctuation marks and/or emoticons are stripped out. One exception is the capitalization feature, where the case of the first letter of the Arabizi word is preserved. The techniques above are then combined together using decision trees. In this approach, the words tagged as *Name* are given a weight that balances their infrequent occurrence in the data.

7.2 Results

Table 3 shows the performance of the *Name* tagging on *Dev* using *Train-S*. The best results are obtained when looking up the MLE value in the training data, with an accuracy and F-score of 97.8% and 56.0%, respectively. When using *Train-L*, the accuracy and F-score given by MLE go up to 98.1% and 63.9%, respectively. See Table 6. The performance of the combined approach

Feature	Accuracy	Recall	Precision	F-Score
Capitalization	85.6	28.3	6.4	10.4
MADAMIRA	95.9	24.8	28.3	26.5
CALIMA	86.3	50.3	10.9	17.9
MLE	**97.8**	46.9	69.4	**56.0**
THARWA	96.3	22.8	33.0	26.9
NAME-LM	84.5	30.3	6.3	10.4
All Combined (Decision Trees)	97.7	49.7	63.2	55.6

Table 3: *Name* tagging results on *Dev* with *Train-S*

does not outperform the most effective single classifier, MLE. This is because adding other features decreases the precision by an amount that exceeds the increase in the recall.

8 Tagging Foreign Words

As shown earlier, around 10% of all words in Arabizi text are foreign, mostly English in our data set. Tagging foreign words is challenging since there are many words that can be either Arabic (in Arabizi) or a word in a foreign languages. For example the Arabizi word *mesh* can refer to the English reading or the Arabic word مش *mš* 'not'. Therefore, simple dictionary lookup is not sufficient to determine whether a word is Arabic or Foreign. Our target in this section is to identify the foreign words in the input Arabizi text .

8.1 Baseline Experiments

We define a foreignness index formula that gives each word a score given its unigram probabilities against Arabic and English language models (LMs).

$$\varepsilon(w) = \alpha P_E(w) + (1-\alpha)(1 - P_A(w_t)) \quad (1)$$

$\varepsilon(w)$ is the foreignness *score* of the Arabizi word w. $P_E(w)$ is the unigram probability of w in the English LM, and $P_A(w_t)$ is the unigram probability in the Arabic LM of the transliteration into Arabic (w_t) proposed by our system for the Arabizi word w. α is a tuning parameter varying from zero to one. From equation 1 we define the minimum and maximum ε values as follows:

$$\begin{array}{l} \varepsilon_{min} = \alpha P_{E_{min}} + (1-\alpha)(1 - P_{A_{max}}) \\ \varepsilon_{max} - \alpha P_{E_{max}} + (1-\alpha)(1 - P_{A_{min}}) \end{array} \quad (2)$$

Where $P_{E_{min}}$ and $P_{E_{max}}$ are the minimum and maximum uni-gram probabilities in the English LM. And $P_{A_{min}}$ and $P_{A_{max}}$ are the minimum and maximum uni-gram probabilities in the Arabic LM. The foreignness index $Foreignness(w)$ is the normalized foreignness *score* derived using equations 1 and 2 as follow:

$$Foreignness\,(w) = \frac{\varepsilon\,(w) - \varepsilon_{min}}{\varepsilon_{max} - \varepsilon_{min}} \quad (3)$$

If the foreignness index of a word is higher than a certain threshold β, we consider the word *Foreign*. We define three baseline experiments as follows:

- **FW-index-manual**: Use brute force search to find the best α and β that maximize the foreign words tagging on *Dev*.
- **FW-index-SVM**: Use the best α from above and train an SVM model using the foreignness index as sole feature. Then use this model to classify each word in *Dev*.
- **LM-lookup**: The word is said to be *Foreign* if it exists in the English LM and does not exist in the Arabic LM.

8.2 Machine Learning Experiments

We conducted a suite of experiments by training different machine learning techniques using WEKA (Hall et al., 2009) on the following groups of features. We performed a two-stage feature exploration, where we did an exhaustive search over all features in each group in the first phase, and then exhaustively searched over all retained feature groups. In addition, we also performed an exhaustive search over all features in the first three groups.

- **Word n-gram features**: Run the input Arabizi word through an English LM and the corresponding Arabic transliteration through an Arabic LM to get the set of features that are defined in "Group1" in Table 4. Then find the best combination of features that maximizes the F-score on *Dev*.
- **FW-char-n-gram features**: Run the input Arabizi word through a character-level n-gram LM of the Arabizi words that are tagged as foreign in the training data. We get the set of features that are defined in "Group2" in Table 4. Then find the best feature combination from this group that maximizes the F-score on *Dev*.
- **AR-char-n-gram features**: Run the input Arabizi word through a character-level n-gram LM of the Arabizi words that are tagged as non-foreign in the training data. We get the set of features that are defined in "Group3" in Table 4. Then find the best feature that maximizes the F-score on *Dev*.
- **Word identity**: Use the input Arabizi word to get all features that are defined in "Group4" in Table 4. Then find the best combination of features that maximizes the F-score on *Dev*.
- **Word properties**: Use the input Arabizi word to get all features that are defined in "Group5" in Table 4. Then find the best combination of features that maximizes the F-score on *Dev*.
- **Best-of-all-groups**: Use the best selected set of features from each of the above experiments. Then find the best combination of these features that maximizes the F-score on *Dev*.
- **All-features**: Use all features from all groups.
- **Probabilistic-features-only**: Find the best combination of features from "Group1", "Group2", and "Group3" in Table 4 that maximizes the F-score on *Dev*.

Group	Description
Group1	Uni and bi-grams probabilities from English and Arabic LMs
Group2	1,2,3,4, and 5 characters level n-grams of foreign words
Group3	1,2,3,4, and 5 characters level n-grams of Arabic words
Group4	Use the Arabizi word itself as a feature
	Was the input Arabizi word tagged as foreign in the gold training data?
	Was the input Arabizi word tagged as Arabic in the gold training data?
Group5	Does the input word has speech effects?
	Word length
	Is the Arabizi word capitalized?

Table 4: List of the different features that are used in the foreign word tagging

8.3 Results

Table 5 shows the results on *Dev* using *Train-S*. It can be seen that the decision tree classifier is doing better than the SVM except in the "Word properties" and "All-features" experiments. The best performing setup is "Probabilistic-features-only" with decision trees which has 87.3% F-score. The best selected features are EN-Unigram, AR-char-2-grams, FW-char-1-grams, FW-char-2-grams, FW-char-5-grams.

Experiment	Recall	Precision	F-Score	Classifier	Selected Features
LM-lookup	7.6	**95.4**	14.1		
FW-index-manual	75.0	51.0	60.7		α =0.8 , β = 0.23
FW-index-SVM	4.0	89.0	7.7	SVM	
Word n-gram features	76.7	73.2	74.9	SVM	AR-unigram, EN-unigram
AR-char-n-gram features	55.4	34.8	42.8		AR-char-4-grams
FW-char-n-gram features	42.4	52.2	46.8		FW-char-3-grams
Word properties	2.4	28.6	4.5		Has-speech-effect, Word-length, Is-capitalized
Word identity	70.3	63.0	66.4		FW-tagged-list
Best-of-all-groups	82.1	76.1	79.0		AR-unigram, EN-unigram, Word-length
All-features	69.4	87.7	77.5		All features from all groups
Probabilistic-features-only	84.5	80.6	82.5		AR-unigram, EN-unigram, AR-char-3-grams, FW-char-3-grams
Word n-gram features	82.8	80.5	81.6	Decision-Tree	AR-unigram, EN-unigram
AR-char-n-gram features	80.6	63.2	70.8		AR-char-5-grams
FW-char-n-gram features	73.8	76.3	75.0		FW-char-3-grams
Word properties	1.9	25.4	3.6		Has-speech-effect, Word-length
Word identity	73.2	60.9	66.5		FW-tagged-list
Best-of-all-groups	87.0	81.5	84.1		AR-unigram, EN-unigram, AR-char-5-grams, FW-char-3-grams
All-features	**92.0**	53.4	67.6		All features from all groups
Probabilistic-features-only	89.9	84.9	**87.3**		**EN-Unigram, AR-char-2-grams, FW-char-1-grams, FW-char-2-grams, FW-char-5-grams**

Table 5: Foreign words tagging results on *Dev* in terms of F-score (%).

9 System Evaluation

9.1 Development and Blind Test Results

We report the results on *Dev* using *Train-L* and with the best settings determined in the previous three sections. Table 6 summarizes the recall, precision and F-score results for the classification of the *Punct*, *Sound*, *Foreign*, *Name* and *Arabic* tags, in addition to emoticon detection.

We report our results on *Test*, our blind test set, using *Train-L* and with the best settings determined in the previous three sections in Table 7.

The punctuation, sounds and emoticons have high F-scores but lower than expected. This is likely due to the limitations of the regular expressions used. The performance on these tags drops further on the test set. A similar drop is seen for the *Foreign* tag. *Name* is the hardest tag overall. But it performs slightly better in test compared to the development set, and so does the *Arabic* tag.

Tag	Accuracy	Recall	Precision	F-Score
Punct	99.8	100.0	88.7	94.0
Sound	99.4	93.5	78.9	85.6
Foreign	95.8	91.6	84.0	87.6
Name	98.1	57.5	71.8	63.9
Arabic	94.5	95.6	97.3	96.4
Emoticon Detection	100.0	97.5	98.7	98.1

Table 6: Tagging results on *Dev* using *Train-L*

Tag	Accuracy	Recall	Precision	F-Score
Punct	99.8	98.2	80.1	88.3
Sound	99.3	87.4	74.2	80.3
Foreign	96.5	92.3	64.3	75.8
Name	98.6	53.7	90.2	67.3
Arabic	95.4	96.3	98.5	97.4
Emoticon Detection	99.2	85.3	93.6	89.3

Table 7: Tagging results on *Test* using *Train-L*

9.2 Overall System Evaluation

In this subsection we report on evaluating the overall system accuracy. This includes the correct tagging and Arabizi to Arabic transliteration. However, since there is no manually annotated gold transliteration for foreign words, punctuation, or sounds into Arabic, we cannot compare the system transliteration of foreign words to the gold transliteration. Thus, we define the following metric to judge the overall system accuracy.

Overall System Accuracy Metric A word is said to be correctly transliterated according to the following rules:

1. If the gold tag is anything other than *Arabic* and *Name*, the produced tag must match the gold tag.

2. If the gold tag is either *Arabic* or *Name*, the produced tag and the produced transliteration must both match the gold.

Data	Baseline Accuracy	System Accuracy
Dev	65.7%	82.5%
Test	76.8%	83.8%

Table 8: Baseline vs. System Accuracy

Tag	Gold Errors		System Errors		Typos
	Not Tagged	Over generated	Not Tagged	Over generated	
Punct	100.0	0.0	0.0	0.0	0.0
Sound	79.3	10.3	10.3	0.0	0.0
Foreign	47.2	1.9	12.3	20.3	18.4
Name	26.3	13.7	45.3	8.4	6.3

Table 9: Error Analysis of tag classification errors

As a baseline, we use the most frequent tag, which is *Arabic* in our case, along with the transliteration of the word using our black box system. Then we apply the above evaluation metric on both *Dev* and *Test*. The results are shown in table 8. The baseline accuracies on *Dev* and *Test* are 65.7% and 76.8% respectively. By considering the actual output of our system, the accuracy on the *Dev* and *Test* data increases to 82.5% and 83.8% respectively.

9.3 Error Analysis

We conducted an error analysis for tag classification on the development set. The analysis is done for the tags that we built models for, which are *Punct*, *Sound*, *Foreign* and *Name*.[2] Table 9 shows the different error types for classifying the tags. Tagging errors could be either gold errors or system errors. These errors could be either due to tag over-generation or because the correct tag is not detected. Additionally, there are typos in the input Arabizi that sometimes prevent the system from assigning the correct tags. Gold errors contribute to a large portion of the tagging errors, representing 100.0%, 89.6%, 49.1% and 40.0% for the *Punct*, *Sound*, *Foreign* and *Name* tags, respectively.

10 Conclusion and Future Work

We presented a system for automatic processing of Arabic social media text written in Roman script, or Arabizi. Our system not only transliterates the Arabizi text in the Egyptian Arabic dialect but also classifies input Arabizi tokens as sounds, punctuation marks, names, foreign words, or Arabic words, and detects emoticons. We define a new task-specific metric for evaluating the complete system. Our best setting achieves an overall performance accuracy of 83.8% on a blind test set.

In the future, we plan to extend our work to other Arabic dialects and other language contexts such as Judeo-Arabic (Arabic written in Hebrew script with code switching between Arabic and Hebrew). We plan to explore the use of this component in the context of specific applications such as machine translation from Arabizi Arabic to English, and sentiment analysis in social media. We also plan to make the system public so it can be used by other people working on Arabic NLP tasks related to Arabizi.

Acknowledgement

This paper is based upon work supported by DARPA Contract No. HR0011-12-C-0014. Any opinions, findings and conclusions or recommendations expressed in this paper are those of the authors and do not necessarily reflect the views of DARPA. Nizar Habash performed most of his contribution to this paper while he was at the Center for Computational Learning Systems at Columbia University.

References

Mohamed Al-Badrashiny, Ramy Eskander, Nizar Habash, and Owen Rambow. 2014. Automatic Transliteration of Romanized Dialectal Arabic. In *Proceedings of the Eighteenth Conference on Computational Natural Language Learning*, pages 30–38, Ann Arbor, Michigan, June. Association for Computational Linguistics.

Ann Bies, Zhiyi Song, Mohamed Maamouri, Stephen Grimes, Haejoong Lee, Jonathan Wright, Stephanie Strassel, Nizar Habash, Ramy Eskander, and Owen Rabmow. 2014. Transliteration of Arabizi into Arabic Orthography: Developing a Parallel Annotated Arabizi-Arabic Script SMS/Chat Corpus. In *Arabic Natural Language Processing Workshop, EMNLP*, Doha, Qatar.

Tim Buckwalter. 2004. Buckwalter Arabic Morphological Analyzer Version 2.0. LDC catalog number LDC2004L02, ISBN 1-58563-324-0.

Achraf Chalabi and Hany Gerges. 2012. Romanized Arabic Transliteration. In *Proceedings of the Second Workshop on Advances in Text Input Methods (WTIM 2012)*.

Eleanor Clark and Kenji Araki. 2011. Text normalization in social media: Progress, problems and applications for a pre-processing system of casual english. *Procedia - Social and Behavioral Sciences*, 27(0):2 – 11. Computational Linguistics and Related Fields.

[2] As mentioned in Section 4, the *Arabic* tag is assigned to any remaining untagged words after running the classification models.

Kareem Darwish, Walid Magdy, and Ahmed Mourad. 2012. Language Processing for Arabic Microblog Retrieval. In *Proceedings of the 21st ACM International Conference on Information and Knowledge Management*, CIKM '12, pages 2427–2430, New York, NY, USA. ACM.

Kareem Darwish. 2013. Arabizi Detection and Conversion to Arabic. *CoRR*.

Kareem Darwish. 2014. Arabizi Detection and Conversion to Arabic . In *Arabic Natural Language Processing Workshop, EMNLP*, Doha, Qatar.

Leon Derczynski, Alan Ritter, Sam Clark, and Kalina Bontcheva. 2013. Twitter part-of-speech tagging for all: Overcoming sparse and noisy data. In *Proceedings of the International Conference Recent Advances in Natural Language Processing RANLP 2013*, pages 198–206, Hissar, Bulgaria, September. INCOMA Ltd. Shoumen, BULGARIA.

Mona Diab, Mohamed Al-Badrashiny, Maryam Aminian, Mohammed Attia, Pradeep Dasigi, Heba Elfardy, Ramy Eskander, Nizar Habash, Abdelati Hawwari, and Wael Salloum. 2014. Tharwa: A Large Scale Dialectal Arabic - Standard Arabic - English Lexicon. In *Proceedings of the Language Resources and Evaluation Conference (LREC)*, Reykjavik, Iceland.

Heba Elfardy, Mohamed Al-Badrashiny, and Mona Diab. 2013. Code Switch Point Detection in Arabic. In *Proceedings of the 18th International Conference on Application of Natural Language to Information Systems (NLDB2013)*, MediaCity, UK, June.

Heba Elfardy, Mohamed Al-Badrashiny, and Mona Diab. 2014. AIDA: Identifying Code Switching in Informal Arabic Text. In *Workshop on Computational Approaches to Linguistic Code Switching, EMNLP*, Doha, Qatar, October.

Ramy Eskander, Nizar Habash, Owen Rambow, and Nadi Tomeh. 2013. Processing Spontaneous Orthography. In *Proceedings of the 2013 Conference of the North American Chapter of the Association for Computational Linguistics: Human Language Technologies (NAACL-HLT)*, Atlanta, GA.

Kevin Gimpel, Nathan Schneider, Brendan O'Connor, Dipanjan Das, Daniel Mills, Jacob Eisenstein, Michael Heilman, Dani Yogatama, Jeffrey Flanigan, and Noah A. Smith. 2011. Part-of-speech tagging for twitter: Annotation, features, and experiments. In *Proceedings of the 49th Annual Meeting of the Association for Computational Linguistics: Human Language Technologies: Short Papers - Volume 2*, HLT '11, pages 42–47, Stroudsburg, PA, USA. Association for Computational Linguistics.

Stephan Gouws, Donald Metzler, Congxing Cai, and Eduard Hovy. 2011. Contextual bearing on linguistic variation in social media. In *Proceedings of the Workshop on Languages in Social Media*, LSM '11, pages 20–29, Stroudsburg, PA, USA. Association for Computational Linguistics.

Nizar Habash, Abdelhadi Soudi, and Tim Buckwalter. 2007. On Arabic Transliteration. In A. van den Bosch and A. Soudi, editors, *Arabic Computational Morphology: Knowledge-based and Empirical Methods*. Springer.

Nizar Habash, Mona Diab, and Owen Rabmow. 2012a. Conventional Orthography for Dialectal Arabic. In *Proceedings of the Language Resources and Evaluation Conference (LREC)*, Istanbul.

Nizar Habash, Ramy Eskander, and Abdelati Hawwari. 2012b. A Morphological Analyzer for Egyptian Arabic. In *Proceedings of the Twelfth Meeting of the Special Interest Group on Computational Morphology and Phonology*, pages 1–9, Montréal, Canada.

Nizar Habash. 2009. REMOOV: A tool for online handling of out-of-vocabulary words in machine translation. In Khalid Choukri and Bente Maegaard, editors, *Proceedings of the Second International Conference on Arabic Language Resources and Tools*. The MEDAR Consortium, April.

Mark Hall, Eibe Frank, Geoffrey Holmes, Bernhard Pfahringer, Peter Reutemann, and Ian H. Witten. 2009. The WEKA data mining software: an update. *SIGKDD Explorations*, 11(1):10–18.

LDC. 2014a. BOLT Phase 2 SMS and Chat Arabic DevTest Data – Source Annotation, Transliteration and Translation. LDC catalog number LDC2014E28.

LDC. 2014b. BOLT Phase 2 SMS and Chat Arabic Training Data – Source Annotation, Transliteration and Translation R1. LDC catalog number LDC2014E48.

LDC. 2014c. BOLT Program: Romanized Arabic (Arabizi) to Arabic Transliteration and Normalization Guidelines. Version 3. Linguistic Data Consortium.

Marco Lui, Jey Han Lau, and Timothy Baldwin. 2014. Automatic detection and language identification of multilingual documents. In *Proceedings of LREC*.

Arfath Pasha, Mohamed Al-Badrashiny, Mona Diab, Ahmed El Kholy, Ramy Eskander, Nizar Habash, Manoj Pooleery, Owen Rambow, and Ryan M. Roth. 2014. MADAMIRA: A Fast, Comprehensive Tool for Morphological Analysis and Disambiguation of Arabic. In *Proceedings of the Language Resources and Evaluation Conference (LREC)*, Reykjavik, Iceland.

Alan Ritter, Sam Clark, Mausam, and Oren Etzioni. 2011. Named entity recognition in tweets: An experimental study. In *Proceedings of the Conference on Empirical Methods in Natural Language Processing*, EMNLP '11, pages 1524–1534, Stroudsburg, PA, USA. Association for Computational Linguistics.

Clare Voss, Stephen Tratz, Jamal Laoudi, and Douglas Briesch. 2014. Finding Romanized Arabic Dialect in Code-Mixed Tweets. In Nicoletta Calzolari (Conference Chair), Khalid Choukri, Thierry Declerck, Hrafn Loftsson, Bente Maegaard, Joseph Mariani, Asuncion Moreno, Jan Odijk, and Stelios

Piperidis, editors, *Proceedings of the Ninth International Conference on Language Resources and Evaluation (LREC'14)*, Reykjavik, Iceland, may. European Language Resources Association (ELRA).

Omar F Zaidan and Chris Callison-Burch. 2011. The Arabic online commentary dataset: an annotated dataset of informal Arabic with high dialectal content. In *Proceedings of ACL*, pages 37–41.

Ines Zribi, Rahma Boujelbane, Abir Masmoudi, Mariem Ellouze, Lamia Belguith, and Nizar Habash. 2014. A Conventional Orthography for Tunisian Arabic. In *Proceedings of the Language Resources and Evaluation Conference (LREC)*, Reykjavik, Iceland.

Code Mixing: A Challenge for Language Identification in the Language of Social Media

Utsab Barman, Amitava Das[†], Joachim Wagner and Jennifer Foster
CNGL Centre for Global Intelligent Content, National Centre for Language Technology
School of Computing, Dublin City University, Dublin, Ireland
[†]Department of Computer Science and Engineering
University of North Texas, Denton, Texas, USA
{ubarman,jwagner,jfoster}@computing.dcu.ie
amitava.das@unt.edu

Abstract

In social media communication, multilingual speakers often switch between languages, and, in such an environment, automatic language identification becomes both a necessary and challenging task. In this paper, we describe our work in progress on the problem of automatic language identification for the language of social media. We describe a new dataset that we are in the process of creating, which contains Facebook posts and comments that exhibit code mixing between Bengali, English and Hindi. We also present some preliminary word-level language identification experiments using this dataset. Different techniques are employed, including a simple unsupervised dictionary-based approach, supervised word-level classification with and without contextual clues, and sequence labelling using Conditional Random Fields. We find that the dictionary-based approach is surpassed by supervised classification and sequence labelling, and that it is important to take contextual clues into consideration.

1 Introduction

Automatic processing and understanding of Social Media Content (SMC) is currently attracting much attention from the Natural Language Processing research community. Although English is still by far the most popular language in SMC, its dominance is receding. Hong et al. (2011), for example, applied an automatic language detection algorithm to over 62 million tweets to identify the top 10 most popular languages on Twitter. They found that only half of the tweets were in English. Moreover, mixing multiple languages together (*code mixing*) is a popular trend in social media users from language-dense areas (Cárdenas-Claros and Isharyanti, 2009; Shafie and Nayan, 2013). In a scenario where speakers switch between languages within a conversation, sentence or even word, the task of automatic language identification becomes increasingly important to facilitate further processing.

Speakers whose first language uses a non-Roman alphabet write using the Roman alphabet for convenience (phonetic typing) which increases the likelihood of code mixing with a Roman-alphabet language. This can be especially observed in South-East Asia and in the Indian subcontinent. The following is a code mixing comment taken from a Facebook group of Indian university students:

> Original: *Yaar tu to*, GOD *hain.* **tui** JU **te ki korchis**? Hail u man!
>
> Translation: Buddy you are GOD. What are you doing in JU? Hail u man!

This comment is written in three languages: English, Hindi (italics), and Bengali (boldface). For Bengali and Hindi, phonetic typing has been used.

We follow in the footsteps of recent work on language identification for SMC (Hughes et al., 2006; Baldwin and Lui, 2010; Bergsma et al., 2012), focusing specifically on the problem of *word-level* language identification for code mixing SMC. Our corpus for this task is collected from Facebook and contains instances of *Bengali(BN)-English(EN)-Hindi(HI)* code mixing.

The paper is organized as follows: in Section 2, we review related research in the area of code mixing and language identification; in Section 3, we describe our code mixing corpus, the data it-

Proceedings of The First Workshop on Computational Approaches to Code Switching, pages 13–23,
October 25, 2014, Doha, Qatar. ©2014 Association for Computational Linguistics

self and the annotation process; in Section 4, we list the tools and resources which we use in our language identification experiments, described in Section 5. Finally, in Section 6, we conclude and provide suggestions for future research on this topic.

2 Background and Related Work

The problem of language identification has been investigated for half a century (Gold, 1967) and that of computational analysis of code switching for several decades (Joshi, 1982), but there has been less work on *automatic language identification for multilingual code-mixed texts*. Before turning to that topic, we first briefly survey studies on the general characteristics of code mixing.

Code mixing is a normal, natural product of bilingual and multilingual language use. Significant studies of the phenomenon can be found in the linguistics literature (Milroy and Muysken, 1995; Alex, 2008; Auer, 2013). These works mainly discuss the sociological and conversational necessities behind code mixing as well as its linguistic nature. Scholars distinguish between *inter-sentence*, *intra-sentence* and *intra-word* code mixing.

Several researchers have investigated the reasons for and the types of code mixing. Initial studies on Chinese-English code mixing in Hong Kong (Li, 2000) and Macao (San, 2009) indicated that mainly linguistic motivations were triggering the code mixing in those highly bilingual societies. Hidayat (2012) showed that Facebook users tend to mainly use inter-sentential switching over intra-sentential, and report that 45% of the switching was instigated by real lexical needs, 40% was used for talking about a particular topic, and 5% for content clarification. The predominance of inter-sentential code mixing in social media text was also noted in the study by San (2009), which compared the mixing in blog posts to that in the spoken language in Macao. Dewaele (2010) claims that 'strong emotional arousal' increases the frequency of code mixing. Dey and Fung (2014) present a speech corpus of English-Hindi code mixing in student interviews and analyse the motivations for code mixing and in what grammatical contexts code mixing occurs.

Turning to the work on automatic analysis of code mixing, there have been some studies on detecting code mixing in speech (Solorio and Liu, 2008a; Weiner et al., 2012). Solorio and Liu (2008b) try to predict the points inside a set of spoken Spanish-English sentences where the speakers switch between the two languages. Other studies have looked at code mixing in different types of short texts, such as information retrieval queries (Gottron and Lipka, 2010) and SMS messages (Farrugia, 2004; Rosner and Farrugia, 2007). Yamaguchi and Tanaka-Ishii (2012) perform language identification using artificial multilingual data, created by randomly sampling text segments from monolingual documents. King and Abney (2013) used weakly semi-supervised methods to perform word-level language identification. A dataset of 30 languages has been used in their work. They explore several language identification approaches, including a Naive Bayes classifier for individual word-level classification and sequence labelling with Conditional Random Fields trained with Generalized Expectation criteria (Mann and McCallum, 2008; Mann and McCallum, 2010), which achieved the highest scores. Another very recent work on this topic is (Nguyen and Doğruöz, 2013). They report on language identification experiments performed on Turkish and Dutch forum data. Experiments have been carried out using language models, dictionaries, logistic regression classification and Conditional Random Fields. They find that language models are more robust than dictionaries and that contextual information is helpful for the task.

3 Corpus Acquisition

Taking into account the claim that code mixing is frequent among speakers who are *multilingual* and *younger in age* (Cárdenas-Claros and Isharyanti, 2009), we choose an Indian student community between the 20-30 year age group as our data source. India is a country with 30 spoken languages, among which 22 are official. code mixing is very frequent in the Indian sub-continent because languages change within very short geo-distances and people generally have a basic knowledge of their neighboring languages.

A Facebook group[1] and 11 Facebook users (known to the authors) were selected to obtain publicly available posts and comments. The Facebook graph API explorer was used for data collection. Since these Facebook users are from West Bengal, the most dominant language is Bengali

[1] https://www.facebook.com/jumatrimonial

(Native Language), followed by English and then Hindi (National Language of India). The posts and comments in Bengali and Hindi script were discarded during data collection, resulting in 2335 posts and 9813 comments.

3.1 Annotation

Four annotators took part in the annotation task. Three were computer science students and the other was one of the authors. The annotators are proficient in all three languages of our corpus. A simple annotation tool was developed which enabled these annotators to identify and distinguish the different languages present in the content by tagging them. Annotators were supplied with 4 basic tags (viz. *sent*ence, *frag*ment, *incl*usion and *wlcm* (word-level code mixing)) to annotate different levels of code mixing. Under each tag, six attributes were provided, viz. *English (en), Bengali (bn), Hindi (hi), Mixed (mixd), Universal (univ) and Undefined (undef)*. The attribute *univ* is associated with symbols, numbers, emoticons and universal expressions (e.g. *hahaha*, *lol*). The attribute *undef* is specified for a sentence or a word for which no language tags can be attributed or cannot be categorized as *univ*. In addition, annotators were instructed to annotate named entities separately. What follows are descriptions of each of the annotation tags.

Sentence (sent): This tag refers to a sentence and can be used to mark *inter-sentential code mixing*. Annotators were instructed to identify a sentence with its base language (e.g. *en*, *bn*, *hi* and *mixd*) or with other types (e.g. *univ*, *undef*) as the first task of annotation. Only the attribute *mixd* is used to refer to a sentence which contains multiple languages in the same proportion. A sentence may contain any number of inclusions, fragments and word-level code mixing. A sentence can be attributed as *univ* if and only if it contains symbols, numbers, emoticons, chat acronyms and no other words (Hindi, English or Bengali). A sentence can be attributed as *undef* if it is not a sentence marked as *univ* and has words/tokens that can not be categorized as Hindi, English or Bengali. Some examples of sentence-level annotations are the following:

1. **English-Sentence:**
   [sent-lang="en"] *what a.....6 hrs long...but really nice tennis....* [/sent]
2. **Bengali-Sentence:**
   [sent-lang="bn"] *shubho nabo borsho.. :)* [/sent]
3. **Hindi Sentence:**
   [sent-lang="hi"] *karwa sachh ..... :(* [/sent]
4. **Mixed-Sentence:**
   [sent-lang="mixd"] [frag-lang="hi"] *oye hoye ..... angreji me kahte hai ke* [/frag] [frag-lang="en"] *I love u.. !!!* [/frag] [/sent]
5. **Univ-Sentence:**
   [sent-lang="univ"] *hahahahahahah....!!!!!* [/sent]
6. **Undef-Sentence:**
   [sent-lang="undef"] *Hablando de una triple amenaza.* [/sent]

Fragment (frag): This refers to a group of foreign words, grammatically related, in a sentence. The presence of this tag in a sentence conveys that *intra-sentential code mixing* has occurred within the sentence boundary. Identification of fragments (if present) in a sentence was the second task of annotation. A *sentence (sent)* with attribute *mixd* must contain multiple *fragments (frag)* with a specific language attribute. In the fourth example above, the sentence contains a Hindi fragment *oye hoye ..... angreji me kahte hai ke* and an English fragment *I love u.. !!!*, hence it is considered as a *mixd* sentence. A fragment can have any number of inclusions and word-level code mixing. In the first example below, *Jio* is a popular Bengali word appearing in the English fragment *Jio.. good joke*, hence tagged as a Bengali inclusion. One can argue that the word *Jio* could be a separate Bengali inclusion (i.e. can be tagged as a Bengali inclusion outside the English fragment). But looking at the syntactic pattern and the sense expressed by the comment, the annotator kept it as a single unit. In the second example below, an instance of word-level code mixing, *typer*, has been found in an English fragment (where the root English word *type* has the Bengali suffix *r*).

1. **Fragment with Inclusion:**
   [sent-lang="mixd"] [frag-lang="en"] [incl-lang="bn"] *Jio..* [/incl] *good joke* [/frag] [frag lang="bn"] *"amar Babin"* [/frag] [/sent]
2. **Fragment with Word-Level code mixing:**
   [sent-lang="mixd"] [frag-lang="en"] *" I will find u and marry you "* [/frag] [frag-lang="bn"] [wlcm-type="en-and-bn-suffix"] *typer* [/wlcm] *hoe glo to! :D* [/frag] [/sent]

Inclusion (incl): An inclusion is a foreign word or phrase in a sentence or in a fragment which is assimilated or used very frequently in native language. Identification of inclusions can be performed after annotating a sentence and fragment (if present in that sentence). An inclusion within a sentence or fragment also denotes *intra-sentential code mixing*. In the example below, *seriously* is an English inclusion which is assimilated in today's colloquial Bengali and Hindi. The only tag that an inclusion may contain is word-level code mixing.

1. <u>**Sentence with Inclusion:**</u>
   [sent-lang="bn"] *Na re* [incl-lang="en"] *seriously* [/incl] *ami khub kharap achi.* [/sent]

Word-Level code mixing (wlcm): This is the smallest unit of code mixing. This tag was introduced to capture *intra-word code mixing* and denotes cases where code mixing has occurred within a single word. Identifying word-level code mixing is the last task of annotation. Annotators were told to mention the type of word-level code mixing in the form of an attribute (Base Language + Second Language) format. Some examples are provided below. In the first example below, the root word *class* is English and *e* is an Bengali suffix that has been added. In the third example below, the opposite can be observed – the root word *Kando* is Bengali, and an English suffix *z* has been added. In the second example below, a named entity *suman* is present with a Bengali suffix *er*.

1. <u>**Word-Level code mixing (EN-BN):**</u>
   [wlcm-type="en-and-bn-suffix"] *classe* [/wlcm]
2. <u>**Word-Level code mixing (NE-BN):**</u>
   [wlcm-type="NE-and-bn-suffix"] *sumaner* [/wlcm]
3. <u>**Word-Level code mixing (BN-EN):**</u>
   [wlcm-type="bn-and-en-suffix"] *kandoz* [/wlcm]

3.1.1 Inter Annotator Agreement

We calculate word-level inter annotator agreement (Cohen's Kappa) on a subset of 100 comments (randomly selected) between two annotators. Two annotators are in agreement about a word if they both annotate the word with the same attribute (*en, bn, hi, univ, undef*), regardless of whether the word is inside an inclusion, fragment or sentence. Our observations that the word-level annotation process is not a very ambiguous task and that annotation instruction is also straightforward are confirmed in a high inter-annotator agreement (IAA) with a Kappa value of 0.884.

3.2 Data Characteristics

Tag-level and word-level statistics of annotated data that reveal the characteristics of our data set are described in Table 1 and in Table 2 respectively. More than 56% of total sentences and almost 40% of total tokens are in Bengali, which is the dominant language of this corpus. English is the second most dominant language covering almost 33% of total tokens and 35% of total sentences. The amount of Hindi data is substantially lower – nearly 1.75% of total tokens and 2% of total sentences. However, English inclusions (84% of total inclusions) are more prominent than Hindi or Bengali inclusions and there are a substantial number of English fragments (almost 52% of total fragments) present in our corpus. This means that English is the main language involved in the code mixing.

Statistics of Different Tags						
Tags	**En**	**Bn**	**Hi**	**Mixd**	**Univ**	**Undef**
sent	5,370	8,523	354	204	746	15
frag	288	213	40	0	6	0
incl	7,377	262	94	0	1,032	1

wlcm	477
Name Entity	3,602
Acronym	691

Table 1: Tag-level statistics

Word-Level Tag	Count
EN	66,298
BN	79,899
HI	3,440
WLCM	633
NE	5,233
ACRO	715
UNIV	39,291
UNDEF	61

Table 2: Word-level statistics

3.2.1 Code Mixing Types

In our corpus, inter- and intra-sentential code mixing are more prominent than word-level code mixing, which is similar to the findings of (Hidayat, 2012) . Our corpus contains every type of code mixing in English, Hindi and Bengali viz. inter/intra sentential and word-level as described in the previous section. Some examples of different types of code mixing in our corpus are presented below.

1. **Inter-Sentential:**
[sent-lang="hi"] *Itna izzat diye aapne mujhe* !!! [/sent]
[sent-lang="en"] *Tears of joy. :'(:'(* [/sent]
2. **Intra-Sentential:**
[sent-lang="bn"] [incl-lang="en"] *by d way* [/incl] *ei* [frag-lang="en"] *my craving arms shall forever remain empty .. never hold u close ..* [/frag] *line ta baddo* [incl-lang="en"] *cheezy* [/incl] :P ;) [/sent]
3. **Word-Level:**
[sent-lang="bn"] [incl-lang="en"] *1st yr* [/incl] *eo to ei* [wlcm-type="en+bnSuffix"] *tymer* [/wlcm] *modhye sobar jute jay ..* [/sent]

3.2.2 Ambiguous Words

Annotators were instructed to tag an English word as English irrespective of any influence of word borrowing or foreign inclusion but an inspection of the annotations revealed that English words were sometimes annotated as Bengali or Hindi. To understand this phenomenon we processed the list of language (EN,BN and HI) word types (total 26,475) and observed the percentage of types that were not always annotated with the one language throughout the corpus. The results are presented in Table 3. Almost 7% of total types are ambiguous (i.e. tagged in different languages during annotation). Among them, a substantial amount (5.58%) are English/Bengali.

Label(s)	Count	Percentage
EN	9,109	34.40
BN	14,345	54.18
HI	1,039	3.92
EN or BN	1,479	5.58
EN or HI	61	0.23
BN or HI	277	1.04
EN or BN or HI	165	0.62

Table 3: Statistics of ambiguous and monolingual word types

There are two reasons why this is happening:

Same Words Across Languages Some words are the same (e.g. *baba*, *maa*, *na*, *khali*) in Hindi and Bengali because both of the languages originated from a single language *Sanskrit* and share a good amount of common vocabulary. It also occurred in English-Hindi and English-Bengali as a result of *word borrowing*. Most of these are commonly used inclusions like *clg*, *dept*, *question*, *cigarette*, and *topic*. Sometimes the annotators were careful enough to tag such words as English and sometimes these words were tagged in the annotators' native languages. During cross checking of the annotated data the same error patterns were observed for multiple annotators, i.e. tagging commonly used foreign words into native language. It only demonstrates that these English words are highly assimilated in the conversational vocabulary of Bengali and Hindi.

Phonetic Similarity of Spellings Due to phonetic typing some words share the same surface form across two and sometimes across three languages. As an example, *to* is a word in the three languages: it has occurred 1209 times as English, 715 times as Bengali and 55 times as Hindi in our data. The meaning of these words (e.g. *to*, *bolo*, *die*) are different in different languages. This phenomenon is perhaps exacerbated by the trend towards short and noisy spelling in SMC.

4 Tools and Resources

We have used the following resources and tools in our experiment.

Dictionaries

1. **British National Corpus (BNC):** We compile a word frequency list from the BNC (Aston and Burnard, 1998).
2. **SEMEVAL 2013 Twitter Corpus (SemevalTwitter):** To cope with the language of social media we use the SEMEVAL 2013 (Nakov et al., 2013) training data for the Twitter sentiment analysis task. This data comes from a popular social media site and hence is likely to reflect the linguistic properties of SMC.
3. **Lexical Normalization List (LexNormList):** Spelling variation is a well-known phenomenon in SMC. We use a lexical normalization dictionary created by Han et al. (2012) to handle the different spelling variations in our data.

Machine Learning Toolkits

1. **WEKA:** We use the Weka toolkit (Hall et al., 2009) for our experiments in decision tree training.
2. **MALLET:** CRF learning is applied using the MALLET toolkit (McCallum, 2002).

3. **Liblinear:** We apply Support Vector Machine (SVM) learning with a linear kernel using the Liblinear package (Fan et al., 2008).

NLP Tools For data tokenization we used the CMU Tweet-Tokenizer (Owoputi et al., 2013).

5 Experiments

Since our training data is entirely labelled at the word-level by human annotators, we address the word-level language identification task in a fully supervised way.

Out of the total data, 15% is set aside as a blind test set, while the rest is employed in our experiments through a 5-fold cross-validation setup. There is a substantial amount of token overlap between the cross-validation data and the test set – 88% of total EN tokens, 86% of total Bengali tokens and 57% of total Hindi tokens of the test set are present in the cross-validation data.[2]

We address the problem of word-level in three different ways:

1. A simple heuristic-based approach which uses a combination of our dictionaries to classify the language of a word
2. Word-level classification using supervised machine learning with SVMs but no contextual information
3. Word-level classification using supervised machine learning with SVMs and sequence labelling using CRFs, both employing contextual information

Named entities and instances of word-level code mixing are excluded from evaluation. For systems which do not take the context of a word into account, i.e. the dictionary-based approach (Section 5.1) and the SVM approach without contextual clues (Section 5.2), named entities and instances of word-level code mixing can be safely excluded from training. For systems which do take context into account, the CRF system (Section 5.3.1) and the SVM system with contextual clues (Section 5.3.2), these are included in training, because to exclude them would result in unrealistic contexts. This means that these systems can classify a word to be a named entity or an instance of word-level code mixing. To avoid this, we implement a post-processor which backs off in these cases to a system which hasn't seen named entities or word-level code mixing in training (see Section 5.3).

[2]We found 25 comments and 17 posts common between the cross-validation data and the test set. The reason for this is that users of social media often express themselves in a concise way. Almost all of these common data consisted of 1 to 3 token(s). In most of the cases these tokens were emoticons, symbols or universal expressions such as *wow* and *lol*. As the percentage of these comments is low, we keep these comments as they are.

5.1 Dictionary-Based Detection

We start with dictionary-based language detection. Generally a dictionary-based language detector predicts the language of a word based on its frequency in multiple language dictionaries. In our data the Bengali and Hindi tokens are phonetically typed. As no such transliterated dictionary is, to our knowledge, available for Bengali and Hindi, we use the training set words as dictionaries. For words that have multiple annotations in training data (ambiguous words), we select the majority tag based on frequency, e.g. the word *to* will always be tagged as English.

Our English dictionaries are those described in Section 4 (*BNC, LexNormList, SemEvalTwitter*) and the training set words. For *LexNormList*, we have no frequency information, and so we consider it as a simple word list. To predict the language of a word, dictionaries with normalized frequency were considered first (BNC, SemEvalTwitter, Training Data), if not found, word list look-up was performed. The predicted language is chosen based on the dominant language(s) of the corpus if the word appears in multiple dictionaries with same frequency or if the word does not appear in any dictionary or list.

A simple rule-based method is applied to predict universal expressions. A token is considered as *univ* if any of the following conditions satisfies:

- All characters of the token are symbols or numbers.
- The token contains certain repetitions identified by regular expressions.(e.g. *hahaha*).
- The token is a hash-tag or an URL or mention-tags (e.g. @*Sumit*).
- Tokens (e.g. *lol*) identified by a word list compiled from the relevant 4/5th of the training data.

Table 4 shows the results of dictionary-based detection obtained from 5-fold cross-validation averaging. We try different combinations and frequency thresholds of the above dictionaries. We find that using a normalized frequency is helpful and that a combination of *LexNormList* and *Training Data* dictionaries is suited best for our data. Hence, we consider this as our baseline language identification system.

Dictionary	Accuracy(%)
BNC	80.09
SemevalTwitter	77.61
LexNormList	79.86
Training Data	90.21
LexNormList+TrainingData (Baseline)	**93.12**

Table 4: Average cross-validation accuracy of dictionary-based detection

5.2 Word-Level Classification without Contextual Clues

The following feature types are employed:

1. **Char-n-grams (G):** We start with a character n-gram-based approach (Cavnar and Trenkle, 1994), which is most common and followed by many language identification researchers. Following the work of King and Abney (2013), we select character n-grams (n=1 to 5) and the word as the features in our experiments.
2. **Presence in Dictionaries (D):** We use presence in a dictionary as a features for all available dictionaries in previous experiments.
3. **Length of words (L):** Instead of using the raw length value as a feature, we follow our previous work (Rubino et al., 2013; Wagner et al., 2014) and create multiple features for length using a decision tree (J48). We use length as the only feature to train a decision tree for each fold and use the nodes obtained from the tree to create boolean features.
4. **Capitalization (C):** We use 3 boolean features to encode capitalization information: whether any letter in the word is capitalized, whether all letters in the word are capitalized and whether the first letter is capitalized.

We perform experiments with an SVM classifier (linear kernel) for different combination of these features.[3] Parameter optimizations (C range 2^{-15} to 2^{10}) for SVM are performed for each feature set and best cross-validation accuracy is found for the GDLC-based run (94.75%) at C=1 (see Table 5 and Fig. 1).

Features	Accuracy	Features	Accuracy
G	94.62	GD	94.67
GL	94.62	GDL	94.73
GC	94.64	GDC	94.72
GLC	94.64	**GDLC**	**94.75**

Table 5: Average cross-validation accuracy for SVM word-level classification (without context), G = char-n-gram, L = binary length features, D = presence in dictionaries and C = capitalization features

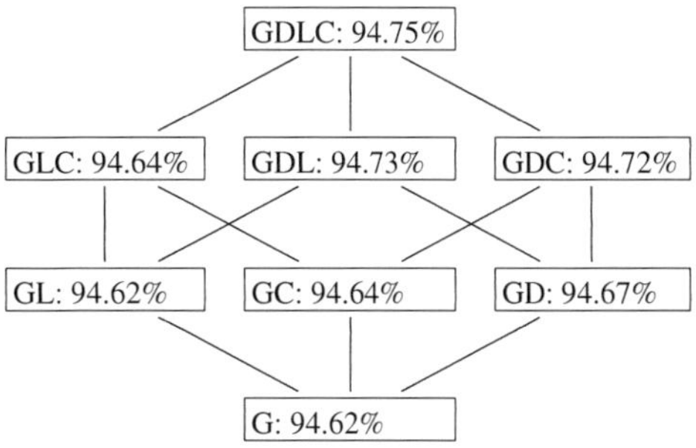

Figure 1: Average cross-validation accuracy for SVM word-level classification (without context), G = char-n-gram, L = binary length features, D = presence in dictionaries and C = capitalization features: cube visualization

We also investigate the use of a dictionary-to-char-n-gram back-off model – the idea is to apply the char-n-gram model SVM-GDLC for those words for which a majority-based decision is taken during dictionary-based detection. However, it does not outperform the SVM. Hence, we select SVM-GDLC for the next steps of our experiments as the best exemplar of our individual word-level classifier (without contextual clues).

5.3 Language Identification with Contextual Clues

Contextual clues can play a very important role in word-level language identification. As an example, a part of a comment is presented from cross-validation fold 1 that contains the word *die* which is wrongly classified by the SVM classifier. The frequency of *die* in the training set of fold 1 is 6 for English, 31 for Bengali and 0 for Hindi.

Gold Data: *..../univ the/en movie/en for/en which/en i/en can/en* ***die/en*** *for/en*

[3]According to (Hsu et al., 2010) the SVM linear kernel with parameter C optimization is good enough when dealing with a large number of features. Though an RBF kernel can be more effective than a linear one, it is possible only after proper optimization of C and γ parameters, which is computational expensive for such a large feature set.

Features	Order-0	Order-1	Order-2
G	92.80	95.16	95.36
GD	93.42	95.59	95.98
GL	92.82	95.14	95.41
GDL	93.47	95.60	95.94
GC	92.07	94.60	95.05
GDC	93.47	95.62	**95.98**
GLC	92.36	94.53	95.02
GDLC	93.47	95.58	95.98

Table 6: Average cross-validation accuracy of CRF-based predictions where G = char-n-gram, L = length feature, D = single dictionary-based labels (baseline system) and C = capitalization features

...../univ

SVM Output: *..../univ the/en movie/en for/en which/en i/en can/en* ***die/bn*** *for/en ...../univ*

We now investigate whether contextual information can correct the mis-classified tags.

Although named entities and word-level code mixing are excluded from evaluation, when dealing with context it is important to consider named entity and word-level code mixing during training because these may contain some important information. We include these tokens in the training data for our context-based experiments, labelling them as *other*. The presence of this new label may affect the prediction for a language token during classification and sequence labelling. To avoid this situation, a 4-way (*bn, hi, en, univ*) backoff classifier is trained separately on English, Hindi, Bengali and universal tokens. During evaluation of any context-based system we discard named entity and word-level code mixing from the prediction of that system. If any of the remaining tokens is predicted as *other* we back off to the decision of the 4-way classifier for that token. For the CRF experiments (Section 5.3.1), the backoff classifier is a CRF system, and, for the SVM experiments (Section 5.3.2), the backoff classifier is an SVM system.

5.3.1 Conditional Random Fields (CRF)

As our goal is to apply contextual clues, we first employ Conditional Random Fields (CRF), an approach which takes history into account in predicting the optimal sequence of labels. We employ a linear chain CRF with an increasing order (Order-0, Order-1 and Order-2) with 200 iterations for different feature combinations (used in SVM-based runs). However, we observe that accuracy of CRF based runs decreases when binarized length features (see Section 5.2 and dictionary features (a feature for each dictionary) are involved. Hence, we use the dictionary-based predictions of the baseline system to generate a single dictionary feature for each token and only the raw length value of a token instead of binarized length features. The results are presented in Table 6 and the second order results are visualized in Fig. 2.

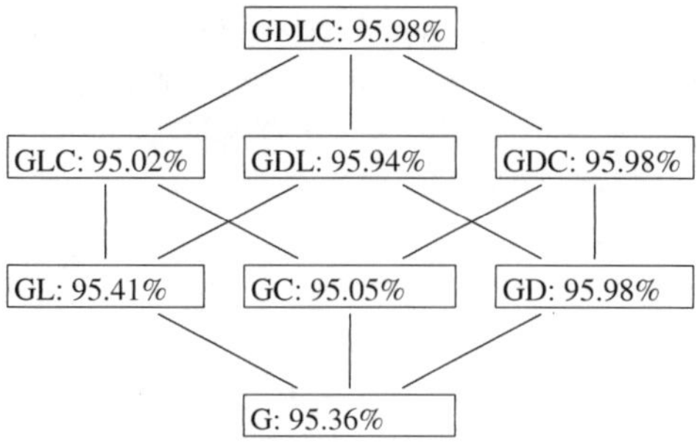

Figure 2: CRF Order-2 results: cube visualisation G = char-n-gram, L = binary length features, D = presence in dictionaries and C = capitalization features

Context	Accuracy (%)
GDLC + P_1	94.66
GDLC + P_2	94.55
GDLC + N_1	94.53
GDLC + N_2	94.37
GDLC + P_1N_1	**95.14**
GDLC + P_2N_2	94.55

Table 7: Average cross-validation accuracy of SVM (GDLC) context-based runs, where P-i = previous i word(s) , N-i = next i word(s)

As expected, the performance increases as the order increases from zero to one and two. The use of a single dictionary feature is also helpful. The results for GDC, GDLC, and GD based runs are almost similar (95.98%). However, we choose the GDC system because it performed slightly better (95.989%) than the GDLC (95.983%) and the GD (95.983%) systems.

5.3.2 SVM with Context

We also add contextual clues to our SVM classifier. To obtain contextual information we include the previous and next two words as features in the SVM-GDLC-based run.[4] All possible com-

[4]We also experimented with extracting all GDLC features for the context words but this did not help.

binations are considered during experiments (Table 7). After C parameter optimization, the best cross-validation accuracy is found for the P_1N_1 (one word previous and one word next) run with C=0.125 (95.14%).

5.4 Test Set Results

We apply our best dictionary-based system, our best SVM system (with and without context) and our best CRF system to the held-out test set. The results are shown in Table 8. Our best result is achieved using the CRF model (95.76%).

5.5 Error Analysis

Manual error analysis shows the limitations of these systems. The word-level classifier without contextual clues does not perform well with Hindi data. The number of Hindi tokens is quite low. Only 2.4% (4,658) of total tokens of the training data are Hindi, out of which 55.36% are bilingually ambiguous and 29.51% are tri-lingually ambiguous tokens. Individual word-level systems often fail to assign proper labels to ambiguous words, but adding context information helps to overcome this problem. Considering the previous example of *die*, both context-based SVM and CRF systems classify it properly. Though the final system CRF-GDC performs well, it also has some limitations, failing to identify the language for the tokens which appear very frequently in three languages (e.g. *are*, *na*, *pic*).

6 Conclusion

We have presented an initial study on automatic language identification with Indian language code mixing from social media communication. We described our dataset of Bengali-Hindi-English Facebook comments and we presented the results of our word-level classification experiments on this dataset. Our experimental results lead us to conclude that character n-gram features are useful for this task, contextual information is also important and that information from dictionaries can be effectively incorporated as features.

In the future we plan to apply the techniques and feature sets that we used in these experiments to other datasets. We have already started this by applying variants of the systems presented here to the Nepali-English and Spanish-English datasets which were introduced as part of the 2014 code mixing shared task (Solorio et al., 2014; Barman et al., 2014).

We did not include word-level code mixing in our experiments – in our future experiments we will explore ways to identify and segment this type of code mixing. It will be also important to find the best way to handle inclusions since there is a fine line between word borrowing and code mixing.

Acknowledgements

This research is supported by the Science Foundation Ireland (Grant 12/CE/I2267) as part of CNGL (www.cngl.ie) at Dublin City University. The authors wish to acknowledge the DJEI/DES/SFI/HEA for the provision of computational facilities and support. Our special thanks to Soumik Mandal from Jadavpur University, India for coordinating the annotation task. We also thank the administrator of JUMatrimonial and the 11 Facebook users who agreed that we can use their posts for their support and permission.

References

Beatrice Alex. 2008. *Automatic detection of English inclusions in mixed-lingual data with an application to parsing*. Ph.D. thesis, School of Informatics, The University of Edinburgh, Edinburgh, UK.

Guy Aston and Lou Burnard. 1998. *The BNC handbook: exploring the British National Corpus with SARA*. Capstone.

Peter Auer. 2013. *Code-Switching in Conversation: Language, Interaction and Identity*. Routledge.

Timothy Baldwin and Marco Lui. 2010. Language identification: The long and the short of the matter. In *Human Language Technologies: The 2010 Annual Conference of the North American Chapter of the Association for Computational Linguistics*, pages 229–237. Association for Computational Linguistics.

Utsab Barman, Joachim Wagner, Grzegorz Chrupała, and Jennifer Foster. 2014. DCU-UVT: Word-level language classification with code-mixed data. In *Proceedings of the First Workshop on Computational Approaches to Code-Switching. EMNLP 2014, Conference on Empirical Methods in Natural Language Processing*, Doha, Qatar. Association for Computational Linguistics.

Shane Bergsma, Paul McNamee, Mossaab Bagdouri, Clayton Fink, and Theresa Wilson. 2012. Language identification for creating language-specific Twitter collections. In *Proceedings of the Second Workshop on Language in Social Media*, pages 65–74. Association for Computational Linguistics.

System	Precision (%)				Recall (%)				Accuracy (%)
	EN	*BN*	*HI*	*UNIV*	*EN*	*BN*	*HI*	*UNIV*	
Baseline (Dictionary)	92.67	90.73	80.64	99.67	92.28	94.63	43.47	94.99	93.64
SVM-GDLC	92.49	94.89	80.31	99.34	96.23	94.28	44.92	97.07	95.21
SVM-P_1N_1	93.51	95.56	83.18	99.42	96.63	95.23	55.94	96.95	95.52
CRF-GDC	94.77	94.88	91.86	99.34	95.65	96.22	55.65	97.73	95.76

Table 8: Test set results for Baseline (Dictionary), SVM-GDLC, SVM-P1N1 and CRF-GDC

MS Cárdenas-Claros and N Isharyanti. 2009. Code-switching and code-mixing in internet chatting: Between'yes,"ya,'and'si'-a case study. *The Jalt Call Journal*, 5(3):67–78.

William B. Cavnar and John M. Trenkle. 1994. N-gram-based text categorization. In Theo Pavlidis, editor, *Proceedings of SDAIR-94, Third Annual Symposium on Document Analysis and Information Retrieval*, pages 161–175.

Jean-Marc Dewaele. 2010. *Emotions in Multiple Languages*. Palgrave Macmillan.

Anik Dey and Pascale Fung. 2014. A Hindi-English code-switching corpus. In *Proceedings of the Ninth International Conference on Language Resources and Evaluation (LREC'14)*, pages 2410–2413, Reykjavik, Iceland. European Language Resources Association (ELRA).

Rong-En Fan, Kai-Wei Chang, Cho-Jui Hsieh, Xiang-Rui Wang, and Chih-Jen Lin. 2008. LIBLINEAR: A library for large linear classification. *Journal of Machine Learning Research*, 9:1871–1874.

Paulseph-John Farrugia. 2004. TTS pre-processing issues for mixed language support. In *Proceedings of CSAW'04, the second Computer Science Annual Workshop*, pages 36–41. Department of Computer Science & A.I., University of Malta.

E Mark Gold. 1967. Language identification in the limit. *Information and control*, 10(5):447–474.

Thomas Gottron and Nedim Lipka. 2010. A comparison of language identification approaches on short, query-style texts. In *Advances in Information Retrieval*, pages 611–614. Springer.

Mark Hall, Eibe Frank, Geoffrey Holmes, Bernhard Pfahringer, Peter Reutemann, and Ian H. Witten. 2009. The WEKA data mining software: An update. *SIGKDD Explor. Newsl.*, 11(1):10–18.

Bo Han, Paul Cook, and Timothy Baldwin. 2012. Automatically constructing a normalisation dictionary for microblogs. In *Proceedings of the 2012 Joint Conference on Empirical Methods in Natural Language Processing and Computational Natural Language Learning*, pages 421–432. Association for Computational Linguistics.

Taofik Hidayat. 2012. An analysis of code switching used by facebookers: a case study in a social network site. Student essay for the study programme "Pendidikan Bahasa Inggris" (English Education) at STKIP Siliwangi Bandung, Indonesia, `http://publikasi.stkipsiliwangi.ac.id/files/2012/10/08220227-taofik-hidayat.pdf`.

Lichan Hong, Gregorio Convertino, and Ed H. Chi. 2011. Language matters in twitter: A large scale study. In *Proceedings of the Fifth International AAAI Conference on Weblogs and Social Media (ICWSM-11)*, pages 518–521, Barcelona, Spain. Association for the Advancement of Artificial Intelligence.

Chih-Wei Hsu, Chih-Chung Chang, and Chih-Jen Lin. 2010. A practical guide to support vector classification. Technical report. Department of Computer Science, National Taiwan University, Taiwan, `https://www.cs.sfu.ca/people/Faculty/teaching/726/spring11/svmguide.pdf`.

Baden Hughes, Timothy Baldwin, Steven Bird, Jeremy Nicholson, and Andrew MacKinlay. 2006. Reconsidering language identification for written language resources. In *Proc. of the 5th edition of the International Conference on Language Resources and Evaluation (LREC 2006)*, pages 485–488, Genoa, Italy.

Aravind K. Joshi. 1982. Processing of sentences with intra-sentential code-switching. In J. Horecký, editor, *Proceedings of the 9th conference on Computational linguistics - Volume 1 (COLING'82)*, pages 145–150. Academia Praha, North-Holland Publishing Company.

Ben King and Steven Abney. 2013. Labeling the languages of words in mixed-language documents using weakly supervised methods. In *Proceedings of the 2013 Conference of the North American Chapter of the Association for Computational Linguistics: Human Language Technologies*, pages 1110–1119, Atlanta, Georgia. Association for Computational Linguistics.

David C. S. Li. 2000. Cantonese-English code-switching research in Hong Kong: a Y2K review. *World Englishes*, 19(3):305–322.

Gideon S. Mann and Andrew McCallum. 2008. Generalized expectation criteria for semi-supervised learning of conditional random fields. In *Proceedings of ACL-08: HLT*, pages 870–878, Columbus, Ohio. Association for Computational Linguistics.

Gideon S. Mann and Andrew McCallum. 2010. Generalized expectation criteria for semi-supervised learning with weakly labeled data. *The Journal of Machine Learning Research*, 11:955–984.

Andrew Kachites McCallum. 2002. Mallet: A machine learning for language toolkit. http://mallet.cs.umass.edu.

Lesley Milroy and Pieter Muysken, editors. 1995. *One speaker, two languages: Cross-disciplinary perspectives on code-switching*. Cambridge University Press.

Preslav Nakov, Sara Rosenthal, Zornitsa Kozareva, Veselin Stoyanov, Alan Ritter, and Theresa Wilson. 2013. Semeval-2013 task 2: Sentiment analysis in twitter. In *Second Joint Conference on Lexical and Computational Semantics (*SEM), Volume 2: Proceedings of the Seventh International Workshop on Semantic Evaluation (SemEval 2013)*, pages 312–320, Atlanta, Georgia, USA. Association for Computational Linguistics.

Dong Nguyen and A. Seza Doğruöz. 2013. Word level language identification in online multilingual communication. In *Proceedings of the 2013 Conference on Empirical Methods in Natural Language Processing (EMNLP 2013)*, pages 857–862, Seattle, Washington, USA. Association for Computational Linguistics.

Olutobi Owoputi, Brendan O'Connor, Chris Dyer, Kevin Gimpel, Nathan Schneider, and Noah A. Smith. 2013. Improved part-of-speech tagging for online conversational text with word clusters. In *Proceedings of the 2013 Conference of the North American Chapter of the Association for Computational Linguistics: Human Language Technologies (NAACL-HLT 2013)*, pages 380–390, Atlanta, Georgia. Association for Computational Linguistics.

Mike Rosner and Paulseph-John Farrugia. 2007. A tagging algorithm for mixed language identification in a noisy domain. In *INTERSPEECH-2007, 8th Annual Conference of the International Speech Communication Association*, pages 190–193. ISCA Archive.

Raphael Rubino, Joachim Wagner, Jennifer Foster, Johann Roturier, Rasoul Samad Zadeh Kaljahi, and Fred Hollowood. 2013. DCU-Symantec at the WMT 2013 quality estimation shared task. In *Proceedings of the Eighth Workshop on Statistical Machine Translation*, pages 392–397, Sofia, Bulgaria. Association for Computational Linguistics.

Hong Ka San. 2009. Chinese-English code-switching in blogs by Macao young people. Master's thesis, The University of Edinburgh, Edinburgh, UK. `http://hdl.handle.net/1842/3626`.

Latisha Asmaak Shafie and Surina Nayan. 2013. Languages, code-switching practice and primary functions of facebook among university students. *Study in English Language Teaching*, 1(1):187–199. `http://www.scholink.org/ojs/index.php/selt`.

Thamar Solorio and Yang Liu. 2008a. Learning to predict code-switching points. In *Proceedings of the Conference on Empirical Methods in Natural Language Processing*, pages 973–981. Association for Computational Linguistics.

Thamar Solorio and Yang Liu. 2008b. Part-of-speech tagging for English-Spanish code-switched text. In *Proceedings of the Conference on Empirical Methods in Natural Language Processing*, pages 1051–1060. Association for Computational Linguistics.

Thamar Solorio, Elizabeth Blair, Suraj Maharjan, Steve Bethard, Mona Diab, Mahmoud Gonheim, Abdelati Hawwari, Fahad AlGhamdi, Julia Hirshberg, Alison Chang, and Pascale Fung. 2014. Overview for the first shared task on language identification in code-switched data. In *Proceedings of the First Workshop on Computational Approaches to Code-Switching. EMNLP 2014, Conference on Empirical Methods in Natural Language Processing*, Doha, Qatar. Association for Computational Linguistics.

Joachim Wagner, Piyush Arora, Santiago Cortes, Utsab Barman, Dasha Bogdanova, Jennifer Foster, and Lamia Tounsi. 2014. DCU: Aspect-based polarity classification for SemEval task 4. In *Proceedings of the International Workshop on Semantic Evaluation (SemEval-2014)*, pages 392–397, Dublin, Ireland. Association for Computational Linguistics.

Jochen Weiner, Ngoc Thang Vu, Dominic Telaar, Florian Metze, Tanja Schultz, Dau-Cheng Lyu, Eng-Siong Chng, and Haizhou Li. 2012. Integration of language identification into a recognition system for spoken conversations containing code-switches. In *Proceedings of the 3rd Workshop on Spoken Language Technologies for Under-resourced Languages (SLTU'12)*, Cape Town, South Africa. International Research Center MICA.

Hiroshi Yamaguchi and Kumiko Tanaka-Ishii. 2012. Text segmentation by language using minimum description length. In *Proceedings of the 50th Annual Meeting of the Association for Computational Linguistics: Long Papers-Volume 1*, pages 969–978. Association for Computational Linguistics.

Detecting Code-Switching in a Multilingual Alpine Heritage Corpus

Martin Volk and Simon Clematide
University of Zurich
Institute of Computational Linguistics
volk|siclemat@cl.uzh.ch

Abstract

This paper describes experiments in detecting and annotating code-switching in a large multilingual diachronic corpus of Swiss Alpine texts. The texts are in English, French, German, Italian, Romansh and Swiss German. Because of the multilingual authors (mountaineers, scientists) and the assumed multilingual readers, the texts contain numerous code-switching elements. When building and annotating the corpus, we faced issues of language identification on the sentence and sub-sentential level. We present our strategy for language identification and for the annotation of foreign language fragments within sentences. We report 78% precision on detecting a subset of code-switches with correct language labels and 92% unlabeled precision.

1 Introduction

In the Text+Berg project we have digitized the yearbooks of the Swiss Alpine Club (SAC) from its first edition in 1864 until today. They contain articles about mountain expeditions, the flora and fauna of the Alpes and other mountain regions, glacier and climate observations, geology and history papers, book reviews, accident and security reports, as well as the protocols of the annual club gatherings. The texts are in the four official languages of Switzerland French, German, Italian and Romansh [1] plus a few in English and Swiss German dialects.

Because of the multilinguality of the authors and readers, many articles are mixed-language texts with inter-sentential and intra-sentential code-switching. This poses a challenge for automatically processing the texts. When we apply Part-of-Speech (PoS) tagging, named entity recognition or parsing, our systems need to know the language that they are dealing with. Therefore we had used a language identifier from the start of the project to mark the language of each sentence. We report on our experiences with sentence-based language identification in section 3. Figure 1 shows an example of a French text with an English appendix title plus an English quote from this book.

Lately we discovered that our corpus also contains many intra-sentential code-switches. For example, we find sentences like

> ... und ich finde es ≪very nice and delightful≫ einen Vortrag halten zu dürfen. (Die Alpen, 1925) *(EN : ... and I find it very nice and delightful to be allowed to give a talk.)*

where the German sentence contains an English phrase in quotation marks. Obviously, a German PoS tagger will produce nonsense tags for the English phrase as the words will be unknown to it. PoS taggers are good at tagging single unknown words based on the surrounding context, but most taggers fail miserably when a sequence of two or more words is unknown. The upper half of figure 2 shows the PoS tagger output for the above example. The words *very, nice, delightful* are senselessly tagged as proper names (NE), only *and* is tagged as foreign word (FM).

Our goal is to detect all intra-sentential code-switches and to annotate them as exemplified in the lower half of figure 2. They shall be framed with the TEI-conformant tag `<foreign>` which also shall specify the language of the foreign language segment. All tokens in the segment shall be tagged as foreign words (e.g. FM in the German STTS tag set, ET in the French Le Monde tag set (Abeillé et al., 2003)), and each lemma shall get

1. Romansh is the 4th official language in Switzerland. It is spoken by around 25,000 people in the mountainous South-Eastern canton of Graubünden.

Proceedings of The First Workshop on Computational Approaches to Code Switching, pages 24–33,
October 25, 2014, Doha, Qatar.

the special symbol @fn@ to set it apart from lemmas of the surrounding sentence. In this paper we report on our experiments towards this goal and suggest an algorithm for detecting code-switching.

We adopt a wide definition of code-switching. We are interested in detecting all instances where a text is in a dominant language and contains words, phrases and sentences in another language. Though our definition is broad, it is clearly more restricted than others, as e.g. the definition by Kracht and Klein (2014) which includes special purpose codes like bank account numbers or shoe sizes.

In this paper we will give an overview of the language mix in the yearbooks of the Swiss Alpine Club over the 150 years, and we will illustrate how we identified inter-sentential and intra-sentential code-switching. We will give a quantitative overview of the number of code-switching candidates that we automatically located.

2 The Text+Berg Corpus

The Text+Berg corpus comprises the annual publications of the Swiss Alpine Club (SAC) from its first edition in 1864 until 2013. From the start until 1923 the official yearbook was called "Jahrbuch des Schweizer Alpen-Club" (EN : yearbook of the Swiss Alpine Club), and it typically consisted of 500 to 700 pages. The articles of these first 60 years were mostly in German (with 86% of the words), but some also in French (13% of the words) and few in Italian and Romansh (Volk et al., 2010).

Interestingly, the German articles contained passages in French and sometimes other languages (e.g. English, Swiss German, Latin) without translations, and vice versa. Obviously, the article authors and yearbook editors assumed that the readers of the yearbook were polyglott at least in English, French, German and Latin during that time. In fact, the members of the SAC in the 19th century came from an academic elite. Mountain exploration was a past-time of the rich and educated.

Still, during that same time the French-speaking sections of the Swiss Alpine Club published their own yearbook in parallel to the official yearbook and called it "Echo des Alpes". It started shortly after the official yearbook in the late 1860s and continued until 1923. Each "Echo des Alpes" yearbook contained between 300 to 600 pages adding up to a total of 22,582 pages with 7.4 million tokens, almost all in French with rare quotes in German.

As of 1925 the official SAC yearbook and the "Echo des Alpes" were merged into a new publication called "Die Alpen. Les Alpes. Le Alpi" (in German, French, Italian) which has been published ever since. Over the years it sometimes appeared as quarterly and sometimes as monthly magazine. Today it appears 12 times per year in magazine format. For the sake of simplicity we continue to call each annual volume a yearbook.

The merger in 1925 resulted in a higher percentage of French texts in the new yearbook. For example, the 1925 yearbook had around 143,000 words in German and 112,000 in French (56% to 44%). The ratio varied somewhat but was still at 64% to 36% in 1956.

From 1957 onwards, the SAC has published parallel (i.e. translated) French and German versions of the yearbooks. At the start of this new era only half of the articles were translated, the rest was printed in the original language in identical versions in the two language copies.

Over the next decade the number of translations increased and as of 1983 the yearbooks were completely translated between German and French. Few Italian articles were still published verbatim in both the French and German yearbooks. As of 2012 the SAC has launched an Italian language version of its monthly magazine so that now it produces French, German and Italian parallel texts.

In its latest release the Text+Berg corpus (comprising the SAC yearbooks, the ALPEN magazine and the Echo des Alpes) contains around 45.8 million tokens (after tokenization). French and German account for around 22 million tokens each, Italian accounts for 0.8 million tokens. The remainder goes to English, Latin, Romansh and Swiss German. The corpus is freely available for research purposes upon request.

3 Language Identification in the Text+Berg Corpus

We compiled the Text+Berg corpus by scanning all SAC yearbooks from 1864 until 2000 (around 100,000+ pages). Afterwards we employed commercial OCR software to convert the scan images into electronic text. We developed and applied techniques to automatically reduce the number of OCR errors (Volk et al., 2011).

We obtained the yearbooks from 2001 to

> de la publication du *Mount Everest 1938* [2] de Tilman. L'*Appendix B*, intitulé: *Antropology* or *Zoology, with Particular Reference to the Abominable Snowman*, reprend la question ab *ovo* [3], en la soumettant, pp. 127–137, à une enquête strictement impartiale.
>
> La conclusion de cette enquête est résumée dans les sept dernières lignes de la page 137:
>
> «I merely affirm that traces for which no adequate explanation is forthcoming have been seen and will continue to be seen in various parts of the Himalaya, and until a worthier claimant is found we may as well attribute them to the ‚Abominable snowman'. *And I think he would be a bold and in some ways an impious sceptic who, after balancing the evidence, does not decide to give him the benefit of the doubt* [4].»
>
> *Conclusion:* Devant l'opinion fortement documentée et motivée de Tilman, peut-être

FIGURE 1 – Example of an English title and an English quote in a French text (Die Alpen, 1955)

```
<w n="23-16-21" lemma="und"      pos="KON">und</w>
<w n="23-16-22" lemma="ich"      pos="PPER">ich</w>
<w n="23-16-23" lemma="finden"   pos="VVFIN">finde</w>
<w n="23-16-24" lemma="es"       pos="PPER">es</w>
<w n="23-16-25" lemma="«"        pos="$(">«</w>
<w n="23-16-26" lemma="unk"      pos="NE">very</w>
<w n="23-16-27" lemma="unk"      pos="NE">nice</w>
<w n="23-16-28" lemma="and"      pos="FM">and</w>
<w n="23-16-29" lemma="unk"      pos="NE">delightful</w>
<w n="23-16-30" lemma="»"        pos="$(">»</w>
<w n="23-16-31" lemma="ein"      pos="ART">einen</w>
<w n="23-16-32" lemma="Vortrag"  pos="NN">Vortrag</w>
<w n="23-16-33" lemma="halten"   pos="VVINF">halten</w>
<w n="23-16-34" lemma="zu"       pos="PTKZU">zu</w>
<w n="23-16-35" lemma="dürfen"   pos="VMINF">dürfen</w>
<w n="23-16-36" lemma="."        pos="$.">.</w>

============= after code-switch detection =============

<w n="23-16-21" lemma="und"      pos="KON">und</w>
<w n="23-16-22" lemma="ich"      pos="PPER">ich</w>
<w n="23-16-23" lemma="finden"   pos="VVFIN">finde</w>
<w n="23-16-24" lemma="es"       pos="PPER">es</w>
<foreign lang="en">
    <w n="23-16-25" lemma="«"     pos="$(">«</w>
    <w n="23-16-26" lemma="@fn@"  pos="FM">very</w>
    <w n="23-16-27" lemma="@fn@"  pos="FM">nice</w>
    <w n="23-16-28" lemma="@fn@"  pos="FM">and</w>
    <w n="23-16-29" lemma="@fn@"  pos="FM">delightful</w>
    <w n="23-16-30" lemma="»"     pos="$(">»</w>
</foreign>
<w n="23-16-31" lemma="ein"      pos="ART">einen</w>
<w n="23-16-32" lemma="Vortrag"  pos="NN">Vortrag</w>
<w n="23-16-33" lemma="halten"   pos="VVINF">halten</w>
<w n="23-16-34" lemma="zu"       pos="PTKZU">zu</w>
<w n="23-16-35" lemma="dürfen"   pos="VMINF">dürfen</w>
<w n="23-16-36" lemma="."        pos="$.">.</w>
```

FIGURE 2 – Example of an annotated German sentence with English segment, before and after code-switch detection (Die Alpen, 1925)

2009 as PDF documents which we automatically converted to text. The subsequent yearbooks from 2010 until 2013 we received as XML files from the SAC.

We have turned the whole corpus into a uniform XML format. For this, the OCR output texts as well as the texts converted from PDF and XML are structured and annotated by automatically marking article boundaries, by tokenization, language identification, Part-of-Speech tagging and lemmatization. Our processing pipeline also includes toponym recognition and geo-coding of mountains, glaciers, cabins, valleys, lakes and towns. Furthermore we recognize and co-reference person names (Ebling et al., 2011), and we annotate temporal expressions (date, time, duration and set) with a variant of HeidelTime (Rettich, 2013). Finally we analyze the parallel parts of our corpus and provide sentence alignment information that is computed via BLEUalign (Sennrich and Volk, 2011).

In order to process our texts with language-specific tools (e.g. PoS tagging and person name recognition) we employed automatic language identification on the sentence level. We used Lingua-Ident[2] (developed by Michael Piotrowski) to determine for each sentence in our corpus whether it is in English, French, German, Italian or Romansh. Lingua-Ident is a statistical language identifier based on letter n-gram frequencies. For long sentences it reliably distinguishes between the languages. Unfortunately it often misclassifies short sentences. Therefore we decided to use it only for sentences with more than 40 characters. Shorter sentences are assigned the language of the article. This can be problematic for mixed language articles. An alternative strategy would be to assign the language of the previous sentence to short sentences.

For sentences that Lingua-Ident judges as German we run a second classifier that distinguishes between Standard German and Swiss German dialect text. Since there are no writing rules for Swiss German dialects, they come in a variety of spellings. We have compiled a list of typical Swiss German words (e.g. Swiss-German : *chli, chlii, chlini, chline* = German : *klein, kleine* = English : *small*) that are not used in Standard German in order to identify Swiss German sentences.[3]

Based on the language tag of each sentence we are able to investigate coarse-grained code-switching. Whenever the language of a sentence deviates from the language of the article, we have a candidate for code-switching. For example, in the yearbook 1867 we find a German text (describing the activities of the club) with a French quote :

> Der Berichterstatter bemerkt darüber : "On peut remarquer à cette occasion qu'il est rare que par un effort de l'esprit on puisse mettre du brouillard en bouteille, et ..." Die etwas ältere Sektion Diablerets, deren Steuer Herr August Bernus mit kundiger Hand ...

Most code-switching occurs with direct speech, quotes and book titles. The communicative goal is obviously to make the text more authentic.

4 Related Work on Detection of Code-Switching

Most previous work on automatically detecting code-switching focused on the switches between two known languages (whereas we have to deal with a mix of 6 languages).

Solorio and Liu (2008) worked on real-time prediction of code-switching points in Spanish-English conversations. This means that the judgement whether the current word is in a different language than the language of the matrix clause can only be based on the previous words. They use the PoS tag and its probability plus the lemma as provided by both the Spanish and the English Tree-Tagger as well as the position of the word in the Beginning-Inside-Outside scheme as features for making the decision. In order to keep the number of experiments manageable they restricted their history to one or two preceding words. As an interesting experiment they generated code-switching sentences Spanish-English based on their different predictors and asked human judges to rate the naturalness of the resulting sentences. This helped them to identify the most useful code-switching predictor.

Vu et al. (2013) and Adel et al. (2013) consider English-Mandarin code-switching in speech recognition. They investigate recurrent neural network language models and factored language models to the task in an attempt to integrate syntactic features. For the experiments they use SEAME,

2. http ://search.cpan.org/dist/Lingua-Ident/

3. We are aware that the Text+Berg corpus contains also occasional sentences (or sentence fragments) in other German dialects (e.g. Austrian German, Bavarian German) and in old German spellings. Since these varieties are rare in the corpus, we do not deal with them explicitly.

the South East Asia Mandarin-English speech corpus compiled from Singaporean and Malaysian speakers. It consists of spontaneous interviews and conversations. The transcriptions were cleaned and each word was manually tagged as English, Mandarin or other. The data consists of an intensive mix of the two languages with the average duration of both English and Mandarin segments to be less than a second (!). In order to assign PoS tags to this mixed language corpus, the authors applied two monolingual taggers and combined the results.

Huang and Yates (2014) also work on the detection of English-Chinese code-switching but not on speech but rather on web forum texts produced by Chinese speakers living in the US. They use statistical word alignment and a Chinese language model to substitute English words in Chinese sentences with suitable Chinese words. Preparing the data in this way significantly improved Machine Translation quality. Their approach is limited to two known languages and to very short code-switching phrases (typically only one word).

Tim Baldwin and his group (Hughes et al., 2006) have surveyed the approaches to language identification at the time. They found a number of missing issues, such as language identification for minority languages, open class language identification (in contrast to identification within a fixed set of languages), sparse training data, varying encodings, and multilingual documents. Subsequently they (Lui and Baldwin, 2011) introduced a system for language identification of 97 languages trained on a mixture of corpora from different domains. They claim that their system Langid is particularly well suited for classifying short input strings (as in Twitter messages). We therefore tested Langid in our experiments for code-switching detection.

5 Exploratory Experiments with the SAC Yearbook 1925

In order to assess the performance of Langid for the detection of code-switching we performed an exploratory experiment with the SAC yearbook 1925. We extracted all word sequences between pairs of quotation marks where at least one token had been assigned the "unknown" lemma by our PoS tagger. The "unknown" lemma indicates that this word sequence may come from a different language.

The word sequence had to be at least 4 characters long, thus skipping single letters and abbreviations. In this way we obtained 333 word sequences that are potential candidates for intra-sentential code-switching. We then ran these word sequences through the Langid language identification system with the restriction that we expect the word sequences only to be either English, French, German, Italian or Latin (Romansh and Swiss German are not included in Langid). For a given string Langid delivers the most likely language together with a confidence score.

We then compared the language predicted by the Langid system with the (automatically) computed language of the complete sentence. In 189 out of the 333 sentences the Langid output predicted a code-switch. We then manually graded all Langid judgements and found that 225 language judgements (67.5%) were correct. But only 89 of the 189 predicted code-switches came with the correct language. 40 of the 100 incorrect judgements were actually code-switches but with a different language. The remaining ones should have been classified with the same language as the surrounding sentence and are thus no examples of code-switching.

A closer inspection of the results revealed that the book contained not only code-switches in the expected 5 languages, but also into Romansh (6), Spanish (4) and Swiss-German (13). Obviously all of these were incorrectly classified. Most (8) of the Swiss-German word sequences were classified as German which could count as half correct, but the others were misclassified as English (among them a variant of the popular Swiss German farewell phrase *uf Wiederluege* spelled as *uf's Wiederluege*).

The Langid system has a tendency to classify word sequences as English. Many of the short, incorrectly classified word sequences were judged as English. It turns out that Langid judges even the empty string as English with a score of 9.06. Therefore all judgements with this score are dubious. We found that 56 short word sequences were classified as English with this score, out of which 35 were erroneously judged as English. Only strings with a length of 15 and more characters that are classified as English should be trusted. All others need to be discarded.

In general, if precision is the most important aspect, then Langid should only be used for strings

SAC yearbooks	candidates	predicted code-sw	correct	wrong lang	no code-sw
1868 to 1878	388	121	88	33	13
1926 to 1935	792	335	266	69	23
Total	1180	456	354	102	36

TABLE 1 – Recognition of code-switches in the Text+Berg corpus

with 20 or more characters. In our test set only 4 strings that were longer than 20 characters were incorrectly classified within the selected language set. Among the errors was the famous Latin phrase *conditio sine qua non* (length : 21 characters including blanks) which Langid incorrectly classified as Italian.

Another reason for the considerable number of misclassifications can be repeated occurrences of a word sequence. Our error count is a token-based count and thus prone to misclassified recurring phrases. In our experiment, Langid misclassified the French book name *Echo des Alpes* as Italian. Unfortunately this name occurs 18 times in our test set and thus accounts for 18 errors. We suspect that an *-o* at the end of a word is a strong indicator for Italian. In a short string like *Echo des Alpes* (14 characters), this can make the difference.

Another interesting observation is that hyphens speak for German. Our test set contains the hyphenated French string *vesse-de-neige* which Langid misclassifies as German with a clear margin over French. When the same string is analyzed without hyphens, then Langid correctly computes a preference for French over German. A similar observation comes from the Swiss German phrase *uf's Wiederluege* being classified as English when spelled with the apostrophe (which is less frequent in German than in English). Without the apostrophe Langid would count the string as German. With short strings like this, special symbols have a visible impact on the language identification.

We also observed that Langid is sensitive to all-caps capitalization. For example, *AUS DEM LEBEN DER GEBIRGSMUNDARTEN* (EN : The Lives of Mountain Dialects) is misclassified as English (with the default score) while *Aus dem Leben der Gebirgsmundarten* is correctly classified as German.

Overall, we found that code-switching within the same article rarely targets different languages. For example, if the article is in German and contains code-switches into English, then it hardly ever contains code-switches into other languages. In analogy to the one-sense-per-discourse hypothesis we might call this the one-code-switch-language-per-discourse hypothesis.

6 Detecting Intra-sentential Code-Switching

Based on exploratory studies and observations we decided on the following algorithm for detecting and annotating intra-sentential foreign language segments in the Text+Berg corpus. We search for sub-sentential token sequences (possibly of length 1) that are framed by a pair of quotation marks and that contain at least one "unknown" lemma. There must be at least two tokens outside of the quotation marks in the same sentence. As a compromise we restrict our detection to strings longer than 15 characters so that we get relatively reliable language judgements by Langid. The strings may consist of one token that is longer than 15 characters (e.g. *Matterhornhochtourist*) or a sequence of tokens whose sum of characters including blanks is more than 15. We feed these candidate strings to Langid for language identification and compare the output language with the language attribute of the surrounding sentence. If the languages are different, then we regard the token sequence as code-switch and mark it accordingly in XML as shown in figure 2.

In order to determine the **precision** of this algorithm, we checked 10 yearbooks from 1868 to 1878 (there was no yearbook in 1870) and from 1926 to 1935. The results are in table 1. From the 1180 code-switch candidates that we computed based on the above restrictions, Langid predicted 456 code-switches (39%). This means that in 39% of the cases Langid predicted a language that was different from the language of the surrounding sentence.

We manually evaluated all 456 predicted code-switches and found that 354 of them (78%) were correctly classified and labeled. These segments were indeed in a different language than the surrounding sentence and their language was correctly determined. For example, the French seg-

SAC yearbooks	> 15 characters without unknowns		≤ 15 characters	
	all	sample : TN/FN	all	sample : TN/FP
1868 to 1878	322	20/1	404	15/8
1926 to 1935	1944	78/1	1136	54/23
Total	2266	(2%) 98/2	1540	(31%) 69/31

TABLE 2 – Estimation of the loss of recall due to the filtering approach based on a random sample of 100 quotations for each filtering category (TN : true negatives, FN : false negatives)

ment in the following German sentence is correctly detected and classified :

> Anschliessend führte Ambros dasselbe Bergsteigertrio ≪dans des circonstances très défavorables≫ auf den Monte Rosa ... (Die Alpen, 1935) *(EN : Afterwards Ambros led the same 3 mountaineers ≪under very unfavorable conditions≫ onto Monte Rosa.)*

Out of the 102 segments whose language was wrongly classified, only 36 were no code-switches. For example, the Latin segment *cum grano salis africani* is indeed a code-switch in a German sentence although Langid incorrectly classifies it as English. In fact, our evaluation showed that Langid is "reluctant" to classify strings as Latin. Latin strings are often misclassified as English or Italian.

Overall this means that only 8% of the predicted code-switches are no code-switches. Therefore we can safely add the module for code-switch detection into our processing and annotation pipeline.

In order to estimate the **recall** of our quotation filtering approach we manually evaluated a sample of the quotations that our algorithm excluded. Table 2 presents the numbers for the two time periods for two cases : first for sequences that are longer than 15 characters and contain only known lemmas, second for sequences that are shorter than 16 characters and contain at least one "unknown" lemma. For both cases we checked 100 instances.

The evaluation for the quotations with more than 15 characters but with all known lemmas (no "unknown" lemma) shows only 2 false negatives. Therefore, we can conclude safely that most of the code-switches with more than 15 characters were included in our candidate set.

Table 2 also shows that there were 1540 quotations with 15 or less characters. The manual inspection of 100 randomly selected quotations revealed that 31 indeed include foreign material. Some of these quotations are geographic names, e.g. the valley *Bergell* (EN/IT : Val Bregaglia), where it is difficult to decide whether this should be regarded as a code-switch. For this evaluation, we sticked to the principle that a foreign geographic name in quotation marks counts as a code-switch. The number of missed code-switches is high (31%). However, due to the limited precision of Langid (and other character-based language identifiers) for short character sequences, we still consider our length threshold appropriate. A different approach to language identification is needed to reliably classify these short quotes.

7 Discussion

The correctly marked code-switches in our test periods can be split by language of the matrix sentence and the language of the sub-sentential segment (= the code-switch segment). Table 3 gives an overview of the types of code-switches for the two periods under investigation. We see clearly that code-switches from German to English were rare in the 19th century (8 out of 89 = 9%) but became much more popular in the 1920s and 1930s (61 out of 265 = 23%). This came at the cost of French which lost ground from 54% (48 out of 89) to 40% (106 out of 265).

One can only compare the code-switch numbers from German with the corresponding numbers from French after normalizing the numbers in relation to the overall amount of text in German and French. During the first period (1868 to 1878) we count roughly 200,000 tokens in French and 1.4 million tokens in German, whereas in the second period (1926 to 1935) we have around 1 million tokens in French and again 1.4 million tokens in German. For the first period we find 87 code-switches (triggered by quotation marks) in the 1.4 million German tokens compared to 189 code-switches in the second period. The num-

sent lang	segm lang	1868 to 1878	1926 to 1935
de	en	8	61
de	fr	48	106
de	it	24	19
de	la	7	3
fr	de	2	35
fr	en	-	20
fr	it	-	11
fr	la	-	2
it	de	-	3
it	en	-	2
it	fr	-	3
Total		89	265

TABLE 3 – Correctly detected code-switches in the Text+Berg corpus

sent lang	segm lang	1868 to 1878	1926 to 1935
de	en	13	23
de	fr	9	5
de	it	8	12
de	la	2	1
fr	de	-	7
fr	en	1	10
fr	it	-	8
fr	la	-	1
it	en	-	2
Total		33	69

TABLE 4 – Incorrectly labeled code-switches in the Text+Berg corpus

correct segm	Langid prediction					
lang	en	it	fr	la	de	Total
la	15	12	3		1	31
de	7	5	5	1		18
fr	7	3				10
it	6					6
es	3	1		2		6
rm		1	2			3
ru	1					1
id	1					1
Total	40	22	10	3	1	76

TABLE 5 – Confusion matrix for incorrectly labeled code-switches in the periods 1868 to 1878 and 1926 to 1935

ber of code-switches have clearly increased. For French we observe the same trend with 2 code-switches in 200'000 words in the first period compared to 68 code-switches in the 1 million tokens in the second period.

There is also a striking difference between French and German with many more code-switches in German than in French. For instance, for German we find 135 code-switches per 1 million tokens in the second period vs. 68 code-switches per 1 million tokens for French.

One surprising finding were the code-switches into Latin. We had not noticed them before, since our corpus does not contain longer passages of Latin text. But this study shows that code-switches into Latin persisted into the 1920s (3 out of German and 2 out of French).

On the negative side (cf. table 4), misclassifying segments as English is the most frequent cause for a wrong language assignment in both periods. Table 5 shows the confusion matrix which contrasts the manually determined segment language with the incorrect language predicted by Langid. This confirms that Langid has a tendency to classify short text segments as English. But there are also a number of errors for Latin being mistaken for Italian, and German being mistaken for Italian or French.

As a general remark, it should be noted that an n-gram-based language identifier has advantages over a lexicon-based language identifier in the face of OCR errors. In the yearbook 1926 we observed the rare case of a whole English sentence having been contracted to one token *Ilovetobemothered.* Still, our code-switch detector recognizes this as an English string.[4]

8 Conclusions

We have described our efforts in language identification in a multilingual corpus of Alpine texts. As part of corpus annotation we have identified the language of each corpus sentence amongst English, French, Standard German, Swiss German,

4. The complete sentence is : *Un long Anglais, avec lequel, dans le hall familial, je m'essaie à échanger laborieusement quelques impressions à ce sujet, me dit : ≪I love to be mothered.≫*

Italian and Romansh. Furthermore we have developed an algorithm to identify intra-sentential code-switching by analyzing sentence parts in quotation marks that contain "unknown" lemmas.

We have shown that token sequences that amount to 15 or more characters can be judged by a state-of-the-art language identifier and will result in 78% correctly labeled code-switches. Another 14% are code-switches but with a language different from the auto-assigned language. Only 8% are not code-switches at all.

There are many ways to continue and extend this research. We have not included language identification for Swiss German nor for Romansh in the intra-sentential code-switch experiments reported in this paper. We will train language models for these two languages and add them to Langid to check the impact on the recognition accuracy. Since code-switches into Romansh are rare, and since Romansh can easily be confused with Italian, it is questionable whether the addition of this language model will have a positive influence.

We have used the "general-purpose" language identifier Langid in these experiments. It will be interesting to investigate language identifiers that are optimized for short text fragments as discussed by Vatanen et al. (2010). Given the relatively high number of short quotations (31%) that contain code-switches, recall could improve considerably.

In this paper we have focused solely on code-switching candidates that are triggered by pairs of quotation marks. In order to increase the recall we will certainly enlarge the set of triggers to other indicators such as parentheses or commas. We have briefly looked at parentheses as trigger symbols and found them clearly less productive than quotation marks. To also find code-switches that have no overt marker remains the ultimate goal.

Finally, we will exploit the parallel parts of our corpus. If a sentence in German contains a French segment, then it is likely that this French segment occurs verbatim in the parallel French sentence. Based on sentence and word alignment we will search for identical phrases in both language versions. We hope that this will lead to high accuracy code-switch data that we can use as training material for machine learning experiments.

Acknowledgments

We would like to thank Michi Amsler and Don Tuggener for useful comments on literature and tools for language identification and code-switching, as well as Patricia Scheurer for comments and suggestions on the language use in the SAC corpus. This research was supported by the Swiss National Science Foundation under grant CRSII2_147653/1 through the project "MODERN : Modelling discourse entities and relations for coherent machine translation".

References

Anne Abeillé, Lionel Clément, and Francois Toussenel. 2003. Building a Treebank for French. In Anne Abeillé, editor, *Building and Using Parsed Corpora*, volume 20 of *Text, Speech and Language Technology*, chapter 10, pages 165–187. Kluwer, Dordrecht.

Heike Adel, Ngoc Thang Vu, and Tanja Schultz. 2013. Combination of recurrent neural networks and factored language models for code-switching language modeling. In *Proceedings of the 51st Annual Meeting of the Association for Computational Linguistics (ACL)*, Sofia.

Sarah Ebling, Rico Sennrich, David Klaper, and Martin Volk. 2011. Digging for names in the mountains : Combined person name recognition and reference resolution for German alpine texts. In *Proceedings of The 5th Language & Technology Conference : Human Language Technologies as a Challenge for Computer Science and Linguistics*, Poznan.

Fei Huang and Alexander Yates. 2014. Improving word alignment using linguistic code switching data. In *Proceedings of the 14th Conference of the European Chapter of the Association for Computational Linguistics*, pages 1–9, Göteborg.

Baden Hughes, Timothy Baldwin, Steven Bird, Jeremy Nicholson, and Andrew Mackinlay. 2006. Reconsidering language identification for written language resources. In *Proceedings of LREC 2006*, pages 485–488, Genoa.

Marcus Kracht and Udo Klein. 2014. The grammar of code switching. *Journal of Logic, Language and Information*, 23(3) :313–329.

Marco Lui and Timothy Baldwin. 2011. Cross-domain feature selection for language identification. In *Proceedings of 5th International Joint Conference on Natural Language Processing*, pages 553–561, Chiang Mai, Thailand. Asian Federation of Natural Language Processing.

Katrin Rettich. 2013. Automatische Annotation von deutschen und französischen temporalen Ausdrücken im Text+Berg-Korpus. Master thesis, Universität Zürich, Institut für Computerlinguistik.

Rico Sennrich and Martin Volk. 2011. Iterative, MT-based sentence alignment of parallel texts.

In *Proceedings of The 18th International Nordic Conference of Computational Linguistics (Nodalida)*, Riga.

Thamar Solorio and Yang Liu. 2008. Learning to predict code-switching points. In *Proceedings of the Conference on Empirical Methods in Natural Language Processing*, pages 973–981, Honolulu. Association for Computational Linguistics.

Tommi Vatanen, Jaakko J. Väyrynen, and Sami Virpioja. 2010. Language identification of short text segments with n-gram models. In *Proceedings of LREC*, pages 3423–3430, Malta.

Martin Volk, Noah Bubenhofer, Adrian Althaus, Maya Bangerter, Lenz Furrer, and Beni Ruef. 2010. Challenges in building a multilingual alpine heritage corpus. In *Proceedings of LREC*, Valletta, Malta.

Martin Volk, Lenz Furrer, and Rico Sennrich. 2011. Strategies for reducing and correcting OCR errors. In C. Sporleder, A. van den Bosch, and K. Zervanou, editors, *Language Technology for Cultural Heritage : Selected Papers from the LaTeCH Workshop Series*, Theory and Applications of Natural Language Processing, pages 3–22. Springer-Verlag, Berlin.

Ngoc Thang Vu, Heike Adel, and Tanja Schultz. 2013. An investigation of code-switching attitude dependent language modeling. In *Statistical Language and Speech Processing*, pages 297–308. Springer.

Exploration of the Impact of Maximum Entropy in Recurrent Neural Network Language Models for Code-Switching Speech

Ngoc Thang Vu[1,2] **and Tanja Schultz**[1]
[1]Karlsruhe Institute of Technology (KIT), [2]University of Munich (LMU), Germany
thangvu@cis.lmu.de, tanja.schultz@kit.edu

Abstract

This paper presents our latest investigations of the jointly trained maximum entropy and recurrent neural network language models for Code-Switching speech. First, we explore extensively the integration of part-of-speech tags and language identifier information in recurrent neural network language models for Code-Switching. Second, the importance of the maximum entropy model is demonstrated along with a various of experimental results. Finally, we propose to adapt the recurrent neural network language model to different Code-Switching behaviors and use them to generate artificial Code-Switching text data.

1 Introduction

The term Code-Switching (CS) denotes speech which contains more than one language. Speakers switch their language while they are talking. This phenomenon appears very often in multilingual communities, such as in India, Hong Kong or Singapore. Furthermore, it increasingly occurs in former monolingual cultures due to the strong growth of globalization. In many contexts and domains, speakers switch more often between their native language and English within their utterances than in the past. This is a challenge for speech recognition systems which are typically monolingual. While there have been promising approaches to handle Code-Switching in the field of acoustic modeling, language modeling is still a great challenge. The main reason is a shortage of training data. Whereas about 50h of training data might be sufficient for the estimation of acoustic models, the transcriptions of these data are not enough to build reliable language models. In this paper, we focus on exploring and improving the language model for Code-switching speech and as a result improve the automatic speech recognition (ASR) system on Code-Switching speech.

The main contribution of the paper is the extensive investigation of jointly trained maximum entropy (ME) and recurrent neural language models (RNN LMs) for Code-Switching speech. We revisit the integration of part-of-speech (POS) tags and language identifier (LID) information in recurrent neural network language models and the impact of maximum entropy on the language model performance. As follow-up to our previous work in (Adel, Vu et al., 2013), here we investigate whether a recurrent neural network alone without using ME is a suitable model for Code-Switching speech. Afterwards, to directly use the RNN LM in the decoding process of an ASR system, we convert the RNN LM into the n-gram language model using the text generation approach (Deoras et al., 2011; Adel et al., 2014); Furthermore motivated by the fact that Code-Switching is speaker dependent (Auer, 1999b; Vu et al., 2013), we first adapt the recurrent neural network language model to different Code-Switching behaviors and then generate artificial Code-Switching text data. This allows us to train an accurate n-gram model which can be used directly during decoding to improve ASR performance.

The paper is organized as follows: Section 2 gives a short overview of related works. In Section 3, we describe the jointly trained maximum entropy and recurrent neural network language models and their extension for Code-Switching speech. Section 4 gives a short description of the SEAME corpus. In Section 5, we summarize the most important experiments and results. The study is concluded in Section 6 with a summary.

2 Related Work

This section gives a brief introduction about the related research regarding Code-Switching and re-

Proceedings of The First Workshop on Computational Approaches to Code Switching, pages 34–41,
October 25, 2014, Doha, Qatar.

current language models.
In (Muysken, 2000; Poplack, 1978; Bokamba, 1989), the authors observed that code switches occur at positions in an utterance following syntactical rules of the involved languages. Code-Switching can be regarded as a speaker dependent phenomenon (Auer, 1999b; Vu et al., 2013). However, several particular Code-Switching patterns are shared across speakers (Poplack, 1980). Furthermore, part-of-speech tags might be useful features to predict Code-Switching points. The authors of (Solorio et al., 2008b; Solorio et al., 2008a) investigate several linguistic features, such as word form, LID, POS tags or the position of the word relative to the phrase for Code-Switching prediction. Their best result is obtained by combining all those features. (Chan et al., 2006) compare four different kinds of n-gram language models to predict Code-Switching. They discover that clustering all foreign words into their POS classes leads to the best performance. In (Li et al., 2012; Li et al., 2013), the authors propose to integrate the equivalence constraint into language modeling for Mandarin and English Code-Switching speech recorded in Hong Kong.

In the last years, neural networks have been used for a variety of tasks, including language modeling (Mikolov et al., 2010). Recurrent neural networks are able to handle long-term contexts since the input vector does not only contain the current word but also the previous hidden layer. It is shown that these networks outperform traditional language models, such as n-grams which only contain very limited histories. In (Mikolov et al., 2011a), the network is extended by factorizing the output layer into classes to accelerate the training and testing processes. The input layer can be augmented to model features, such as POS tags (Shi et al., 2011; Adel, Vu et al., 2013). Furthermore, artificial text can be automatically generated using recurrent neural networks to enlarge the amount of training data (Deoras et al., 2011; Adel et al., 2014).

3 Joint maximum entropy and recurrent neural networks language models for Code-Switching

3.1 Recurrent neural network language models

The idea of RNN LMs is illustrated in Figure 1. Vector $w(t)$ forms the input of the recurrent neural network. It represents the current word using 1-of-N coding. Thus, its dimension equals the size of the vocabulary. Vector $s(t)$ contains the state of the network - 'hidden layer'. The network is trained using back-propagation through time (BPTT), an extension of the back-propagation algorithm for recurrent neural networks. With BPTT, the error is propagated through recurrent connections back in time for a specific number of time steps t. Hence, the network is able to capture a longer history than a traditional n-gram LM. The matrices U, V and W contain the weights for the connections between the layers. These weights are learned during the training phase.

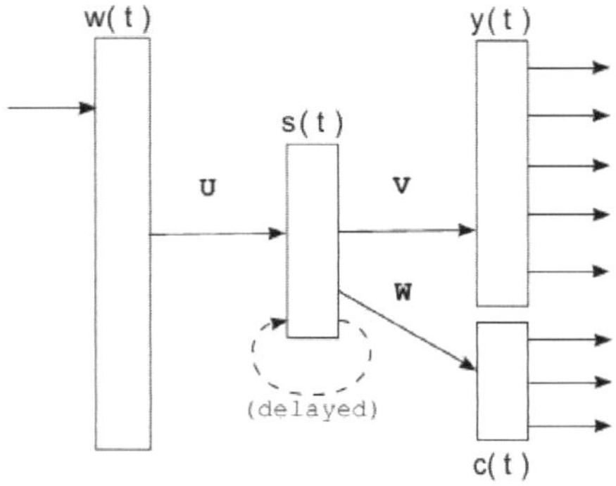

Figure 1: RNN language model

To accelerate the training process, (Mikolov et al., 2011a) factorized the output layer into classes based on simple frequency binning. Every word belongs to exactly one class. Vector $c(t)$ contains the probabilities for each class and vector $w(t)$ provides the probabilities for each word given its class. Hence, the probability $P(w_i|history)$ is computed as shown in equation 1.

$$P(w_i|history) = P(c_i|s(t))P(w_i|c_i, s(t)) \quad (1)$$

Furthermore in (Mikolov et al., 2011b), the authors proposed to jointly train the RNN with ME - *RMM-ME* - to improve the language model and also ASR performance. The ME can be seen as a weight matrix which directly connects the input with the output layer as well as the input with the class layer. This weight matrix can be trained jointly with the recurrent neural network. "Direct-order" and "direct connection" are the two important parameters which define the length of history and the number of the trained connections.

3.2 Code-Switching language models

To adapt RNN LMs to the Code-Switching task, (Adel, Vu et al., 2013) analyzed the SEAME corpus and observed that there are words and POS tags which might have a high potential to predict Code-Switching points. Therefore, it has been proposed to integrate the POS and LID information into the RNN LM. The idea is to factorize the output layer into classes which provide language information. By doing that, it is intended to not only predict the next word but also the next language. Hence according to equation 1, the probability of the next language is computed first and then the probability of each word given the language. In that work, four classes were used: English, Mandarin, other languages and particles. Moreover, a vector $f(t)$ which contains the POS information is added to the input layer. This vector provides the corresponding POS of the current word. Thus, not only the current word is activated but also its features. Since the POS tags are integrated into the input layer, they are also propagated into the hidden layer and back-propagated into its history $s(t)$. Hence, not only the previous features are stored in the history but also features from several time steps in the past.

In addition to that previous work, the experiments in this paper aim to explore the source of the improvements observed in (Adel, Vu et al., 2013). We now clearly distinguish between the impacts due to the long but unordered history of the RNN and the effects of the maximum entropy model which also captures information about the most recent word and POS tag in the history.

4 SEAME corpus

To conduct research on Code-Switching speech we use the SEAME corpus (South East Asia Mandarin-English). It is a conversational Mandarin-English Code-Switching speech corpus recorded by (D.C. Lyu et al., 2011). Originally, it was used for the research project "Code-Switch" which was jointly performed by Nanyang Technological University (NTU) and Karlsruhe Institute of Technology (KIT) from 2009 until 2012. The corpus contains 63 hours of audio data which has been recorded and manually transcribed in Singapore and Malaysia. The recordings consist of spontaneously spoken interviews and conversations. The words can be divided into four language categories: English words (34.3% of all tokens), Mandarin words (58.6%), particles (Singaporean and Malayan discourse particles, 6.8% of all tokens) and others (other languages, 0.4% of all tokens). In total, the corpus contains 9,210 unique English and 7,471 unique Mandarin words. The Mandarin character sequences have been segmented into words manually. The language distribution shows that the corpus does not contain a clearly predominant language. Furthermore, the number of Code-Switching points is quite high: On average, there are 2.6 switches between Mandarin and English per utterance. Additionally, the duration of the monolingual segments is rather short: More than 82% of the English segments and 73% of the Mandarin segments last less than one second. The average duration of English and Mandarin segments is only 0.67 seconds and 0.81 seconds, respectively. This corresponds to an average length of monolingual segments of 1.8 words in English and 3.6 words in Mandarin.

For the task of language modeling and speech recognition, the corpus has been divided into three disjoint sets: training, development and evaluation set. The data is assigned to the three different sets based on the following criteria: a balanced distribution of gender, speaking style, ratio of Singaporean and Malaysian speakers, ratio of the four language categories, and the duration in each set. Table 1 lists the statistics of the SEAME corpus.

	Training	Dev	Eval
# Speakers	139	8	8
Duration(hours)	59.2	2.1	1.5
# Utterances	48,040	1,943	1,029
# Words	575,641	23,293	11,541

Table 1: Statistics of the SEAME corpus

5 Experiments and Results

This section presents all the experiments and results regarding language models and ASR on the development and the evaluation set of the SEAME corpus. However, the parameters were tuned only on the development set.

5.1 LM experiments

5.1.1 Baseline n-gram

The n-gram language model served as the baseline in this work. We used the SRI language model toolkit (Stolcke, 2002) to build the CS 3-gram baseline from the SEAME training transcriptions containing all words of the transcriptions. Modified Kneser-Ney smoothing (Rosenfeld, 2000) was applied. In total, the vocabulary size is around 16k words. The perplexities (PPLs) are 268.4 and 282.9 on the development and evaluation set respectively.

5.1.2 Exploration of ME and of the integration of POS and LID in RNN

To investigate the effect of POS and LID integration into the RNN LM and the importance of the ME, different RNN LMs were trained.

The first experiment aims at investigating the importance of using LID information for output layer factorization. All the results are summarized in table 2. The first RNNLM was trained with a hidden layer of 50 nodes and without using output factorization and ME. The PPLs were 250.8 and 301.1 on the development and evaluation set, respectively. We observed some gains in terms of PPL on the development set but not on the evaluation set compared to the n-gram LM. Even using ME and factorizing the output layer into four classes based on frequency binning (fb), the same trend could be noticed - only the PPL on the development set was improved. Four classes were used to have a fair comparison with the output factorization with LID. However after including the LID information into the output layer, the PPLs were improved on both data sets. On top of that, using ME provides some additional gains. The results indicate that LID is a useful information source for the Code-Switching task. Furthermore, the improvements are independent of the application of ME.

Model	Dev	Eval
CS 3-gram	268.4	282.9
RNN LM	250.8	301.1
RNN-ME LM	246.6	287.9
RNN LM with fb	246.0	287.3
RNN-ME LM with fb	256.0	294.0
RNN LM with LID	241.5	274.4
RNN-ME LM with LID	**237.9**	**269.3**

Table 2: Effect of output layer factorization

In the second experiment we investigated the use of POS information and the effect of the ME. The results in Table 3 show that an integration of POS without ME did not give any further improvement compared to RNN LM. The reason could lie in the fact that a RNN can capture a long history but not the information of the word order. Note that in the syntactic context, the word order is one of the most important information. However using ME allows using the POS of the previous time step to predict the next language and also the next word, the PPL was improved significantly on development and evaluation set. These results reveal that POS is a reasonable trigger event which can be used to support Code-Switching prediction.

Model	Dev	Eval
CS 3-gram	268.4	282.9
RNN LM	250.8	301.1
RNN-ME LM	246.6	287.9
RNN LM with POS	250.6	298.3
RNN-ME LM with POS	**233.5**	**268.0**

Table 3: Effect of ME on the POS integration into the input layer

Finally, we trained an LM by integrating the POS tags and factorizing the output layer with LID information. Again without applying ME, we observed that POS information is not helpful to improve the RNN LM. Using the ME provides a big gain in terms of PPL on both data sets. We obtained a PPL of 219.8 and 239.2 on the development and evaluation set respectively.

Model	Dev	Eval
CS 3-gram	268.4	282.9
RNN LM	250.8	301.1
RNN-ME LM	246.6	287.9
RNN LM with POS + LID	243.9	277.1
RNN-ME LM with POS+ LID	**219.8**	**239.2**

Table 4: Effect of ME on the integration of POS and the output layer factorization using LID

5.1.3 Training parameters

Moreover, we investigated the effect of different parameters, such as the backpropagation through time (BPTT) step, the direct connection order and the amount of direct connections on the performance of the RNN-ME LMs. Therefore, different LMs were trained with varying values for these parameters. For each parameter change, the remaining parameters were fixed to the most suitable value which has been found so far.

First, we varied the BPTT step from 1 to 5. The BPTT step defines the length of the history which is incorporated to update the weight matrix of the

RNN. The larger the BPTT step is, the longer is the history which is used for learning. Table 5 shows the perplexities on the SEAME development and evaluation sets with different BPTT steps. The results indicate that increasing BPTT might improve the PPL. The best PPL can be obtained with a BPTT step of 4. The big loss in terms of PPL by using a BPTT step of 5 indicates that too long histories might hurt the language model performance. Another reason might be the limitation of the training data.

BPTT	1	2	3	4	5
Dev	244.7	224.6	222.8	**219.8**	266.8
Eval	281.1	241.4	242.8	**239.2**	284.5

Table 5: Effect of the BPTT step

It has been shown in the previous section, that ME is very important to improve the PPL especially for the Code-Switching task, we also trained several RNN-ME LMs with various values for "direct order" and "direct connection". Table 6 and 7 summarize the PPL on the SEAME development and evaluation set. The results reveal that the larger the direct order is, the lower is the PPL. We observed consistent PPL improvement by increasing the direct order. However, the gain seems to be saturated after a direct order of 3 or 4. In this paper, we choose to use a direct order of 4 to train the final model.

Direct order	1	2	3	4
Dev	238.6	231.7	220.5	**219.8**
Eval	271.8	261.4	240.7	**239.2**

Table 6: Effect of the direct order

Since the "direct order" is related to the length of the context, the size of the "direct connection" is a trade off between the size of the language model and also the amount of the training data. Higher "direct connection" leads to a larger model and might improve the PPL if the amount of training data is enough to train all the direct connection weights. The results with four different data points (50M, 100M, 150M and 200M) show that the best model can be obtained on SEAME data set by using 100M of direct connection.

5.1.4 Artificial Code-Switching text generation using RNN

The RNN LM demonstrates a great improvement over the traditional n-gram language model. However, it is inefficient to use the RNN LM directly in the decoding process of an ASR system. In order to convert the RNN into a n-gram language model, a text generation method which was proposed in (Deoras et al., 2011) can be applied. Moreover, it allows to generate more training data which might be useful to improve the data sparsity of the language modeling task for Code-Switching speech. In (Deoras et al., 2011), the authors applied the Gibb sampling method to generate artificial text based on the probability distribution provided by the RNNs. We applied that technique in (Adel et al., 2014) to generate Code-Switching data and were able to improve the PPL and ASR performance on CS speech. In addition to that previous work, we now propose to use several Code-Switching attitude dependent language models instead of the final best RNN LM.

#Connection	50M	100M	150M	200M
Dev	226.2	**219.8**	224.7	224.6
Eval	244.7	**239.2**	243.7	242.0

Table 7: Effect of the number of direct connections

Code-Switching attitude dependent language modeling Since POS tags might have a potential to predict Code-Switch points, (Vu et al., 2013) performed an analysis of these trigger POS tags on a speaker level. The CS rate for each tag was computed for each speaker. Afterwards, we calculated the minimum, maximum and mean values as well as standard deviations. We observed that the spread between minimum and maximum values is quite high for most of the tags. It indicates that although POS information may trigger a CS event, it is rather speaker dependent.

Motivated by this observation, we performed k-mean clustering of the training text into three different portions of text data which describe different Code-Switching behaviors (Vu et al., 2013). Afterwards, the LM was adapted with each text portion to obtain Code-Switching attitude dependent language models. By using these models, we could improve both PPL and ASR performance for each speaker.

Artificial text generation To generate artificial text, we first adapted the best RNN-ME LM described in the previous section to three different Code-Switching attitudes. Afterwards, we generated three different text corpora based on these specific Code-Switching attitudes. Each corpus contains 100M tokens. We applied the SRILM toolkit (Stolcke, 2002) to train n-gram language model and interpolated them linearly with the weight $= \frac{1}{3}$. Table 8 shows the perplexity of the resulting n-gram models on the SEAME development and evaluation set. To make a comparison, we also used the unadapted best RNN-ME LM to generate two different texts, one with 300M tokens and another one with 235M tokens (Adel et al., 2014). The results show that the n-gram LMs trained with only the artificial text data can not outperform the baseline CS 3-gram. However they provide some complementary information to the baseline CS 3-gram LM. Therefore, when we interpolated them with the baseline CS 3-gram, the PPL was improved all the cases. Furthermore by using the Code-Switching attitude dependent language models to generate artificial CS text data, the PPL was slightly improved compared to using the unadapted one. The final 3-gram model (*Final 3-gram*) was built by interpolating all the Code-Switching attitude dependent 3-gram and the baseline CS 3-gram. It has a PPL of 249.3 and 266.9 on the development set and evaluation set.

Models	Dev	Eval
CS 3-gram	268.4	282.9
300M words text	391.3	459.5
+ CS 3-gram	250.0	270.9
235M words text	385.1	454.6
+ CS 3-gram	249.5	270.5
100M words text I	425.4	514.4
+ CS 3-gram	251.4	274.5
100M words text II	391.8	421.6
+ CS 3-gram	251.6	266.4
100M words text III	390.3	428.1
+ CS 3-gram	250.6	266.9
Interpolation of I, II and III	377.5	416.1
+ CS 3-gram (Final n-gram)	**249.3**	**266.9**
RNN-ME LM + POS + LID	**219.8**	**239.2**

Table 8: PPL of the N-gram models trained with artificial text data

5.2 ASR experiments

For the ASR experiments, we applied BioKIT, a dynamic one-pass decoder (Telaar et al., 2014). The acoustic model is speaker independent and has been trained with all the training data. To extract the features, we first trained a multilayer perceptron (MLP) with a small hidden layer with 40 nodes. The output of this hidden layer is called *bottle neck features* and is used to train the acoustic model. The MLP has been initialized with a multilingual multilayer perceptron as described in (Vu et al., 2012). The phone set contains English and Mandarin phones, filler models for continuous speech (+noise+, +breath+, +laugh+) and an additional phone +particle+ for Singaporean and Malayan particles. The acoustic model applied a fully-continuous 3-state left-to-right HMM. The emission probabilities were modeled with Gaussian mixture models. We used a context dependent acoustic model with 3,500 quintphones. Merge-and-split training was applied followed by six iterations of Viterbi training. To obtain a dictionary, the CMU English (CMU Dictionary, 2014) and Mandarin (Hsiao et al., 2008) pronunciation dictionaries were merged into one bilingual pronunciation dictionary. Additionally, several rules from (Chen et al., 2010) were applied which generate pronunciation variants for Singaporean English.

As a performance measure for decoding Code-Switching speech, we used the mixed error rate (MER) which applies word error rates to English and character error rates to Mandarin segments (Vu et al., 2012). With character error rates for Mandarin, the performance can be compared across different word segmentations. Table 9 shows the results of the baseline CS 3-gram LM, the 3-gram LM trained with 235M artificial words interpolated with CS 3-gram LM and the final 3-gram LM described in the previous section. Compared to the baseline system, we are able to improve the MER by up to 3% relative. Furthermore, a very small gain can be observed by using the Code-Switching attitude dependent language model compared to the unadapted best RNN-ME LM.

Model	Dev	Eval
CS 3-gram	40.0%	34.3%
235M words text + CS-3gram	39.4%	33.4%
Final 3-gram	**39.2%**	**33.3%**

Table 9: ASR results on SEAME data

6 Conclusion

This paper presents an extensive investigation of the impact of maximum entropy in recurrent neural network language models for Code-Switching speech. The experimental results reveal that factorization of the output layer of the RNN using LID always improved the PPL independent whether the ME is used. However, the integration of the POS tags into the input layer only improved the PPL in combination with ME. The best LM can be obtained by jointly training the ME and the RNN LM with POS integration and factorization using LID. Moreover, using the RNN-ME LM allows generating artificial CS text data and therefore training an n-gram LM which carries the information of the RNN-ME LM. This can be directly used during decoding to improve ASR performance on Code-Switching speech. On the SEAME development and evaluation set, we obtained an improvement of up to 18% relative in terms of PPL and 3% relative in terms of MER.

7 Acknowledgment

This follow-up work on exploring the impact of maximum entropy in recurrent neural network language models for Code-Switching speech was motivated by the very useful comments and suggestions of the SLSP reviewers, for which we are very grateful.

References

H. Adel, N.T. Vu, F. Kraus, T. Schlippe, and T. Schultz. *Recurrent Neural Network Language Modeling for Code Switching Conversational Speech* In: Proceedings of ICASSP 2013.

H. Adel, K. Kirchhoff, N.T. Vu, D.Telaar, T. Schultz *Comparing Approaches to Convert Recurrent Neural Networks into Backoff Language Models For Efficient Decoding* In: Proceedings of Interspeech 2014.

P. Auer *Code-Switching in Conversation* Routledge 1999.

P. Auer *From codeswitching via language mixing to fused lects toward a dynamic typology of bilingual speech* In: International Journal of Bilingualism, vol. 3, no. 4, pp. 309-332, 1999.

E.G. Bokamba *Are there syntactic constraints on code-mixing?* In: World Englishes, vol. 8, no. 3, pp. 277-292, 1989.

J.Y.C. Chan, PC Ching, T. Lee, and H. Cao *Automatic speech recognition of Cantonese-English code-mixing utterances* In: Proceeding of Interspeech 2006.

W. Chen, Y. Tan, E. Chng, H. Li *The development of a Singapore English call resource* In: Proceedings of Oriental COCOSDA, 2010.

Carnegie Mellon University *CMU pronouncation dictionary for English* Online: http://www.speech.cs.cmu.edu/cgi-bin/cmudict, retrieved in July 2014

D.C. Lyu, T.P. Tan, E.S. Cheng, H. Li *An Analysis of Mandarin-English Code-Switching Speech Corpus: SEAME* In: Proceedings of Interspeech 2011.

A. Deoras, T. Mikolov, S. Kombrink, M. Karafiat, S. Khudanpur *Variational approximation of long-span language models for LVCSR* In: Proceedings of ICASSP 2011.

R. Hsiao, M. Fuhs, Y. Tam, Q. Jin, T. Schultz *The CMU-InterACT 2008 Mandarin transcription system* In: Procceedings of ICASSP 2008.

Y. Li, P. Fung *Code-Switch Language Model with Inversion Constraints for Mixed Language Speech Recognition* In: Proceedings of COLING 2012.

Y. Li, P. Fung *Improved mixed language speech recognition using asymmetric acoustic model and language model with Code-Switch inversion constraints* In: Proceedings of ICASSP 2013.

M.P. Marcus, M.A. Marcinkiewicz, and B. Santorini. *Building a large annotated corpus of english: The penn treebank* In: Computational Linguistics, vol. 19, no. 2, pp. 313-330, 1993.

T. Mikolov, M. Karafiat, L. Burget, J. Jernocky and S. Khudanpur. *Recurrent Neural Network based Language Model* In: Proceedings of Interspeech 2010.

T. Mikolov, S. Kombrink, L. Burget, J. Jernocky and S. Khudanpur. *Extensions of Recurrent Neural Network Language Model* In: Proceedings of ICASSP 2011.

T. Mikolov, A. Deoras, D. Povey, L. Burget, J.H. Cernocky *Strategies for Training Large Scale Neural Network Language Models* In: Proceedings of ASRU 2011.

P. Muysken *Bilingual speech: A typology of code-mixing* In: Cambridge University Press, vol. 11.

S. Poplack *Syntactic structure and social function of code-switching* , Centro de Estudios Puertorriquenos, City University of New York.

S. Poplack *Sometimes i'll start a sentence in spanish y termino en espanol: toward a typology of code-switching* In: Linguistics, vol. 18, no. 7-8, pp. 581-618.

D. Povey, A. Ghoshal, et al. *The Kaldi speech recognition toolkit* In: Proceedings of ASRU 2011.

R. Rosenfeld *Two decades of statistical language modeling: Where do we go from here?* In: Proceedings of the IEEE 88.8 (2000): 1270-1278.

T. Schultz, P. Fung, and C. Burgmer, Detecting code-switch events based on textual features.

Y. Shi, P. Wiggers, M. Jonker *Towards Recurrent Neural Network Language Model with Linguistics and Contextual Features* In: Proceedings of Interspeech 2011.

T. Solorio, Y. Liu *Part-of-speech tagging for English-Spanish code-switched text* In: Proceedings of the Conference on Empirical Methods in Natural Language Processing. Association for Computational Linguistics, 2008.

T. Solorio, Y. Liu *Learning to predict code-switching points* In: Proceedings of the Conference on Empirical Methods in Natural Language Processing. Association for Computational Linguistics, 2008.

A. Stolcke *SRILM-an extensible language modeling toolkit.* In: Proceedings of Interspeech 2012.

D. Telaar, et al. *BioKIT - Real-time Decoder For Biosignal Processing* In: Proceedings of Interspeech 2014.

N.T. Vu, D.C. Lyu, J. Weiner, D. Telaar, T. Schlippe, F. Blaicher, E.S. Chng, T. Schultz, H. Li *A First Speech Recognition System For Mandarin-English Code-Switch Conversational Speech* In: Proceedings of Interspeech 2012.

N.T. Vu, H. Adel, T. Schultz *An Investigation of Code-Switching Attitude Dependent Language Modeling* In: In Statistical Language and Speech Processing, First International Conference, 2013.

N.T. Vu, F. Metze, T. Schultz *Multilingual bottleneck features and its application for under-resourced languages* In: Proceedings of SLTU, 2012.

Predicting Code-Switching in Multilingual Communication for Immigrant Communities

Evangelos E. Papalexakis
Carnegie Mellon University
Pittsburgh, USA
epapalex@cs.cmu.edu

Dong Nguyen
University of Twente
Enschede, The Netherlands
d.nguyen@utwente.nl

A. Seza Doğruöz
Netherlands Institute
for Advanced Study
Wassenaar, The Netherlands
a.s.dogruoz@gmail.com

Abstract

Immigrant communities host multilingual speakers who switch across languages and cultures in their daily communication practices. Although there are in-depth linguistic descriptions of code-switching across different multilingual communication settings, there is a need for automatic prediction of code-switching in large datasets. We use emoticons and multi-word expressions as novel features to predict code-switching in a large online discussion forum for the Turkish-Dutch immigrant community in the Netherlands. Our results indicate that multi-word expressions are powerful features to predict code-switching.

1 Introduction

Multilingualism is the norm rather than an exception in face-to-face and online communication for millions of speakers around the world (Auer and Wei, 2007). 50% of the EU population is bilingual or multilingual (European Comission, 2012). Multilingual speakers in immigrant communities switch across different languages and cultures depending on the social and contextual factors present in the communication environment (Auer, 1988; Myers-Scotton, 2002; Romaine, 1995; Toribio, 2002; Bullock and Toribio, 2009). Example (1) illustrates Turkish-Dutch code-switching in a post about video games in an online discussion forum for the Turkish immigrant community in the Netherlands.

Example (1)
user1: <dutch>vette spellllllllll </dutch>.. <turkish>bir girdimmi cikamiyomm .. yendikce yenesi geliyo insanin</turkish>
Translation: <dutch> awesome gameeeee </dutch>.. <turkish>once you are in it, it is hard to leave .. the more you win, the more you want to win</turkish>

Mixing two or more languages is not a random process. There are in-depth linguistic descriptions of code-switching across different multilingual contexts (Poplack, 1980; Silva-Corvalán, 1994; Owens and Hassan, 2013). Although these studies provide invaluable insights about code-switching from a variety of aspects, there is a growing need for computational analysis of code-switching in large datasets (e.g. social media) where manual analysis is not feasible. In immigrant settings, multilingual/bilingual speakers switch between minority (e.g. Turkish) and majority (e.g. Dutch) languages. Code-switching marks multilingual, multi-cultural (Luna et al., 2008; Grosjean, 2014) and ethnic identities (De Fina, 2007) of the speakers. By predicting code-switching patterns in Turkish-Dutch social media data, we aim to raise consciousness about mixed language communication patterns in immigrant communities. Our study is innovative in the following ways:

- We performed experiments on the longest and largest bilingual dataset analyzed so far.
- We are the first to predict code-switching in social media data which allow us to investigate features such as emoticons.
- We are the first to exploit multi-word expressions to predict code-switching.
- We use automatic language identification at the word level to create our dataset and features that capture previous language choices.

The rest of this paper is structured as follows: we discuss related work on code-switching and multilingualism in Section 2, our dataset in Section 3, a qualitative analysis in Section 4, our experimental setup and features in Section 5, our results in Section 6 and our conclusion in Section 7.

Proceedings of The First Workshop on Computational Approaches to Code Switching, pages 42–50,
October 25, 2014, Doha, Qatar.

2 Related Work

Code-switching in sociolinguistics There is rarely any consensus on the terminology about mixed language use. Wei (1998) considers alternations between languages at or above clause levels as *code-mixing*. Romaine (1995) refers to both inter-sentential and intra-sentential switches as code-switching. Bilingual speakers may shift from one language to another entirely (Poplack et al., 1988) or they mix languages partially within the single speech (Gumperz, 1982). In this study, we focus on code-switching within the same post in an online discussion forum used by Turkish-Dutch bilinguals.

There are different theoretical models which support (Myers-Scotton, 2002; Poplack, 1980) or reject (MacSwan, 2005; Thomason and Kaufman, 2001) linguistic constraints on code-switching. According to (Thomason and Kaufman, 2001; Gardner-Chloros and Edwards, 2004) linguistic factors are mostly unpredictable since social factors govern the multilingual environments in most cases. Bhatt and Bolonyai (2011) have an extensive study on socio-cognitive factors that lead to code-switching across different multilingual communities.

Although multilingual communication has been widely studied through spoken data analyses, research on online communication is relatively recent. In terms of linguistic factors Cárdenas-Claros and Isharyanti (2009) report differences between Indonesian-English and Spanish-English speakers in their amount of code-switching on MSN (an instant messaging client). Durham (2003) finds a tendency to switch to English over time in an online multilingual (German, French, Italian) discussion forum in Switzerland.

The media (e.g. IRC, Usenet, email, online discussions) used for multilingual conversations influence the amount of code-switching as well (Paolillo, 2001; Hinrichs, 2006). Androutsopoulos and Hinnenkamp (2001), Tsaliki (2003) and Hinnenkamp (2008) have done qualitative analyses of switch patterns across German-Greek-Turkish, Greek-English and Turkish-German in online environments respectively.

In terms of social factors, a number of studies have investigated the link between topic and language choices qualitatively (Ho, 2007; Androutsopoulos, 2007; Tang et al., 2011). These studies share the similar conclusion that multilingual speakers use minority languages to discuss topics related to their ethnic identity and reinforcing intimacy and self-disclosure (e.g. homeland, cultural traditions, joke telling) whereas they use the majority language for sports, education, world politics, science and technology.

Computational approaches to code-switching Recently, an increasing number of research within NLP has focused on dealing with multilingual documents. For example, corpora with multilingual documents have been created to support studies on code-switching (e.g. Cotterell et al. (2014)) To enable the automatic processing and analysis of documents with mixed languages, there is a shift in focus toward language identification at the word level (King and Abney, 2013; Nguyen and Doğruöz, 2013; Lui et al., 2014). Most closely related to our work is the study by Solorio and Liu (2008) who predict code-switching in recorded English-Spanish conversations. Compared to their work, we use a large-scale social media dataset that enables us to explore novel features.

The task most closely related to automatic prediction of code-switching is automatic language identification (King and Abney, 2013; Nguyen and Doğruöz, 2013; Lui et al., 2014). While automatic language detection uses the words to identify the language, automatic prediction of code-switching involves predicting whether the language of the next word is the same *without* having access to the next word itself.

Language practices of the Turkish community in the Netherlands Turkish has been in contact with Dutch due to labor immigration since the 1960s and the Turkish community is the largest minority group (2% of the whole population) in the Netherlands (Centraal Bureau voor de Statistiek, 2013). In addition to their Dutch fluency, second and third generations are also fluent in Turkish through speaking it within the family and community, regular family visits to Turkey and watching Turkish TV through satellite dishes. These speakers grow up speaking both languages simultaneously rather than learning one language after the other (De Houwer, 2009). In addition to constant switches between Turkish and Dutch, there are also literally translated Dutch multi-word expressions (Doğruöz and Backus, 2007; Doğruöz and Backus, 2009). Due to the religious backgrounds of the Turkish-Dutch community, Arabic words and phrases (e.g. greetings) are part of daily communication. In addition, English words and phrases are used both in Dutch and Turkish due to the exposure to American and British media.

Although the necessity of studying immigrant languages in Dutch online environments has been voiced earlier (Dorleijn and Nortier, 2012), the current study is the first to investigate mixed language communication patterns of Turkish-Dutch bilinguals in online environments.

3 Dataset

Our data comes from a large online forum (Hababam) used by Turkish-Dutch speakers. The forum is active since 2000 and contains 28 subforums on a variety of topics (e.g. sports, politics, education). Each subforum consists of multiple threads which start with a thread title (e.g. a statement or question) posted by a moderator or user. The users are Turkish-Dutch bilinguals who reside in the Netherlands. Although Dutch and Turkish are used dominantly in the forum, English (e.g. fixed expressions) and Arabic (e.g. prayers) are occasionally used (less than 1%) as well. We collected the data between June 2005 and October 2012 by crawling the forum. Statistics of our data are shown in Table 1.

	Frequency
Number of posts	4,519,869
Number of users	14,923
Number of threads	113,517
Number of subforums	29

Table 1: Dataset Statistics

The subforums *Chit-Chat* (1,671,436), *Turkish youth & love* (447,436), and *Turkish news & updates* (418,135) have the highest post frequency whereas *Columns* (4727), *Science & Philosophy* (5083) and *Other Beliefs* (6914) have the lowest post frequency.

An automatic language identification tagger is used to label the language of the words in posts and titles of the threads. The tagger distinguishes between Turkish and Dutch using logistic regression (Nguyen and Doğruöz, 2013) and achieves a word accuracy of approximately 97%. We use the language labels to train our classifier (since given the labels we can determine whether there is a switch or not), and to evaluate our model.

4 Types of Code-Switching

In this section, we provide a qualitative analysis of code-switching in the online forum. We differentiate between two types of code-switching: code-switching across posts and code-switching within the same post.

4.1 Code-switching across posts

Within the same discussion thread, users react to posts of other users in different languages. In example (2), user 1 posts in Dutch to tease User 2. User 2 reacts to this message with a humorous idiomatic expression in Turkish (i.e. [*adim cikmis*] "I made a name") to indirectly emphasize that there is no reason for her to defend herself since she has already become famous as the *perfect* person in the online community. This type of humorous switch has also been observed for Greek-English code-switching in face-to-face communication (Gardner-Chloros and Finnis, 2003). The text is written with Dutch orthography instead of conventional Turkish orthography (i.e. [*adım çıkmış*]). It is probably the case that the user has a Dutch keyboard without Turkish characters. However, writing with non-Turkish characters in online environments is also becoming popular among monolingual Turkish users from Turkey.

Example (2)
User1: <dutch> je hoefde niet gelijk in de verdediging te schieten hoor </dutch> :P
Tra: "you do not need to be immediately defensive dear"

User2: <turkish> zaten adim cikmis mukemmel sahane kusursuz insana, bi de yine cikmasin </turkish> :(
Tra: "I already have established a name as a great amazing perfect person, I do not need it to spread around once more"

Example (3) is taken from a thread about breakfast traditions. The users have posted what they had for breakfast that day. The first user talks about his breakfast in Turkish and describes the culture specific food items (e.g. *borek* "Turkish pastry") prepared by his mother. The second user describes a typical Dutch breakfast and therefore switches to Dutch.

Example (3)
User1: <turkish>annemin peynirli borekleri ve cay</turkish>
Tra: "the cheese pastries of my mom and tea"

User2: <dutch>Twee sneetjes geroosterd bruin brood met kipfilet en een glas thee.</dutch>
Tra: "Two pieces of roasted brown bread with chicken filet and a cup of tea"

4.2 Code-switching within the same post

In addition to code-switching across posts, we encountered code-switching within the same post of a user as well. Manual annotation of a subset of the posts in Nguyen and Doğruöz (2013), suggests that less than 20% of the posts contain a switch. Example (4) is taken from a thread about Mother's Day and illustrates an intra-sentential switch. The user starts the post in Dutch (*vakantie boeken* "to book a vacation") and switches to Turkish since booking a vacation through internet sites or a travel agency is a typical activity associated with the Dutch culture.

Example (4)
<dutch>vakantie boeken</dutch>
<turkish> yaptim annecigimee </turkish>
Tra[1]:"(I) <dutch>booked a holiday</dutch>
<turkish>for my mother.</turkish>"

Example (5) is taken from a thread about Turkish marriages and illustrates an inter-sentential switch. The user is advising the other users in Turkish to be very careful about choosing their partners. Since most Turkish community members prefer Turkish partners and follow Turkish traditions for marriage, she talks about these topics in Turkish. However, she switches to Dutch when she talks about getting a diploma in the Dutch school system. Similar examples of code-switching for emphasizing different identities based on topic have been observed for other online and face-to-face communication as well (Androutsopoulos, 2007; Gardner-Chloros, 2009).

Example (5)
<turkish>Allah korusun yani. Kocani iyi sec diyim=) evlilik evcilik degildir.</turkish>
<dutch>Al zou ik wanneer ik getrouwd ben een HBO diploma op zak hebben, zou ik hem dan denk ik niet verlaten.</dutch>
Tra:"<turkish> May God protect you. Choose your husband carefully. Marriage is not a game </turkish> <dutch> Even if I am married and have a university diploma, I don't think I will leave him </dutch>"

Code-switching through greetings, wishes and formulaic expressions are commonly observed in bilingual face-to-face communication and online immigrant forums as well (Androutsopoulos, 2007; Gardner-Chloros, 2009).

5 Experimental Setup

The focus of this paper is on code-switching within the same post. We discuss the setup and features of our experiment in this section.

5.1 Goal

We cast the prediction of the code-switch point within the post as a binary classification problem. We define the i-th token of the post as an instance. If the $i + 1$th token is in a different language, the label is 1. Otherwise, the label is 0.

Obtaining language labels In order to label each token of a post, we rely on the labels obtained using automatic language identification at the word level (see Section 3). This process may not be the most accurate way of labeling each token of a post at a large scale. One particular artifact of this procedure is that an automatic tagger may falsely tag the language of a token in longer posts. As a result, some lengthy posts might appear to have one or more code-switches by accident. However, since the accuracy of our tagger is high (approx. 97% accuracy), we expect the amount of such spurious code-switches to be low. For future work, we plan to experiment on a dataset based on automatic language identification as well as a smaller dataset using manual annotation.

5.2 Creating train and test sets

Before we attempt to train a classifier on our data, we eliminate the biases and imbalances. The majority of posts do not contain any switches. As a consequence, the number of instances that belong to the '0' class (i.e. no code-switching occurring after the current word) grossly outnumber the instances of class '1', where code-switching takes place. In order to alleviate this class imbalance, for all our experiments, we sample an *equal* amount of instances from '0' and '1' classes randomly [2], both for our training and testing data. This way the result will not favor the '0' class even if we randomly decide on the class label for each instance. The average number of training and testing

[1]It is possible to drop the subject pronoun in Turkish. As typical in bilingual speech, an additional Turkish verb *yapmak* follows the Dutch verb *boeken* "to book".

[2]We do 100 iterations and average the results of all these independent samples.

instances per iteration was 4000 and 80000 respectively. By drawing 100 independent samples from the entire dataset, we cover a reasonable portion of the full data and do not sacrifice the balance of the two classes, which is crucially important for the validity of our results.

5.3 Feature selection

We use the following features (see Table 2) to investigate code-switching within a post.

5.3.1 Non-linguistic features

Emoticons Emoticons are iconic symbols that convey emotional information along with language use in online environments (Dresner and Herring, 2014). Emoticons have mostly been used in the context of sentiment analysis (e.g. Volkova et al. (2013), Chmiel et al. (2011)). Park et al. (2014) studied how the use of emoticons differ across cultures in Twitter data. Panayiotou (2004) studied how bilinguals express emotions in face-to-face environments in different languages. We are the first to investigate the role of emoticons as a non-linguistic factor in predicting code-switching on social media.

Emoticons in our data are either signified by a special tag `[smiley:smiley_type]` or can appear in any of the common ASCII emoticon forms (e.g. `:)`, `:-)` etc.). In order to detect the emoticons, we used a hand picked list of ASCII emoticons as our dictionary, as well as a filter that searched for the special emoticon tag. Since we rely on an automatic language tagger, the language label of a particular emoticon depends on its surrounding tokens. If an emoticon is within a block of text that is tagged as Turkish, then the emoticon will automatically obtain a Turkish label (and accordingly for Dutch). For future work, we will experiment with labeling emoticons differently (e.g. introducing a third, neutral label).

To assess the strength of emoticons as predictors of code-switching, we generate 4 different features (see Table 2). These features capture whether or not there is an emoticon *at* or *before* the token that we want to classify as the switch boundary between Dutch and Turkish. We record whether there was an emoticon at token i (i.e. the token we want to classify), token $i-1$ and token $i-2$.

The last emoticon feature records whether there is any emoticon *after* the current token. We note that this feature looks ahead (after the i-th token), and therefore cannot be implemented in a real time system which predicts code-switching on-the-fly. However, we included the feature for exploratory purposes.

5.3.2 Linguistic features

Language around the switch point We also investigate whether the knowledge of the language of a couple of tokens before the token of interest, as well as the language at the token of interest, hold some predictive strength. These features correspond to #1-3 in Table 2. Generally, the language label is binary. However, if there are no tokens in positions $i-2$ or $i-1$ for features #1 and #2, we assign a third value to represent this non-existence. Additionally, we explore whether a previous code-switching in a post triggers a second code-switching later in the same post. We test this hypothesis by recording feature #4 which represents the existence of code-switching before token i.

Single word versus multi-word switch There is an on-going discussion in multilingualism about the classification of switched tokens (Poplack, 2004; Poplack, 2013) and whether there are linguistic constraints on the switches (Myers-Scotton, 2002). In addition to switches across individual lexical tokens, multilingual speakers also switch across multi-word expressions.

Automatic identification of multi-word expressions in monolingual language use have been widely discussed (Baldwin et al., 2003; Baldwin and Kim, 2010) but we know little about how to predict switch points that include multi-word expressions. We are the first to include multi-word expressions as a feature to predict code-switching. We are mostly inspired by (Schwartz et al., 2013) in identifying MWEs.

More specifically, we built a corpus of 3-gram MWEs (2,241,484 in total) and selected the most frequent 100 MWEs. We differentiate between two types of MWEs: Let the i-th token of a post be the switch point. For *type 1*, we take 3 tokens (all in the same language) right before the switch token (i.e. terms $i-3$, $i-2$, $i-1$). [*Allah razi olsun*] "May the Lord be with you" and [*met je eens*] "agree with you" are the two of the most frequent MWEs (in Turkish and Dutch respectively).

For *type 2*, we take the tokens $i-2$, $i-1$, i and the last token is in a different language (e.g. [*Turkse premier Recep*] "Turkish prime-minister

Table 2: Features

Feature #	Feature Description
1	Language of token in position $i-2$
2	Language of token in position $i-1$
3	Language of token in position i (current token)
4	Was there code-switching before the current token?
5	Is there an emoticon in position $i-2$?
6	Is there an emoticon in position $i-1$?
7	Is there an emoticon in position i?
8	Are there any emoticons in positions after i?
9	Is the i-th token the first word of a 3-word multi-word expression?
10	Is the i-th token the second word of a 3-word multi-word expression?
11	Is the i-th token the third word of a 3-word multi-word expression?

Recep").

The first type of MWEs captures whether an MWE (all three words in the same language), signifies code-switching for token i or not.

The second type investigates whether there are MWEs that "spill over" the code-switching point (i.e. the first two tokens of an MWE are in the same language, but the third token is in another language). In order to get a good estimate of the MWEs in our corpus, we count the occurrences of all these 3-grams and keep the top scoring ones in terms of frequency, which end up as our dictionary of MWEs.

6 Results

To evaluate the predictive strength of our features, we conduct experiments using a Naive Bayes classifier.

In order to measure the performance, we train the classifiers for various combinations of the features shown in Table 2. As we described in the previous section, we train on randomly chosen, class-balanced parts of the data and we test on randomly selected balanced samples (disjoint from the training set), averaging over 100 runs. For each combination of features, we measure and report average precision, recall, and F1-score, with respect to positively predicting code-switching.

Table 3 illustrates the performance of individual features used in our classifier. Features that concern the language of the previous tokens (i.e. features #1 & #2) seem to perform better than chance in predicting code-switching. On the other hand, features #3 (*language of the token in position i*) and #4 (*previous code-switching*) have the worst performance. In fact, the obtained classifier always predicts *no code-switching* regardless of the value of the feature. Therefore, both precision and recall are 0. Features #1 & #2 behave differently from features #3 & #4 because #1 & #2 have ternary values (the token language, or *non-existing*). This probably forces the classifiers to produce a non-constant decision. For instance, the model for feature #1 decides positively for code-switching if the language label is either *Turkish* or *Dutch* and decides negatively if the label is *non-existing*.

Table 3: Performance of individual features

Feature #	Precision	Recall	F1 score
1	0.6305	1	0.7733
2	0.6362	1	0.7776
3	0	0	-
4	0	0	-
5	0.704	0.2116	0.3254
6	0.7637	0.2324	0.3564
7	0.8025	0.1339	0.0954
8	0.4879	0.3214	0.3875
9	0.5324	0.7819	0.6335
10	0.5257	0.8102	0.6376
11	0.5218	0.8396	0.6436

The rest of the individual features perform similarly but worse than #1 and #2. Therefore, it is necessary to use a combination of features instead of single ones.

After examining how features perform individually, we further investigate how features behave in groups. We first group the features into homogeneous categories (e.g. #1-#3 focus on the language of tokens, #5-#8 record the presence of emoticons and #9-#11 refer to MWEs). Subsequently, we test the performance of these categories in different combinations, and finally measure the effect of

Table 4: Performance of groups of features

	Features	Precision	Recall	F1 score
1-3	Language of tokens	0.6362	1	0.7777
1-4	Language + previous code-switching	0.6663	0.1312	0.6663
5-8	Emoticons	0.6638	0.397	0.2766
9-11	MWEs	0.5384	0.7476	0.626
5-11	Emoticons + MWEs	0.52	0.8718	0.6466
1-8	Language + previous code-switching + emoticons	0.6932	0.5114	0.4634
1-4, 9-11	Language + previous code-switching + MWEs	0.712	0.7297	0.7113
1-11	All	0.6847	0.8034	0.7106

using all our features for the task. Table 4 shows the combinations of the features we used, as well as the average precision, recall, and F1-score.

According to Table 4, the combination of the language of the tokens (features #1-#3) and the previous code-switching earlier in the post (features #1-#4), and MWEs (features #9-#11) perform the highest in terms of precision/recall. Features #3 and #4 have rather low performances on their own but they yield a strong classifier in combination with other features.

When we use features that record emoticons (#5-#8) or MWEs (#9-#11) alone, the performance of our classifier decreases. In general, MWEs outperform emoticons. We observe this performance boost when we combine emoticon features with other features (e.g. #1-#8) and with MWEs together in the same subset (#1-#4, #9-#11).

7 Conclusion

We focused on predicting code-switching points for a mixed language online forum used by the Turkish-Dutch immigrant community in the Netherlands. For the first time, a long term data set was used to investigate code-switching in social media. We are also the first to test new features (e.g. emoticons and MWEs) to predict code-switching and to identify the features with significant predictive strength. For future work, we will continue our investigation with exploring the predictive value of these new features within the Turkish-Dutch immigrant community as well as others.

8 Acknowledgements

The first author was supported by the National Science Foundation (NSF), Grant No. IIS-1247489. The second author was supported by the Netherlands Organization for Scientific Research (NWO) grant 640.005.002 (FACT). The third author was supported by a Digital Humanities Research Grant from Tilburg University and a research fellowship from Netherlands Institute for Advanced Study.

References

Jannis Androutsopoulos and Volker Hinnenkamp. 2001. Code-switching in der bilingualen chatkommunikation: ein explorativer blick auf# hellas und# turks. *Beisswenger, Michael (ed.)*, pages 367–401.

Jannis Androutsopoulos, 2007. *The Multilingual Internet*, chapter Language choice and code-switching in German-based diasporic web forums, pages 340–361. Oxford University Press.

Peter Auer and Li Wei, 2007. *Handbook of multilingualism and multilingual communication.*, chapter Introduction: Multilingualism as a problem? Monolingualism as a problem, pages 1–14. Berlin: Mouton de Gruyter.

Peter Auer. 1988. A conversation analytic approach to code-switching and transfer. *Codeswitching: Anthropological and sociolinguistic perspectives*, 48:187–213.

Timothy Baldwin and Su Nam Kim. 2010. Multiword expressions. *Handbook of Natural Language Processing, second edition. Morgan and Claypool.*

Timothy Baldwin, Colin Bannard, Takaaki Tanaka, and Dominic Widdows. 2003. An empirical model of multiword expression decomposability. In *Proceedings of the ACL 2003 workshop on Multiword expressions: analysis, acquisition and treatment-Volume 18*, pages 89–96. Association for Computational Linguistics.

Rakesh M Bhatt and Agnes Bolonyai. 2011. Code-switching and the optimal grammar of bilingual language use. *Bilingualism: Language and Cognition*, 14(04):522–546.

Barbara E Bullock and Almeida Jacqueline Toribio. 2009. *The Cambridge handbook of linguistic code-switching*, volume 1. Cambridge University Press Cambridge.

Monica S. Cárdenas-Claros and Neny Isharyanti. 2009. Code-switching and code-mixing in internet chatting: Between'yes,"ya,'and'si'-a case study. *The Jalt Call Journal*, 5(3):67–78.

Centraal Bureau voor de Statistiek. 2013. Bevolking, generatie, geslacht, leeftijd en herkomstgroepering. 2013.

Anna Chmiel, Julian Sienkiewicz, Mike Thelwall, Georgios Paltoglou, Kevan Buckley, Arvid Kappas, and Janusz A Hołyst. 2011. Collective emotions online and their influence on community life. *PloS one*, 6(7):e22207.

Ryan Cotterell, Adithya Renduchintala, Naomi Saphra, and Chris Callison-Burch. 2014. An algerian arabic-french code-switched corpus. In *LREC*.

Anna De Fina. 2007. Code-switching and the construction of ethnic identity in a community of practice. *Language in Society*, 36(03):371–392.

Annick De Houwer. 2009. *Bilingual first language acquisition*. Multilingual Matters.

A Seza Doğruöz and Ad Backus. 2007. Postverbal elements in immigrant Turkish: Evidence of change? *International Journal of Bilingualism*, 11(2):185–220.

A. Seza Doğruöz and Ad Backus. 2009. Innovative constructions in Dutch Turkish: An assessment of ongoing contact-induced change. *Bilingualism: Language and Cognition*, 12(01):41–63.

Margreet Dorleijn and Jacomine Nortier, 2012. *The Cambridge Handbook of Linguistic Code-switching*, chapter Code-switching and the internet, pages 114–127. Cambridge University Press.

Eli Dresner and Susan C Herring. 2014. Emoticons and illocutionary force. In *Perspectives on Theory of Controversies and the Ethics of Communication*, pages 81–90. Springer.

Mercedes Durham. 2003. Language choice on a Swiss mailing list. *Journal of Computer-Mediated Communication*, 9(1):0–0.

European Comission. 2012. Europeans and their languages: Special barometer 386. Technical report, European Comission.

Penelope Gardner-Chloros and Malcolm Edwards. 2004. Assumptions behind grammatical approaches to code-switching: When the blueprint is a red herring. *Transactions of the Philological Society*, 102(1):103–129.

Penelope Gardner-Chloros and Katerina Finnis. 2003. How code-switching mediates politeness: Gender-related speech among London Greek-Cypriots. *Sociolinguistic Studies*, 4(2):505–532.

Penelope Gardner-Chloros, 2009. *Handbook of Code-switching*, chapter Sociolinguistic Factors in Code-Switching, pages 97–114. Cambridge University Press.

Francois Grosjean. 2014. Bicultural bilinguals. *International Journal of Bilingualism*, xx(xx):1–15.

John J Gumperz. 1982. *Discourse strategies*, volume 1. Cambridge University Press.

Volker Hinnenkamp. 2008. Deutsch, Doyc or Doitsch? Chatters as languagers–The case of a German–Turkish chat room. *International Journal of Multilingualism*, 5(3):253–275.

Lars Hinrichs. 2006. *Codeswitching on the Web: English and Jamaican Creole in E-mail Communication (Pragmatics & Beyond, Issn 0922-842x)*. John Benjamins.

Judy Woon Yee Ho. 2007. Code-mixing: Linguistic form and socio-cultural meaning. *The International Journal of Language Society and Culture*, 21.

Ben King and Steven P Abney. 2013. Labeling the languages of words in mixed-language documents using weakly supervised methods. In *HLT-NAACL*, pages 1110–1119.

Marco Lui, Jey Han Lau, and Timothy Baldwin. 2014. Automatic detection and language identification of multilingual documents. *Transactions of the Association for Computational Linguistics*, 2:27–40.

David Luna, Torsten Ringberg, and Laura A Peracchio. 2008. One individual, two identities: Frame switching among biculturals. *Journal of Consumer Research*, 35(2):279–293.

Jeff MacSwan. 2005. Codeswitching and generative grammar: A critique of the mlf model and some remarks on "modified minimalism". *Bilingualism: language and cognition*, 8(01):1–22.

Carol Myers-Scotton. 2002. *Contact linguistics: Bilingual encounters and grammatical outcomes*. Oxford University Press Oxford.

Dong Nguyen and A. Seza Doğruöz. 2013. Word level language identification in online multilingual communication. In *Proceedings of EMNLP 2013*.

Jonathan Owens and Jidda Hassan, 2013. *Information Structure in Spoken Arabic*, chapter Conversation markers in Arabic-Hausa code-switching, pages 207–243. Routledge Arabic Linguistics. Routledge.

Alexia Panayiotou. 2004. Switching codes, switching code: Bilinguals' emotional responses in english and greek. *Journal of multilingual and multicultural development*, 25(2-3):124–139.

John C Paolillo. 2001. Language variation on internet relay chat: A social network approach. *Journal of sociolinguistics*, 5(2):180–213.

Jaram Park, Young Min Baek, and Meeyoung Cha. 2014. Cross-cultural comparison of nonverbal cues in emoticons on twitter: Evidence from big data analysis. *Journal of Communication*, 64(2):333–354.

Shana Poplack, David Sankoff, and Christopher Miller. 1988. The social correlates and linguistic processes of lexical borrowing and assimilation. *Linguistics*, 26(1):47–104.

Shana Poplack. 1980. Sometimes i'll start a sentence in spanish y termino en espanol: toward a typology of code-switching1. *Linguistics*, 18(7-8):581–618.

Shana Poplack, 2004. *Soziolinguistik. An international handbook of the science of language*, chapter Codeswitching, pages 589–597. Walter de Gruyter, 2nd edition.

Shana Poplack. 2013. "sometimes i'll start a sentence in spanish y termino en español": Toward a typology of code-switching. *Linguistics*, 51(Jubilee):11–14.

Suzanne Romaine. 1995. Bilingualism (2nd edn). *Malden, MA: Blackwell Publishers.*

H Andrew Schwartz, Johannes C Eichstaedt, Margaret L Kern, Lukasz Dziurzynski, Stephanie M Ramones, Megha Agrawal, Achal Shah, Michal Kosinski, David Stillwell, Martin EP Seligman, et al. 2013. Personality, gender, and age in the language of social media: The open-vocabulary approach. *PloS one*, 8(9):e73791.

Carmen Silva-Corvalán. 1994. *Language Contact and Change: Spanish in Los Angeles.* ERIC.

Thamar Solorio and Yang Liu. 2008. Learning to predict code-switching points. In *Proceedings of the Conference on Empirical Methods in Natural Language Processing*, pages 973–981. Association for Computational Linguistics.

Dai Tang, Tina Chou, Naomi Drucker, Adi Robertson, William C Smith, and Jeffery T Hancock. 2011. A tale of two languages: strategic self-disclosure via language selection on facebook. In *Proceedings of the ACM 2011 conference on Computer supported cooperative work*, pages 387–390. ACM.

Sarah Grey Thomason and Terrence Kaufman. 2001. *Language contact.* Edinburgh University Press Edinburgh.

Almeida Jacqueline Toribio. 2002. Spanish-english code-switching among us latinos. *International journal of the sociology of language*, pages 89–120.

Liza Tsaliki. 2003. Globalization and hybridity: the construction of greekness on the internet. *The Media of Diaspora, Routledge, London.*

Svitlana Volkova, Theresa Wilson, and David Yarowsky. 2013. Exploring demographic language variations to improve multilingual sentiment analysis in social media. In *EMNLP*, pages 1815–1827.

Li Wei, 1998. *Codeswitching in conversation: Language, interaction and identity*, chapter The 'why' and 'how' questions in the analysis of conversational codeswitching, pages 156–176. Routledge.

Twitter Users #CodeSwitch Hashtags! #MoltoImportante #wow #한글

David Jurgens, Stefan Dimitrov, Derek Ruths
School of Computer Science
McGill University
Montreal, Canada
jurgens@cs.mcgill.ca, stefan.dimitrov@mail.mcgill.ca,
druths@networkdynamics.org

Abstract

When code switching, individuals incorporate elements of multiple languages into the same utterance. While code switching has been studied extensively in formal and spoken contexts, its behavior and prevalence remains unexamined in many newer forms of electronic communication. The present study examines code switching in Twitter, focusing on instances where an author writes a post in one language and then includes a hashtag in a second language. In the first experiment, we perform a large scale analysis on the languages used in millions of posts to show that authors readily incorporate hashtags from other languages, and in a manual analysis of a subset the hashtags, reveal prolific code switching, with code switching occurring for some hashtags in over twenty languages. In the second experiment, French and English posts from three bilingual cities are analyzed for their code switching frequency and its content.

1 Introduction

Online platforms enable individuals from a wide variety of linguistic backgrounds to communicate. When individuals share multiple languages in common, their communication will occasionally include linguistic elements from multiple languages (Nilep, 2006), a practice commonly referred to as code switching. Typically, during code switching, the text or speech in a language retains its syntactic and morphological constraints for that language, rather than having text from both languages conform to one of the language's grammatical rules. This requirement enables code switching to be separated from borrowing, where foreign words are integrated into a native language's lexicon and morphology (Gumperz, 1982; Poplack et al., 1988; Sankoff et al., 1990).

While work on code switching began with conversational analyses, recent work has examined the phenomena in electronic communication, finding similar evidence of code switching (Climent et al., 2003; Lee, 2007; Paolillo, 2011). However, these investigations into code switching have largely examined interpersonal communication or settings where the number of participants is limited. In contrast, social media platforms such as Twitter offer individuals the ability to write a text that is decoupled from direct conversation but may be read widely.

Twitter enables users to post messages with special markers known as hashtags, which can serve as a side channel to comment on the post itself (Davidov et al., 2010). As a result, multilingual authors have embraced using hashtags from languages other than the language of their post. Consider the following real examples:

- Eating an apple for lunch while everyone around me eats cheeseburgers and fries. #yoquiero
- Jetzt gibt's was vernünftiges zum essen! #salad #turkey #lunch #healthy #healthylifestyle #loveit
- Hasta mañana a todo mundo. Que tengan linda noche. #MarketerosNocturnos #MarketingDigital #BlackVirs #SocialMedia
- 1% มันสำคัญมากนะ เพราะมันอาจเปลี่ยนจากD+ เป็น C และ B+เป็นA เกรดเฉลี่ยคงดีกว่านี้อ่ะ #พลาด #เสียดาย #fail

Here, the first author posted in English with a Spanish hashtag reflecting the author's envious disposition. In the second, the author comments in German on sensible food, using multiple English hashtags to describe the meal and their attitude. In the third and fourth, the authors comment

Proceedings of The First Workshop on Computational Approaches to Code Switching, pages 51–61,
October 25, 2014, Doha, Qatar. ©2014 Association for Computational Linguistics

on sleep and school, respectively, and then each use hashtags with similar meanings in both their native language and English.

Hashtags provide authors with a communication medium that also has broader social utility by embedding their post within global discussion of other posts using the same hashtag (Letierce et al., 2010) or by becoming a part of a virtual community (Gupta et al., 2010). These social motivations resemble those seen for why individuals may code switch, such as to assimilate into a group or make discussions easier (Urciuoli, 1995). Twitter and other hashtag-supporting platforms such as Instagram and Facebook offer a unique setting for code switching hashtags for two reasons: (1) potential readers are disconnected from the author, who may not know of their language fluency, and (2) text translation is built into the platform, which enables readers to translate a post into their native language. As such, authors may be motivated to include a hashtag of another language to increase their potential audience size or to appear as a member of a multilingual virtual community.

Despite the prevalence of non-English tweets, which are approaching 50% of the total volume (Liu et al., 2014), no study has examined the prevalence of hashtag code switching. We propose an initial study of hashtag code switching in Twitter focusing on three central questions: (1) for which language pairs do authors write in the first language and then incorporate a hashtag of the second language, (2) when tweets include a hashtag of a different language, which instances signal code switching behavior, and (3) the degree to which bilingual populations code switch hashtags. Here, we adopt a general definition of code switching as instances where an individual establishes a linguistic context in one language and then includes elements (such as words) from one or more other languages different from the first. Two experiments are performed to answer these questions. In the first, we test general methods to identify which languages adopt the same hashtags and whether those shared hashtags are examples of code switching. In the second, we focus on three bilingual cities to examine hashtag code switching behavior in French and English speakers.

Our study provides three main contributions. First, we demonstrate that hashtag code switching is widespread in Twitter. Second, we show that Twitter as a platform includes multiple phenomena that can be falsely interpreted as code switching and therefore must be accounted for in future analyses. Third, in a study of French and English tweets from three cities, we find that an increased rate of bilinguality decreases the frequency of including hashtags from another language but increases the overall rate of code switching when such hashtags are present. Furthermore, all data for the experiments is made publicly available.

2 Related Work

Research on code switching is long standing, with many theories proposed for the motivations behind code switching and how the two languages interact linguistically (Poplack and Sankoff, 1984; Myers-Scotton, 1997; Auer, 1998). Most related to the present work are those studies examining code switching in online communications.

Climent et al. (2003) examined the use of Spanish and Catalan in newsgroups, finding it occurs 2.2% and 4.4% of the Catalan and Spanish contexts, respectively. Lee (2007) analyzed a corpus of Cantonese and English emails and ICQ instant messages and surveyed Hong Kong users of each form of communication. She found that the users preferred mixed-language communication, with no user indicating that they communicated in only Cantonese. Furthermore, the shorter, more informal ICQ messages were more likely to be code switched (99.4%) than emails (41.3%).

Paolillo (2011) measured code switching amongs English, Hindi, and Punjabi in both IRC and Usenet forum posts, finding similar to Climent et al. (2003) that the shorter, more conversational IRC posts had higher rates of code switching. Paolillo (2011) also note that code switching rates differed between Hindi and Punjabi speakers.

The present work differs significantly from these three studies in two aspects. First, we assess code switching across all language communities on Twitter, rather than examining individual groups of bilingual speakers. Second, we focus our analysis only on the code switching of a post's hashtag due to its unique role in microtext (Gupta et al., 2010), which has yet to be examined in this context.

3 Hashtag Use in Twitter

Hashtags provide general functionality on Twitter and prior works have proposed that they serve

Name	Description	Examples
ANNOTATION	Serves as an annotation about the author's feelings or comments on the content of a tweet.	#happy #fail #cute #joking #YoloSwaggins
COMMUNITY	A topical entity that links the tweet with an external community, which is commonly topical but also includes "team-like" groups	#music #friends #BecauseItIs-TheCup #TeamEdward
NAMED ENTITY	Refers to a specific entity that has a universally recognized name.	#Glee #TeenChoiceAwards #WorldCup2014
PLATFORM	Refer to some feature or behavior specific to the Twitter platform.	#followback #lasttweet #oomf
APPLICATION	Generated by a third-party application, which automatically includes its hashtag in the message.	#AndroidGames #NowPlaying #iPhone #Android
VOTING	Created as a result of certain real-world phenomena asking individuals to tweet with specific hashtags as a way of voting.	#MtvHottest #iHeartAwards
ADVERTISING	Promoting an item, good, or service, which can be sought out by interested parties.	#forsale #porn
SPAM	Used by adversarial parties to appear on trending lists and to make spam accounts appear real.	#NanaLoveLingga #681team #LORDJASONJEROME

Table 1: A taxonomy of hashtag according to their intended use.

a dual role as (1) bookmarking content with the tag's particular expression and (2) functioning as a method for ad hoc community formation and discussion around a tag's topic (Gupta et al., 2010; Davidov et al., 2010; Yang et al., 2012). However, the diverse user base of the Twitter platform has given rise to additional roles for hashtags beyond these two. For example, many popular hashtags focus on promoting users to follow each other,[1] such as #followback and #openfollow. Similarly, contests are run on Twitter, which have individuals vote by posting using a specific hashtag, e.g., #MtvHottest.

Given hashtags' flexible roles, some may be used in multiple languages without being examples of code switching, such as the contest-based or follower-promotion hashtags noted above. Therefore, we first propose a taxonomy for classifying all types of hashtags according to their primary observed use in order to disentangle potential code switching behavior from Twitter-specific behavior. To construct the taxonomy, two annotators independently reviewed several thousand hashtags of different frequency to assess the differences in how the tag was used in practice. Each annotator then proposed their own taxonomy. The final taxonomy was produced from a discussion of differences, with both annotators initially proposing highly similar taxonomies.[2]

Table 1 shows the proposed taxonomy, containing eight broad types of hashtags. The first two types of hashtags correspond to the main hashtag roles proposed in Yang et al. (2012). The NAMED ENTITY tags also serve as method for individuals to link their content with a specific audience like the COMMUNITY type; however, NAMED ENTITY tags were treated as a separate group for the purposes of this study because the entities typically have a common name which is used in all languages and therefore would not be translated; in contrast, COMMUNITY hashtags refer to more general topics such as #soccer, which may be translated, e.g., #futbol. Hashtags of the five remaining types would likely not be observed in instances of code switching, with such hashtags often being used for purposes other than interpersonal communication.

4 Experiment 1: Popular Hashtags

Persistently popular hashtags reflect established norms of communication on Twitter. We hypothesize that these hashtags may be adopted by the speakers of multiple languages for joining a global discussion. Therefore, the first experiment examines the most-used hashtags over a five month period to measure two aspects: (1) which languages adopt the hashtags of other languages and (2) which hashtags used in multiple languages are evidence of code switching.

[1]In Twitter, following denotes creating a directional social relation from one account to another.

[2]We note that a small number of hashtags did not fit this taxonomy due to their idiosyncratic use. These hashtags were typically single-letter hashtags used when spelling out words, e.g., "tonight is going to be #f #u #n," or when the author has mistakenly used punctuation, which is not included in Twitter's definition of a hashtag, e.g., "#I'mAwesome," which has the hashtag #I rather than the full expression.

4.1 Experimental Setup

Data Hashtag frequencies were calculated from 981M tweets spanning March 2014 to July 2014. Frequencies were calculated over this five month period in order to focus on widely-used hashtags, rather than bursty hashtags that are popular only for a short time, such as those studied in Huang et al. (2010) and Lin et al. (2013). For each hashtag, up to 10K non-retweet posts containing that hashtag were retained, randomly sampling from the time period studied when more than 10K were observed. To enable a more reliable estimate of the language distribution, we restrict our analysis to only those hashtags with more than 1000 posts, for a total number of 19.4M posts for 4624 hashtags, with an average of 4204 posts per hashtag.

Language Identification The languages of tweets were identified using a two-step procedure. First, message content was filtered to remove content such as usernames, URLs, emoji, and hashtags. Tweets with fewer than three remaining tokens were excluded (e.g., a message with only hashtags). Second, the remaining content was processed using `langid.py` (Lui and Baldwin, 2012), a state of the art language identification program that supports the diversity of languages found on Twitter.

Determining the language of a hashtag in a general setting for all languages is difficult due to the presence of acronyms, abbreviations, and slang. Therefore, we adopt a heuristic where a hashtag's language is set as the language used by the majority of its tweets. To quantify the accuracy of this heuristic, two annotators inspected the tweets of 200 hashtags to identify the language of the hashtag and for the majority of the tweets. This analysis showed that the heuristic correctly identifies the hashtag's language in 96.5% of the instances.

4.2 Hashtag Sharing by Languages

The adoption of a hashtag by a second language was measured by calculating the frequency with which tweets using a hashtag with language l_1 were labeled with language l_2. The noisy nature of microtext is known to make language identification difficult (Bergsma et al., 2012; Goldszmidt et al., 2013) and can create spurious instances of second-language hashtag adoption. Therefore, we impose a minimum frequency of hashtag use where l_2 is only said to use a hashtag of l_1 if at least 20 tweets using that hashtag were labeled with l_2. To quantify the accuracy of our hashtag adoption measure, two annotators inspected the second-language tweets of 200 hashtags, sampled from the data and representing 40 language pair combinations; this analysis showed that with the filtering the assertion that at least one author from language l_1 used a hashtag of language l_2 was correct in 67% of the instances.

Hashtag	# Langs.	Primary Lang.	Type
#lastfm	39	en	APPLICATION
#WaliSupitKEPO	32	id	SPAM
#RenggiTampan-DanKece	32	id	SPAM
#NP	32	en	APPLICATION
#Np	32	en	APPLICATION
#MTVHottest	31	en	VOTING
#SidikLoveTini	30	id	SPAM
#np	30	en	APPLICATION
#GER	29	en	NAMED ENTITY
#User_Indonesia	29	id	APPLICATION
#Soccer	29	en	COMMUNITY
#RobotKepo	29	id	APPLICATION
#KeePO	27	id	APPLICATION
#NowPlaying	28	en	APPLICATION
#Hot	28	en	ADVERTISEMENT

Table 3: The hashtags associated with the most number of languages having at least 20 tweets using that hashtag

Table 2 shows the frequency with which authors using the 15 most-commonly observed languages (shown as columns using their ISO 639-1 language codes) adopt a hashtag from another of the most-common languages (shown as rows), revealing widespread sharing of hashtags between languages. English hashtags are the most frequently used in other languages, likely due to it being the most common language in Twitter. However, other languages' hashtags are also adopted, with Spanish, Japanese, and Indonesian being the most common after English.

Despite the strong evidence of using of a single hashtag in multiple languages, the results in Table 2 should not be interpreted as evidence of code switching. Table 3 shows the 15 hashtags used in the most number of languages. The majority of these hashtags are generated by either (1) Twitter-based applications that automatically write a tweet in a user's native language and then append a fixed English-language hashtag or (2) spam-like accounts that use the same hashtag and include random text snippets in various languages, neither of which signal code switching behavior.

Furthermore, given the noise introduced by language misidentification and spam behavior on the

	Language of tweet														
	de	ru	ko	pt	en	it	fr	zh	es	ar	th	ja	id	nl	tr
de		2	1	4	15	6	9	4	9			1	4	6	1
ru	3		3	3	25	7	5	8	7	2	1	7	7	7	1
ko	4	2			13	3	6	5	10	3	10	11	4	2	
pt	14	3			64	45	40	13	63		2	4	3	15	10
en	1705	532	155	1235		1735	2183	1171	2482	362	176	742	1097	1101	342
it	5	2	1	10	29		15	4	22	5		3	6	3	1
fr	38	2	3	36	87	49		28	67	8	1	12	19	29	6
zh	3	4	2	2	12	1	2		4		1	11	1		1
es	67	17	3	321	435	264	206	105		29	5	32	66	66	31
ar	6	2			38	4	9	6	7			8	5	1	2
th	3		7	1	24	5	4	8	8	2		6	4	1	
ja	17	18	11	11	123	17	24	132	45	2	2		14	12	4
id	84	2	6	25	131	88	58	14	92	6	5	11		52	17
nl	13		1	3	17	6	11	2	9			1	1		
tr	17	1		3	28	9	7	7	13	3		1	22	9	

Table 2: The frequency with which a hashtag is used by multiple languages. Columns denote the language in which the tweet is written; rows denote the hashtag's language; and cell values report the number of hashtags where the column's language has used the hashtag in at least 20 tweets. Diagonal same-language values are omitted for clarity.

Twitter platform, we view the initial results in Table 2 an overestimate of hashtag adoption by languages other than the hashtag's source language. A further inspection of language classification errors revealed four common factors: (1) the lack of accents on characters,[3] (2) the use of short words, which appeared ambiguous to `langid.py`, (3) the use of non-Latin characters for emoticons or visual affect, and (4) proper names originating from a language different from the tweet's. Nevertheless, the observed trends do provide some guidance as to which language pairs might share hashtags and also may code switch.

Among the hashtags in Table 3, two are legitimately used by authors in multiple languages: #soccer and #GER, the latter corresponding to the German soccer team. Both hashtags were popular due to the World Cup, which occurred during the time period studied. For both, authors included these hashtags while taking part in a global conversation about the games and event. The hashtag #soccer is a clear case of code switching, where individuals are communicating their interests in multiple languages, even when equivalent hashtags in the tweet's language are actively being used. Indeed, over half of the languages using #football had at least one tweet containing both #football and #futbol. The example of #GER highlights a boundary case of code switching. Here, GER is an abbreviation for the country's name, making it a highly-recognized marker, rather than an example of a language change that results in code switching; however, the country has different names depending on the language used (e.g., Deutschland), which does point to an active choice on an author's part when selecting a particular name and its abbreviation.

4.3 Analysis by Hashtag Type

In a second analysis, we focus specifically on hashtags classified as COMMUNITY and ANNOTATION, which are more associated with intentional communication actions and therefore more likely to be used in instances of code switching. Performing such an analysis at scale would require automated methods for classifying hashtags by their use, which is beyond the scope of this initial investigation. Therefore, we performed a manual analysis of the 100 most-common, 100 least-common, and 100 median-frequency hashtags in our dataset to assess the distribution of hashtag types and cases of code switching among the COMMUNITY and ANNOTATION hashtags. Two annotators labeled each hashtag, achieving 64.6% agreement on the type annotations; disagreements were largely due to mistaken assignments rather that disputed classifications.[4] An adjudication step resolved all disagreements. Additionally, eleven hashtags were excluded from analysis due being made of common words (e.g., #go, #be) which had

[3] In particular, the lack of character accents caused significant difficulties in distinguish between Spanish and Catalan.

[4] In particular, mistakes were more common when analyzing hashtags used in languages outside the annotators' fluency, which required a more careful assessment of why the hashtag was being used.

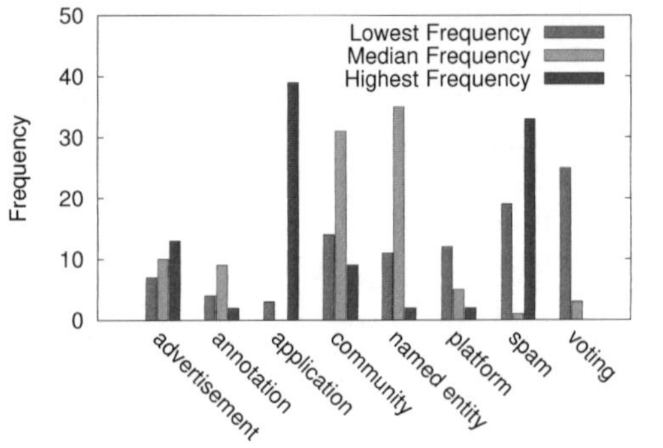

Figure 1: Type distributions of the sets of 100 highest, median, and lowest frequency hashtags used in our dataset

Hashtag	Lang.	Lang. of Code Switched Tweet
#Noticias	es	en
#Facts	en	id th fr es ru
#simple	en	id es fr ms tr tl sw zh ja ko
#bitch	en	ar cs de es fr id it ja ms nl pt ru sv tl tr zh
#delicious	en	ca de es fr id it ja ko ms nl ru th tr zh
#Design	en	ar de es fr ja kr pt th tl zh
#Felicidad	es	ca en
#SWAG	en	de es fr id it pl pt ru
#fresh	en	es fr id it ms nl sv
#BoludecesNO	es	en
#truth	en	ar bs bu es fr hi id ja it ms pa pt ru tl zh
#Hadith	ar	nl en
#Quran	ar	fa ms id sw az it de en
#hadith	ar	fr en
#tech	en	de es nl ar el fr ro id it ja ms no pl pt ru sq sv zh
#RemajaIndonesia	jv	ms
#class	en	ar tr es bg de fr pt he hr id it ja lt lv ms nl ru sw tl uk zh
#animals	en	ar ca de es fr pt it ms ja mk pl pt ro ru tl tr ur vi
#cine	es	ca de en fr ja pt ro ru
#sunday	en	es ar tr fr ca de el gl hu id it ja ms ko pt nl nn no pl ro ru sl sv th tl zh
#Energy	en	ru es de fr it pt tr
#change	en	ar nl es cs de el eu fr pt id it ja ko jv lv ms nb no pl ro uk ru sv ta th tl tr ur zh
#magic	en	nl fr ar ru ca cs de el it es hu id ja jv ko lv ru ms nn pl pt ro sq sv sw sl tl tr zh

Table 4: Code switched hashtags and the languages of the tweets in which they were seen (ANNOTATION types top, COMMUNITY types bottom).

no meaningful interpretation for their use. Following, we describe the results of the analysis and then highlight several types of hashtags.

Figure 1 shows the distribution of hashtag types observed in the three samples. SPAM and APPLICATION hashtags were most common among highest frequency hashtags, whereas the lowest frequency tags in the dataset were also either SPAM or VOTING. Surprisingly, the median frequency hashtags had the majority of the discussion-related hashtag types

Within the ANNOTATION and COMMUNITY types, we selected thirteen hashtags each to manually evaluate if code switching behavior was observed. For each hashtag, two annotators reviewed all associated tweets that were identified as using a different language than that of the hashtag. Annotators were instructed to consider the tweet an instance of code switching only in cases where (1) there was sufficient text to determine the message's actual language and (2) the message was an act of communication (in contrast to spam-like or nonsensical messages).

Code switching behavior was observed for eleven of the ANNOTATION hashtags and twelve of the COMMUNITY hashtags. Table 4 shows those code switched hashtags and the languages in which they were seen, highlighting the varying frequency with which hashtags were used in multiple languages. For example, the primarily Arabic hashtag #Hadith was used in English and Dutch tweets; similarity, all three Spanish hashtags were used in English tweets.

Many hashtags are used primarily with languages that are associated with countries known to have bilingual speakers fluent in English. However, several hashtags were used in a variety of diverse languages. For example, #truth was used with languages such as Arabic, Bosnian, Bulgarian Hindi, and Punjabi. The most widely code switched hashtag was #magic. In English, the hashtag is commonly used with content on magic tricks; however, in other languages, the hashtag often connotes surprise. For example, the Latvian tweet "Es izmeklēju visu plauktu, nekur nav. Mamma piejiet ne sekunde nepagāja, kad viņa atrada. #magic" comments on having an item on the shelf disappear when looking for it, only for it to reappear like magic.

During annotation, we observed that authors were highly productive in their code switching, using these hashtags to generate the types of emotional and sarcastic messages typically seen in same-language messages. For example, in the Swedish tweet "Bussen luktar spya och öl. #fresh" the author is sarcastically commenting on a bus that smells of vomit and beer.

4.4 Discussion

The process of annotating code switching for hashtags revealed four notable trends in author behavior that occurred with multiple hashtags. First, authors fluent in non-Latin writing systems will often use Latin-transliterated hashtags, which are then adopted by authors of Latin-based systems. For example, the hashtag #aikatsu describes a collectible card game and anime and is heavily used by both Japanese and English authors. Similarity, the transliterated hashtags #Hadith and #Quran are commonly associated with Arabic-language tweets, which rarely include an Arabic-script version of those hashtags even when the tweets include other hashtags in Arabic.

Second, when two or more languages share the same written form of a word (i.e., homographs), the resulting hashtags become conflated and appear as false examples of code switching. For example, #Real was widely used in both English and Spanish, but with two meanings: the English usages denoting something existent (i.e., not fake) and the Spanish usages referring to Real Madrid FC, a soccer club. The hashtag #cine also posed a challenge due to abbreviation. While many Spanish-language tweets include #cine (cinema), tweets in other languages include #cinema and its abbreviated form #cine, which matches the Spanish term, creating false evidence of code switching.

Third, multilingual individuals may adopt a common hashtag for reasons other than code switching, which we highlight with two examples. The hashtag #1DWelcomeToBrazil is used in a large number of English and Portuguese tweets. This hashtag is associated with the travel arrival of the English-speaking band One Direction to Brazil. Similarly, the #100happydays hashtag was spawned from a movement where individuals describe positive aspects of their day. These global phenomena increases the difficulty of automatically identifying code switching instances.

Fourth, spam accounts will occasionally latch onto a hashtag and use it in a variety of languages. For example, the popular hashtag #1000ADAY is used to attract new followers, which resulted in adult content services also using the hashtag to post spam advertisements. Surprisingly, nearly a third of tweets for this hashtag are in Russian and feature fully-grammatical text that appears to be randomly sampled from other sources, such as lists of proverbs. After examining multiple accounts, we speculate that these messages are actually bot accounts who need to generate sufficient number of messages to avoid Twitter's spam filters. Work on detecting fake accounts has largely been done in English (Benevenuto et al., 2010; Grier et al., 2010; Ghosh et al., 2012) and so may benefit from detecting this cross-lingual hashtag use in accounts.

5 Experiment 2: Bilingual Cities

The second experiment measures the prevalence of hashtag code switching in tweets from three cities with different populations of English and French speakers: Montreal, Canada, Quebec City, Canada and Paris, France. All three cities are known to contain bilingual speaker as well, who have been shown to actively code switch (Heller, 1992). To test for differences in the code switching behavior of populations, each city is analyzed according to the degree to which Anglophone and Francophone speakers incorporate hashtags of other languages into their tweets and whether translations of the code switched hashtags are used in the original language.

5.1 Experimental Setup

Data Tweets were gathered for each city by using the method of Jurgens (2013) to identify Twitter users with a home location within each city's greater metropolitan area. Tweets were then extracted for these users over a three year sample of 10% of Twitter. This process yielded 4.4M tweets for Montreal, 203K for Quebec City, and 58.1M for Paris. For efficiency, we restricted the Paris dataset to 5M tweets, randomly sampled across the time period.

Language Identification The language of a tweet was identified using a similar process as in Experiment 1. Because this setting restricts the analysis to only English and French, a different method was used to determine the language of a hashtag. Given a tweet in language l_1, the text of a hashtag is tested to see if it wholly occurs within the dictionary for l_1; if not, a greedy tokenization algorithm is run to attempt to split a hashtag into constituent words that are in the dictionary of l_1. If either the dictionary-lookup and tokenization steps

French hashtags on English tweets			English hashtags on French tweets		
Quebec City	Montreal	Paris	Quebec City	Montreal	Paris
imfc	imfc	comprendraquipourra	lasttweet	gohabsgo	bbl
rilive	charte	sachezle	bbl	fail	teaminsomniaque
relev	seriea	nian	mtvhottest	ind	teamportugal
ceta	bel	hollande	gohabsgo	mtvhottest	ps
preorderproblemonitunes	brasil2014	federer	not	not	findugame
derpatrash	touspourgagner	tropa	fail	soccer	adp
villequebec	2ne1	guillaumeradio	100factsaboutme	wow	lasttweet
tufnations	ma	vousetespaspret	herbyvip	podcast	follow
ta	lavoixtva	bel	foodies	ukraine	teamom
rougeetor	passionforezria	retouraupensionnat	electionsqc2014	int	thebest

Table 5: The ten most frequent hashtags occurring in French and English tweets

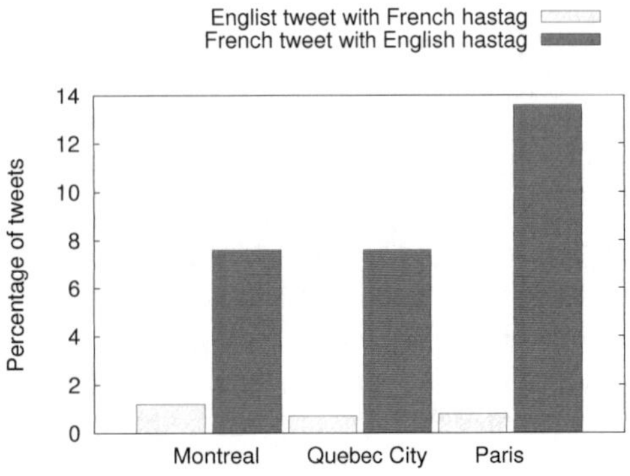

Figure 2: Percentages of tweets with any hashtag that include a hashtag from the other language

succeed, the hashtag is said to be in l_1. Otherwise, the tests are repeated with the second language l_2. If the hashtag cannot be recognized in l_1 or l_2, it is assumed to be in the language of its tweet. The `aspell` dictionaries were used to recognize words. Furthermore, after analyzing the errors made due to missing words, dictionaries were augmented to include common social media terms in each language (e.g., "selfie"). A manual analysis of 100 hashtags each for French and English showed that this language assignment method was correct for 91% of the instances.

5.2 Results

Francophone authors were much more likely to use English hashtags than Anglophone authors were for French hashtags. For tweets in each locale and language, Figure 2 shows the percentage containing a hashtag in the other language relative to the total number in that city using a hashtag in either language. Notably, Paris has a higher rate of using English hashtags than both Canadian cities. We speculate that this difference is due to the high rate of bilingualism in Montreal and Quebec City; because authors are fully fluent in both languages, should Francophone authors need to express themselves with an English hashtag, they may write the entire tweet in English, rather than code switching. In contrast, Parisian authors are less likely to be fully fluent in English (though functional) and therefore express themselves primarily in French with English hashtags as desired. An analogous trend may be seen for French hashtags in the English tweets from Montreal, which has a higher population of primarily Anglophone speakers who might be less willing to communicate entirely in French but will still use French hashtags to connect their content with the dominant language used in the city.

For each language and city, Table 5 shows the ten most popular hashtags incorporated into tweets of the other language. Examining the most popular English tags in French tweets shows a clear distinction in the two populations; French Parisian tweets include more universal English hashtags or those generated by applications, which are not generally instances of code switching. In contrast, the Canadian cities include more ANNOTATION type hashtags, including the sarcasm-marking #not, which are more indicative of code switching behavior.

An established linguistic convention within a population can also motivate authors to prefer one language's expression over another (Myers-Scotton, 1997). To test whether a high-frequency concept was equally expressed in French and English or whether one language's expression was preferred, we created pairs of equivalent English and French hashtags expressing the same concept (e.g., #happy/#heureux) by translating the 50 most-popular English hashtags used in French tweets. Then, the tweets for each city were analyzed to identify which languages were used in expressing each concept as a hashtag. The results in Figure 3 reveal that for nearly half of the hash-

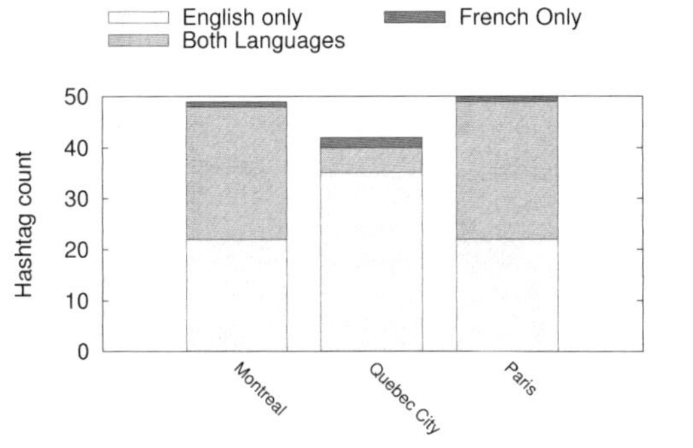

Figure 3: For 50 most-common concepts expressed in equivalent French and English translations, the frequency with which the hashtags for a concept were seen in each language.

tags, equivalent French language versions are in use; however, examining the relative frequencies shows that in all cases, the English version is still preferred, despite the presence of a large Francophone population. For hashtags that were only seen in English, many were of the COMMUNITY type, e.g., #50factsaboutme, which may not have an equivalent French-language version. However, we observed that when both an English hashtag and its French translation were attested, the use of the English hashtag in French was most often an instance of code switching. Hence, testing for the presence hashtag translation pairs may serve as a helpful heuristic for identifying hashtags whose use signals code switching behavior.

6 Discussion

Typically, code switching is distinguished from the related phenomena of borrowing by testing whether the word is being fluently mixed into the utterance instead of simply functioning as a loan word (Poplack, 2001). Hashtags present a unique challenge for distinguishing between the two phenomena due their brief content and unstructured usage: a hashtag may occur anywhere in a tweet and its general content lacks grammatical constraints. Examining the hashtags seen in our study, we find evidence spanning both types of uses. Common hashtags such as #win or #fail are widely recognized outside of English and their uses could easily be interpreted instances of borrowing. However, the complexity of other hashtags gives the appearance that their uses go beyond that of borrowing, e.g., #goingbacktoschool in "Nadie dijo que sería fácil, pero cómo cuesta estudiar después de 4 años de no tener nada académico cerquita #goingbacktoschool" where the author is commenting on the difficulty of returning for a degree. Still other posts include multiple single-token hashtags from a second language, e.g., the earlier example of "Jetzt gibt's was vernünftiges zum essen! #salad #turkey #lunch #healthy #healthylifestyle #loveit." Although individually these hashtags may be widely recognized and operate as interlingual markers, their combined presence suggests an intentional language shift on the part of the author that could be interpreted as code switching. Together, the examples point to hashtag use by multiple languages as a complex phenomena where shared hashtag entities exist on a graded scale from simple borrowing to fully signaling code switching. Our study is intended as a starting point for analyzing this practice and all our data is made available to support future discussions on the roles these hashtags play and how they facilitate communication both within and across language communities.

7 Conclusion

The present work has provided an initial study of code switching in Twitter focusing on instances where an author produces a message in one language and then includes a hashtag from a second language. Our work provides three main contributions. First, using state-of-the-art language identification techniques, we show that hashtags are widely shared across languages, though the challenges of correctly classifying the language of tweets limits our ability to quantify the exact scale. Second, in a manual analysis of ANNOTATION and COMMUNITY hashtags, we show that authors readily code switch with these types of hashtags, using them just as they would in single language tweets (e.g., indicating sarcasm). Third, in a case study of French and English tweets from three Francophone cities with bilingual speakers, we find that the cities with more bilingual speakers tended to have fewer occurrences English hashtags in French tweets, which we speculate is due to authors being more likely to write such tweets entirely in English, rather than code switch; however, when English hashtags were observed in French tweets from these more bilingual cities, they were much more likely to be used in instances of code switching. Data for all of the experiments is available at http://www.networkdynamics.org/datasets/.

Our work raises several avenues for future work. First, we plan to examine how to improve language identification in microtext in order to gain a more accurate estimation of hashtag sharing and code switching rates for languages. Second, the Twitter platform enables measuring additional factors that may influence an individual's rate of code switching; specifically, we plan to investigate (1) a user's historical tweets to estimate the degree of bilinguality and (2) the impact of a user's social network with respect to homophily and language use.

References

Peter Auer. 1998. *Code-switching in conversation: Language, interaction and identity*. Routledge.

Fabrıcio Benevenuto, Gabriel Magno, Tiago Rodrigues, and Virgılio Almeida. 2010. Detecting spammers on twitter. In *Collaboration, electronic messaging, anti-abuse and spam conference (CEAS)*, volume 6, page 12.

Shane Bergsma, Paul McNamee, Mossaab Bagdouri, Clayton Fink, and Theresa Wilson. 2012. Language identification for creating language-specific twitter collections. In *Proceedings of the Second Workshop on Language in Social Media*, pages 65–74. Association for Computational Linguistics.

S. Climent, J. Moré, A. Oliver, M. Salvatierra, I. Sànchez, M. Taulé, and L. Vallmanya. 2003. Bilingual newsgroups in catalonia: A challenge for machine translation. *Journal of Computer-Mediated Communication*, 9(1).

Dmitry Davidov, Oren Tsur, and Ari Rappoport. 2010. Semi-supervised recognition of sarcastic sentences in twitter and amazon. In *Proceedings of the Fourteenth Conference on Computational Natural Language Learning (CoNLL)*, pages 107–116. Association for Computational Linguistics.

Saptarshi Ghosh, Bimal Viswanath, Farshad Kooti, Naveen Kumar Sharma, Gautam Korlam, Fabricio Benevenuto, Niloy Ganguly, and Krishna Phani Gummadi. 2012. Understanding and combating link farming in the twitter social network. In *Proceedings of the 21st international conference on World Wide Web (WWW)*, pages 61–70. ACM.

Moises Goldszmidt, Marc Najork, and Stelios Paparizos. 2013. Boot-strapping language identifiers for short colloquial postings. In *Proceedings of the European Conference on Machine Learning and Principles and Practice of Knowledge Discovery in Databases (ECMLPKDD 2013)*. Springer Verlag, September.

Chris Grier, Kurt Thomas, Vern Paxson, and Michael Zhang. 2010. @ spam: the underground on 140 characters or less. In *Proceedings of the 17th ACM conference on Computer and communications security (CCS)*, pages 27–37. ACM.

John Joseph Gumperz. 1982. *Discourse strategies*. Cambridge University Press.

Manish Gupta, Rui Li, Zhijun Yin, and Jiawei Han. 2010. Survey on social tagging techniques. *ACM SIGKDD Explorations Newsletter*, 12(1):58–72.

Monica Heller. 1992. The politics of codeswitching and language choice. *Journal of Multilingual & Multicultural Development*, 13(1-2):123–142.

Jeff Huang, Katherine M Thornton, and Efthimis N Efthimiadis. 2010. Conversational tagging in twitter. In *Proceedings of the 21st ACM conference on Hypertext and hypermedia*, pages 173–178. ACM.

David Jurgens. 2013. That's what friends are for: Inferring location in online social media platforms based on social relationships. In *Proceedings of the 7th International Conference on Weblogs and Social Media (ICWSM)*. AAAI.

Carmen K. M. Lee. 2007. Linguistic features of email and icq instant messaging in hong kong. In Brenda Danet and Susan C. Herring, editors, *The Multilingual Internet: Language, Culture, and Communication Online*. Oxford University Press.

Julie Letierce, Alexandre Passant, John Breslin, and Stefan Decker. 2010. Understanding how twitter is used to spread scientific messages. In *WebSci10: Extending the Frontiers of Society On-Line*.

Yu-Ru Lin, Drew Margolin, Brian Keegan, Andrea Baronchelli, and David Lazer. 2013. # bigbirds never die: Understanding social dynamics of emergent hashtags. In *Seventh International Conference on Weblogs and Social Media (ICWSM)*. AAAI.

Yabing Liu, Chloe Kliman-Silver, and Alan Mislove. 2014. The tweets they are a-changin': Evolution of twitter users and behavior. In *Proceedings of the 8th International Conference on Weblogs and Social Media (ICWSM)*. AAAI.

Marco Lui and Timothy Baldwin. 2012. langid. py: An off-the-shelf language identification tool. In *Proceedings of the ACL 2012 System Demonstrations*, pages 25–30. Association for Computational Linguistics.

Carol Myers-Scotton. 1997. *Duelling Languages: Grammatical Structure in Codeswitching*. Clarendon Press.

Chad Nilep. 2006. Code switching in sociocultural linguistics. *Colorado Research in Linguistics*, 19(1):1–22.

John C. Paolillo. 2011. Conversational codeswitching on usenet and internet relay chat. *Language@Internet*, 8.

Shana Poplack and David Sankoff. 1984. Borrowing: the synchrony of integration. *Linguistics*, 22(1):99–136.

Shana Poplack, David Sankoff, and Christopher Miller. 1988. The social correlates and linguistic processes of lexical borrowing and assimilation. *Linguistics*, 26(1):47–104.

Shana Poplack. 2001. Code-switching (linguistic). In *International Encyclopedia of the Social and Behavioral Sciences*, pages 2062–2065. Elsevier Science Ltd., 2nd edition.

David Sankoff, Shana Poplack, and Swathi Vanniarajan. 1990. The case of the nonce loan in tamil. *Language variation and change*, 2(01):71–101.

Bonnie Urciuoli. 1995. Language and borders. *Annual Review of Anthropology*, 24:pp. 525–546.

Lei Yang, Tao Sun, Ming Zhang, and Qiaozhu Mei. 2012. We know what@ you# tag: does the dual role affect hashtag adoption? In *Proceedings of the 21st international conference on World Wide Web (WWW)*, pages 261–270. ACM.

Overview for the First Shared Task on Language Identification in Code-Switched Data

Thamar Solorio
Dept. of Computer Science
University of Houston
Houston, TX, 77004
solorio@cs.uh.edu

Elizabeth Blair, Suraj Maharjan, Steven Bethard
Dept. of Computer and Information Sciences
University of Alabama at Birmingham
Birmingham, AL, 35294
{eablair, suraj, bethard}@uab.edu

Mona Diab, Mahmoud Gohneim, Abdelati Hawwari, Fahad AlGhamdi
Dept. of Computer Science
George Washington University
Washington, DC 20052
{mtdiab, mghoneim, abhawwari, fghamdi}@gwu.edu

Julia Hirschberg and **Alison Chang**
Dept. of Computer Science
Columbia University
New York, NY 10027
julia@cs.columbia.edu
ayc2135@columbia.edu

Pascale Fung
Dept. of Electronic & Computer Engineering
Hong Kong University of Science and Technology
Clear Water Bay, Kowloon, Hong Kong
pascale@ece.ust.hk

Abstract

We present an overview of the first shared task on language identification on code-switched data. The shared task included code-switched data from four language pairs: Modern Standard Arabic-Dialectal Arabic (MSA-DA), Mandarin-English (MAN-EN), Nepali-English (NEP-EN), and Spanish-English (SPA-EN). A total of seven teams participated in the task and submitted 42 system runs. The evaluation showed that language identification at the token level is more difficult when the languages present are closely related, as in the case of MSA-DA, where the prediction performance was the lowest among all language pairs. In contrast, the language pairs with the higest F-measure where SPA-EN and NEP-EN. The task made evident that language identification in code-switched data is still far from solved and warrants further research.

1 Introduction

The main goal of this language identification shared task is to increase awareness of the outstanding challenges in the automated processing of Code-Switched (CS) data and motivate more research in this direction. We define CS broadly as a communication act, whether spoken or written, where two or more languages are being used interchangeably. In its spoken form, CS has probably been around ever since different languages first came in contact. Linguists have studied this phenomenon since the mid 1900s. In contrast, the Natural Language Processing (NLP) community has only recently started to pay attention to CS, with the earliest work in this area dating back to Joshi's theoretical work proposing an approach to parsing CS data (Joshi, 1982) based on the Matrix and Embedded language framework. With the wide-spread use of social media, CS is now being used more and more in written language and thus we are seeing an increase in published papers dealing with CS. We are specifically interested in intrasentential code switched phenomena. As a result of this task, we have successfully created the first set of annotated data for several language pairs with a coherent set of labels across the languages. As the shared task results show, CS poses new research questions that warrant new NLP approaches, and thus we expect to see a significant increase in NLP work in the coming years addressing CS phenomena in data.

The shared task covers four language pairs and is focused on social media data. We provided participants with annotated data from Twitter for the

Proceedings of The First Workshop on Computational Approaches to Code Switching, pages 62–72,
October 25, 2014, Doha, Qatar.

language pairs: Modern Standard Arabic-Arabic dialects (MSA-DA), Mandarin-English (MAN-EN), NEP-EN (NEP-EN), and SPA-EN (SPA-EN). These language pairs represent a good variety in terms of language typology and relatedness among pairs. They also cover languages with different representation in terms of number of speakers world wide. Participants were asked to make predictions on unseen Twitter data for each language pair. We also provided participants with test data from a "surprise genre" with the objective of assessing the robustness of language identification systems to genre variation.

2 Task Description

The task consists of labeling each token/word in the input file with one of six labels: *lang1*, *lang2*, *other*, *ambiguous*, *mixed*, and named entities NE. The *lang1*, *lang2* labels refer to the two languages addressed in the subtask, for example for the language pair MSA-DA, *lang1* would be an MSA and *lang2* is DA. The *other* category is a label used to tag all punctuation marks, emoticons, numbers, and similar tokens that do not represent actual words in any of the given languages. The *ambiguous* label is for instances where it is not possible to assign a language with certainty, for example, a lexical form that belongs to both languages, appearing in a context that does not indicate one language over the other. The *mixed* category is for words composed of CS morphemes, such as the word snap*chateando* 'to chat' from SPA-EN, the word over*ai* from NEP-EN, or the word *hayqwlwn*[1] 'they will say', from MSA-DA, where the 'ha' is a DA future morpheme and the stem 'yqwlwn' is MSA.The *NE* label is included in this task in an effort to allow for a more focused analysis of CS data with the exclusion of proper nouns. NEs have a very different behavior than most other words in a language vocabulary and thus from our perspective they need to be identified to be handled properly.

Table 1 shows Twitter examples taken from the training data. The annotation guidelines are posted on the workshop website[2]. We post the ones used for SPA-EN as for the other language pairs the only differences are the examples provided.

[1]We use Buckwalter transliteration scheme http://www.qamus.org/transliteration.htm

[2]http://emnlp2014.org/workshops/CodeSwitch/call.html

Language Pair	Example
MSA-DA	*AlnhArdp AlsAEp 11 hAkwn Dyf >. HAfZ AlmyrAzy ElY qnAp drym* llHdyv En >wlwyAt Alvwrp fy AlmrHlp Al-HAlyp wqDyp tSHyH msAr Alvwrp Al<ElAmy (Today O'Clock 11 I_will_be [a_]guest[_of] Mr. Hafez AlMirazi on Channel Dream to_talk about [the_]priorities[_of] the_revolution in the_stage the_current and_[the_]issue[_of] correcting [the_]path[_of] the_revolution Media)
NEP-EN	My car at the workshop for a much needed repairs... *ABA pocket khali hune bho* (My car at the workshop for a much needed repairs... now my pocket will be empty)
SPA-EN	*Por primera vez veo a* @username actually being hateful! it was beautiful:) (For the first time I get to see @username actually being hateful! it was beautiful:)

Table 1: Examples of Twitter data used in the shared task.

3 Related Work

In the past, most language identification research has been done at the document level. Some researchers, however, have developed methods to identify languages within multilingual documents (Singh and Gorla, 2007; Nguyen and Doğruöz, 2013; King and Abney, 2013). Their test data comes from a variety of sources, including web pages, bilingual forum posts, and jumbled data from monolingual sources, but none of them are trained on code-switched data, opting instead for a monolingual training set per language. This could prove to be a problem when working on code-switched data, particularly in shorter samples such as social media data, as the code-switching context is not present in training material.

One system tackled both the problems of code-switching and social media in language and code-switched status identification (Lignos and Marcus, 2013). Lignos and Marcus gathered millions of monolingual tweets in both English and Spanish in order to model the two languages, and used crowd-sourcing to annotate tens of thousands of Spanish tweets, approximately 11% of which contained code-switched content. This system was able to achieve 96.9% word-level accuracy and a 0.936 F-measure in identifying code-switched tweets.

The issue still stands that relatively little code-switching data, such as that used in Lignos and

Marcus' research, is readily available. Even in their data, the percentage of code-switched tweets was barely over a tenth of the total test data. There have been other corpora built, particularly for other language pairs such as Mandarin-English (Li et al., 2012; Lyu et al., 2010), but the amount of data available and the percentage of code-switching data within that data are not up to the standards of other areas of the natural language processing field. With this in mind, we sought to provide corpora for multiple language pairs, each with a better distribution of code-switching phenomena.

4 Data Sets

Most of the data for the shared task comes form Twitter. However, we also collected and annotated data from other social media sources, including Facebook, web forums, and blogs. These additional sources of data were used as the surprise data. In this section we describe briefly the corpora curated for the shared task.

Language-pair	Training	Test	Surprise
MAN-EN	1000	313	n/a
MSA-DA	5,838	2332, 1,777	12,017
NEP-EN	9,993	3,018 (2,874)	1,087
SPA-EN	11,400	3,060 (1,626)	1,102

Table 2: Statistics of the shared task data sets per language pairs. The numbers are according to what was actually annotated, numbers in parenthesis show what the participating systems were able to crawl from Twitter. The Surprise genre comes from various sources, other than Twitter.

Table 2 shows some statistics about the different datasets used in this task. We strive to provide dataset sizes that would allow a robust analysis of results. However, an unexpected challenge was the rate at which tweets became unavailable. Different language pairs had different attrition rates with SPA-EN being the most affected language and MSA-DA and NEP-EN the least affected. Note that we provided two test datasets for MSA-DA. Since we separated the data on a per user basis, the first test set had a highly skewed distribution. The second test set was distributed to participants to allow a comparison with a data set having a class distribution more similar to the training set.

4.1 SPA-EN data

Developing the corpus involved two primary steps: locating code-switching tweets and using crowdsourcing to annotate their tokens with language tags. A small portion of the tweets were annotated in-lab and this was used as the gold data for quality control in the crowdsourcing annotation.

To avoid biasing the data used in this task, we used a two step process to select the tweets: first we identified CS tweets by doing a keyword search on Twitter's API. We selected a few frequently used English words and restricted the search to tweets identified by Twitter as Spanish from users in California and Texas. An additional set of tweets was then collected by using frequent Spanish words in an all English tweet, from users in the same locations. We filtered these tweets to remove tweets containing URLs, duplicates, spam tweets and retweets.

In-lab annotators labeled the filtered tweets using the guidelines referenced above. From this set of labeled data we then ranked the users in this set by the percentage of CS tweets. We selected the 12 most prolific CS users and then pulled all of their available tweets. These 12 users contributed the tweets used in the shared task. The tweets were labeled using CrowdFlower[3]. After analyzing the number and content distribution of the tweets, the SPA-EN data was split into a 11,400 tweet training set and a 3,014 tweet test set.

The SPA-EN Surprise Genre (SPA-EN-SG) included Facebook comments from the Veteranas community[4] and the Chicanas community[5] and blog data from the Albino Bean [6]. Data was collected using Python scripts that implemented the Beautiful Soup library and the third-party Python Facebook SDK (for Blogger and Facebook respectively). Post and comment IDs were used to identify Facebook posts, and URLs were used to identify Blogger posts. The collected posts were formatted to match those collected from Twitter. In-lab annotators were used to annotate approximately 1K tokens. All the data we collected in this manner was released as surprise data to all participants.

4.2 NEP-EN data

The collection of NEP-EN data followed a similar approach to that of SPA-EN. We first focused on finding users that switched frequently between

[3]http://www.crowdflower.com/

[4]https://www.facebook.com/VeteranaPinup

[5]https://www.facebook.com/pages/Chicanas/444483772293893

[6]http://thealbinobean.blogspot.com/

Nepali and English. In addition, the users must not be using Devnagari script as done by Nepalese to write Nepali, but must have used its Romanized form. We started by manually reading tweets from some of our Nepali friends. We then crawled their followers who corresponded with them using code-switched tweets or replies. We found that a lot of these users were regular code-switchers themselves. We repeated the same process with the followers and collected nearly 30 such users. We then collected about 2,000 tweets each from these users using the Twitter API. We filtered out all the retweets and the tweets with URLs, following the same process that was used for SPA-EN.

For the surprise test data, we crawled code-switched data from Facebook comments and posts. We found that most Nepalese comments had a rich amount of code-switched data. However, we could not crawl their data because of privacy issues. Nevertheless, we could crawl data from public Facebook pages. We identified some public Nepali Facebook pages where anyone could comment. These pages include FM, news and public figures' public Facebook pages. We crawled the latest 10 feeds from these public pages using the Facebook API and gathered about 12,000 comments and posts for the shared task.

Initially, we sought out help from Nepali graduate students at the University of Alabama at Birmingham to annotate 100 tweets (1739 tokens). We gave the same annotation file to two annotators to do the annotation. We found that they agreed with an accuracy of 95.34%. These tweets were then reviewed and used as initial gold data in Crowdflower to annotate the first 1000 tweets. The annotation job was enabled only in Nepal and Bhutan. We disabled India, even though people living in some regions of India (Darjeeling, Sikkim) also speak and write in Nepali, as most spammers were coming from India. We then ran two batches of 5000 tweets and one batch of 3000 tweets along with the initial 1,000 tweets as the gold data. This NEP-EN data was then split into a 9,993 tweet training set and a 2,874 tweet test set. No Twitter user appeared in both sets.

4.3 MAN-EN data

The MAN-EN tweets were collected from Twitter with the Twitter API. Users were selected from lists of most followed Twitter accounts in Taiwan (where Mandarin Chinese is the official language). These users' tweets were checked for Mandarin English bilingualism and added to our data collection if they contained both languages.

The next round of usernames came from the lists of users that our original top accounts were following. The tweets written by this new set of users were then examined for Mandarin English code switching and stored as data if they matched the criteria.

The jieba tokenizer[7] was used to segment the Mandarin sections of the tweets and compute offsets of each segment. We format the code switching tweets into columns including language type, labels, and offsets. Named entities were labeled manually by a single annotator.

The data was split by user into 1000 tweets for training and 313 for testing. No MAN-EN surprise data for the current shared task.

4.4 MSA-DA data

For the MSA-DA language pair, we selected Egyptian Arabic (EGY) as the Arabic dialect. We harvested data from two social media sources: Twitter [TWT] and Blog commentaries [COM]. The TWT data served as the main gold standard data for the task where we provided fully annotated data for Training/Tuning and Test. We provided two TWT data sets for the test data that exemplified different tag distributions. The COM data set comprised only test data and it served as the Arabic surprise data set.

To reduce the potential of TWT data attrition from users deleting their accounts or tweets, we selected tweets that are less prone to deletion and/or change. Thereby we harvested tweets by a select set of Egyptian Public Figures. The percentage of deleted tweets and deactivated accounts among those users is significantly lower if we compare it to the tweets crawled from random Egyptian users.

We used the "Tweepy" library to crawl the timelines of 12 Public Figures. Similar to other language pairs, we excluded all re-tweets, tweets with URLs, tweets mentioning other users, and tweets containing Latin characters. We accepted 9,947 tweets, for each we extracted the tweet-id and user-id. Using these IDs, we retrieved the tweets text, tokenized it and assigned character offsets. To guarantee consistency and avoid any misalignment issues, we compiled the full pipeline into the "Arabic Tweets Token Assigner" package which is made

[7]`https://github.com/fxsjy/jieba`

available through the workshop website[8].

For COM, we selected 6723 commentaries (half MSA and half DA) from "youm7"[9] commentaries provided by the Arabic Online Commentary Dataset (Zaidan and Callison-Burch, 2011). The COM data set was processed (12017 total tokens) using the same pipeline created for the task. We also provided the participants with the data formatted with character offsets to maintain consistency across data sets in the Arabic subtask.

The annotation of MSA-DA language pair data is based on two sets of guidelines. The first set is a generic set of guidelines for code switching in general across different language pairs. These guidelines provide the overarching framework for annotating code switched data on the morphological, lexical, syntactic, and pragmatic levels. The second set of guidelines is language pair specific. We created the guidelines for the Arabic language specifically. We enlisted the help of 3 annotators in addition to a super annotator, hence resulting in 4 annotators overall for the whole collection of the data. All the annotators are native speakers of Egyptian Arabic with excellent proficiency in MSA. The super annotator only annotated 10% of the overall data and served as the adjudicator. The annotation process was iterative with several repetitions of the cycle of training, annotation, revision, adjudication until we approached a stable Inter Annotator Agreement (IAA) of over 90% pairwise agreement.

5 Survey of Shared Task Systems

We received submissions from seven different teams. Each participating system had the freedom to submit responses to any of the language pairs covered in the shared task. All seven participants submitted system responses for SPA-EN, making this language pair the most popular in this shared task and MAN-EN the least popular.

All but one participating system used a machine learning algorithm or language models, or even a combination of both, as part of their configuration. A couple of the participating systems used handcrafted rules of some sort, either at the intermediate steps or as the final post-processing step. We also observed a good number of systems using external resources, in the form of labeled monolingual corpora, language specific gazetteers, off the shelf tools (NE recognizers, language id systems, or morphological analyzers) and even unsupervised data crawled from the same users present in the data sets provided. Affixes were also used in some form by different systems.

The architecture of the different systems ranged from a simple approach based on frequencies of character n-grams combined in a rule-based system, to more complex approaches using word embeddings, extended Markov Models, and CRF autoencoders. The majority of the systems that participated in more than one language pair did little to no customization to account for the morphological differences of the specific language pairs beyond language specific parameter-tuning, which probably reflects participants' goal to develop a multilingual id system.

Due to the presence of the NE label, several systems included a component for NE recognition where there was one available for the specific language. In addition, many systems also included case information. One unexpected finding from the shared task was that no participating system tried to embed in their models some form of linguistic theory or framework about CS. Only one system made an explicit reference to CS theories (Chittaranjan et al., 2014) in their motivation to use contextual information, which can be considered as a loose embedding of CS theory. While system performance was competitive (see next section), there is still room for improvement and perhaps some of that improvement can come out of adding this kind of knowledge into the models. Lastly, we were surprised to see that not all systems made use of character encoding information, even though for Mandarin-English that would have been a strong indicator. In Table 3 we present a summary highlighting some of the design choices of participating systems.

6 Results

We used the following evaluation metrics: Accuracy, Precision, Recall, and F-measure. We use F-measure to provide a ranking of systems. In the evaluation at the tweet level we use the standard f-measure. For the evaluation at the token level we use instead the average weighted f-measure to account for the highly imbalanced distribution of classes.

To provide a fair evaluation, we only scored pre-

[8] `http://emnlp2014.org/workshops/CodeSwitch/call.html`

[9] An Egyptian newspaper, `www.youm7.com`

System	Machine Learning	Rules	Case	Character Encoding	External Resources	LM	Affixes	Context
(Chittaranjan et al., 2014)	CRF		✔	✔	dbpedia dumps, online sources			± 3
(Shrestha, 2014)		✔		✔	spell checker			
(Jain and Bhat, 2014)	CRF		✔	✔	English dictionary	✔	✔	± 2
(King et al., 2014)	eMM				ANERgazet, TwitterNLP, Stanford NER	✔	✔	✔
(Bar and Dershowitz, 2014)	SVM		✔		Illocution Twitter Lexicon, monolingual corpora (NE lists)	✔	✔	± 2
(Lin et al., 2014)	CRF		✔	✔	Hindi-Nepali Wikipedia, JRC, CoNLL 2003 shared task, lang id predictors: cld2 and ldig		✔	✔
(Barman et al., 2014)	kNN, SVM	✔	✔		BNC, LexNorm		✔	± 1

Table 3: Comparison of shared task participating system algorithm choices. CRF stands for Conditional Random Fields, SVM for Support Vector Machines and LM for Language Models.

dictions on tweets submitted by all teams. All systems were compared to a simple lexicon-based baseline. The lexicon was gathered from the training data for classes *lang1* and *lang2* only. Emoticons, punctuation marks, usernames and URLs are by default tagged as *other*. In the case of a tie or a new token, the baseline system assigns the majority class for that language pair.

Figure 1 shows prediction performance on the Twitter test data for each language pair at the tweet level. The system predictions for this task are taken directly from the individual token predictions in the following manner: if the system predictions for the same tweet contain at least one tag from each language (lang1 and lang2), the tweet is labeled as code-switched, otherwise it is labeled as monolingual. As illustrated, each language pair shows different patterns. Comparing the systems that participated in all language pairs, there is no clear winner across the board. However, (Chittaranjan et al., 2014) was in the top three places in at least one test file for each language pair. Table 4 shows the results at the token level by label. Here again the figures show F-measure per class label and the last column is the weighted average f-measure (Avg-F). One of the few general trends on these results is that most participating systems were not able to correctly identify the minority classes "ambiguous" and "other". There are only few instances of these labels in the training set and some test sets did not have one of these classes present. The impact on final system performance from these classes is not significant. However, to study CS patterns we will need to have these labels identified properly.

The MAN-EN pair received four system responses and all four of them reached an F-measure >80% and outperformed the simple baseline by a considerable margin. We expected this language pair to be the easiest one for the shared task since each language uses a different encoding script. A very rough but accurate distinction between Mandarin and English could be achieved by looking at the character encoding. However, according to the system descriptions provided, not all systems used encoding information. The best performing systems for MAN-EN are (King et al., 2014) and (Chittaranjan et al., 2014). The former slightly outperformed the latter at the Tweet level (see Figure 1a) task while the opposite was true at the token level (see Table 4 rows 4 and 5).

In the case of SPA-EN, all seven systems outperformed the simple baseline. The best performing system in all SPA-EN tasks was (Bar and Dershowitz, 2014). This system achieved an F-measure of 82.2%, 2.9 percentage points above the second best system (Lin et al., 2014) on the tweet level task (see Figure 1(d)). In the token level evaluation, (Bar and Dershowitz, 2014) reached an Avg. F-measure of 94%. This top performing system uses a sequential classification approach where the labels from the preceding words are used as features in the model. Another design choice that might have given the edge to this system is the fact that their model combines character- and word-based language models in what the authors call "intra- and inter-word level" features. Both types of language models are trained on large amounts of monolingual data and NE lists, which again provides additional knowledge that other systems are not exploiting. For instance, the NE lexicons might account for the best results in the NE class in both the Twitter data and the Surprise genre (see Table 4 last row for SPA-EN and second to last for SPA-EN Surprise). Most systems showed considerable

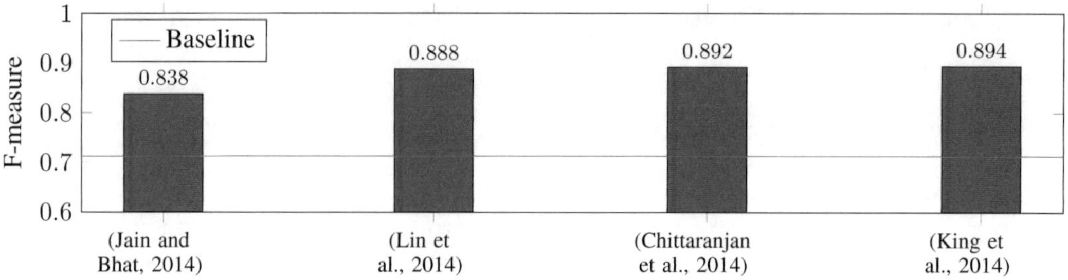

(a) MAN-EN

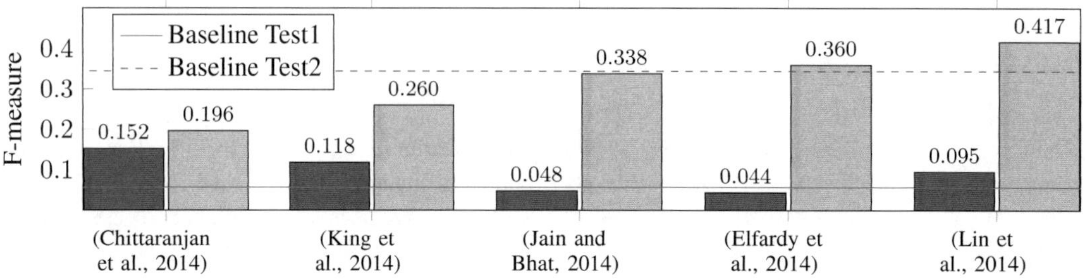

(b) MSA-DA. Dark gray bars show performance on Test1 and light gray bars show performance for Test2

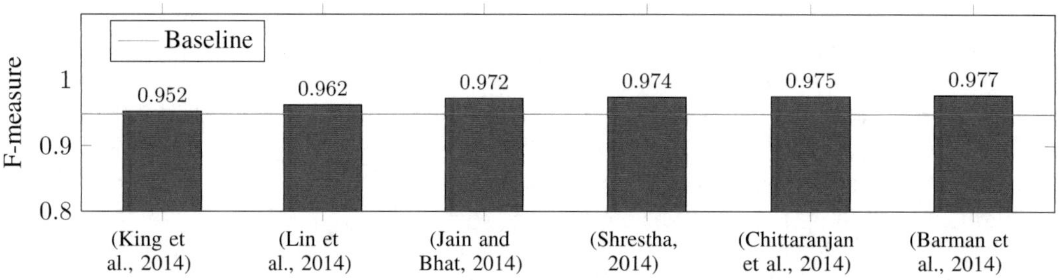

(c) NEP-EN

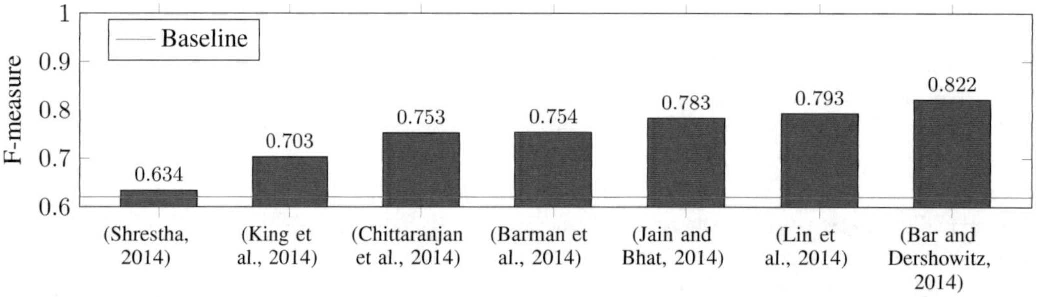

(d) SPA-EN

Figure 1: Prediction results on language identification at the tweet level. This is a binary task to distinguish between a monolingual and a CS tweet. We show performance of participating systems using F-measure as the evaluation metric. The solid line shows the lexicon baseline performance.

differences in prediction performance in both genres. In all cases the Avg. F-measure was higher on the Twitter test data than on the surprise genre. Although the surprise genre is too small to draw strong conclusions, all language pairs with surprise genre test data showed a decrease in performance of around 10%.

We analyzed system outputs and found some consistent sources of error. Lexical forms that exist in both languages were frequently mislabeled by most systems. For example the word for "he" was frequently mislabeled by at least one system. In most of the cases systems were predicting EN as label when the target language was SPA. Cases like this were even more prone to errors when these words fell in the CS point, as in this tweet: *ni el* header ***he*** *hecho* (I haven't even done the header). Tweets like this one, with just one token from the other language, were difficult for most systems. Named entities were also frequent sources of error, especially when they were spelled with lower cases letters.

By far the hardest language pair in this shared task was MSA-DA, as anticipated. Especially when considering the typological similarities between MSA and DA. This is mainly due to the fact that DA and MSA are close variants of one another and hence they share considerable amount of lexical items. The shared lexical items could be simple cognates of one another, or *faux amis* where they are homographs or homophones, but have completely different meaning. Both categories constitute a significant challenge. Accordingly, the baseline system had the lowest performance from all language pairs in both test sets. We note challenges in this language pair on each linguistic level where CS occurs especially for the shared lexical items.

On the phonological level, DA writers tend to mimic the MSA script for DA words even if they are pronounced differently. For example: "heart" is pronounced in DA *Alob* and in MSA as *qalob* but commonly written in MSA as "qalob" in DA data. Also many phonological differences are in short vowels that are underspecified in written Arabic, adding another layer of ambiguity.

On the morphological level, there is no available morphological analyzer able to recognize such shared words and hence they are mostly misclassified. Language identification for MSA-DA CS text highly depends on the context. Typically some Arabic variety word serves as a marker for a context switch such as *mElh$* for DA or *mn∗* for MSA. But if shared lexical items are used, it is challenging to identify the Arabic variant. An example from the training data is *qlb* meaning either *heart* as a noun or *change* as a verb in the phrase *lw qlb mjrm*, corresponding to 'If the heart of a criminal' or 'if he changes into a criminal'. These challenges render language identification for CS MSA-DA data far from solved as evident by the fact that the highest scoring system reached an F-measure of only 41.7% in Test2 for CS identification. Moreover, this is the only language pair where at least one system was not able to outperform the baseline and in the case of Test2 only one system (Lin et al., 2014) outperformed the baseline.

Most teams did well for the NEP-EN shared task, and all teams outperformed the baseline. The reason for the high performance might be the high number of codeswitched tweets in the training and test data for NEP-EN (much higher than other language pairs). This allowed systems to have more samples of CS instances. The other reason for good performance by most participants in both evaluations might be that Nepali and English are two very different languages. The structure of the words and syntax of word formation are very different. We suspect, for instance, that there is a much lower overlap of character n-grams in this language pair than in SPA-EN, which makes for an easier task. At the Tweet level, system performance ranged over a small set of values, the lowest F-measure was 95.2% while the highest was 97.7%. Looking at the numbers in Table 4, we can see that even NE recognition seemed to be a much easier task for this language pair than for SPA-EN (compare results for the NE category in both SPA-EN sets to those of both NEP-EN data sets). The best performing system for the Twitter test data is (Barman et al., 2014) with an F-measure of 97.7%. The results trend in the surprise genre is not consistent with what we observed for the Twitter test data. The top ranked system for Twitter sunk to the 4th place with an F-measure or 59.6%, a considerable drop of almost 40 percentage points. In this case, the overall numbers indicate a much wider difference in the genres than what we observed for other languages, such as SPA-EN, for example. We should note that the class distribution in the surprise data is considerably different from what the models used for training, and from that of the test data as well. In the Twitter data there was a larger number of CS tweets than monolingual ones, while in the surprise genre the majority class was monolingual. This will account for a good portion of the differences in performance. But here as well, the small number of labeled instances makes it hard to draw strong conclusions.

Test Set	System	lang1	lang2	NE	other	ambiguous	mixed	Avg-F
MAN-EN	Baseline	0.9	0.47	0	0.29	-	0	0.761
	(Jain and Bhat, 2014)	0.97	0.66	0.52	0.33	-	0	0.871
	(Lin et al., 2014)	0.98	0.73	0.62	0.34	-	0	0.886
	(King et al., 2014)	0.98	0.74	0.58	0.30	-	0	0.884
	(Chittaranjan et al., 2014)	0.98	0.76	0.66	0.34	-	0	**0.892**
MSA-DA Test 1	(King et al., 2014)	0.88	0.14	0.05	0	0	-	0.720
	Baseline	0.92	0.06	0	0.89	0	-	0.819
	(Chittaranjan et al., 2014)	0.94	0.15	0.57	0.91	0	-	0.898
	(Jain and Bhat, 2014)	0.93	0.05	0.73	0.87	0	-	0.909
	(Lin et al., 2014)	0.94	0.09	0.74	0.98	0	-	0.922
	(Elfardy et al., 2014)*	0.94	0.05	0.85	0.99	0	-	**0.936**
MSA-DA Test 2	Baseline	0.54	0.27	0	0.94	0	0	0.385
	(King et al., 2014)	0.59	0.59	0.13	0.01	0	0	0.477
	(Chittaranjan et al., 2014)	0.58	0.50	0.42	0.43	0.01	0	0.513
	(Jain and Bhat, 2014)	0.62	0.49	0.67	0.75	0	0	0.580
	(Elfardy et al., 2014)*	0.73	0.73	0.91	0.98	0	0.01	0.777
	(Lin et al., 2014)	0.76	0.81	0.73	0.98	0	0	**0.799**
MSA-DA Surprise	(King et al., 2014)	0.48	0.60	0.05	0.02	0	0	0.467
	(Jain and Bhat, 2014)	0.53	0.61	0.62	0.96	0	0	0.626
	(Chittaranjan et al., 2014)	0.56	0.69	0.33	0.96	0	0	0.654
	(Lin et al., 2014)	0.68	0.82	0.61	0.97	0	0	0.778
	(Elfardy et al., 2014)*	0.66	0.81	0.87	0.99	0	0	**0.801**
NEP-EN	Baseline	0.67	0.76	0	0.61	-	0	0.678
	(King et al., 2014)	0.87	0.80	0.51	0.34	-	0.03	0.707
	(Lin et al., 2014)	0.93	0.91	0.49	0.95	-	0.02	0.917
	(Jain and Bhat, 2014)	0.94	0.96	0.52	0.94	-	0	0.942
	(Shrestha, 2014)	0.94	0.96	0.57	0.95	-	0	0.944
	(Chittaranjan et al., 2014)	0.94	0.96	0.45	0.97	-	0	0.948
	(Barman et al., 2014)	0.96	0.97	0.58	0.97	-	0.06	**0.959**
NEP-EN Surprise	(Lin et al., 2014)	0.83	0.73	0.46	0.65	-	-	0.712
	(King et al., 2014)	0.82	0.88	0.43	0.12	-	-	0.761
	(Chittaranjan et al., 2014)	0.78	0.87	0.37	0.80	-	-	0.796
	(Jain and Bhat, 2014)	0.83	0.91	0.50	0.87	-	-	0.850
	(Barman et al., 2014)	0.87	0.90	0.61	0.74	-	-	0.853
	(Shrestha, 2014)	0.85	0.92	0.53	0.78	-	-	**0.855**
SPA-EN	Baseline	0.72	0.56	0	0.75	0	0	0.704
	(Shrestha, 2014)	0.88	0.85	0.35	0.92	0	0	0.873
	(Jain and Bhat, 2014)	0.92	0.92	0.36	0.90	0	0	0.905
	(Lin et al., 2014)	0.93	0.93	0.32	0.91	0.03	0	0.913
	(Barman et al., 2014)	0.93	0.92	0.47	0.93	0.03	0	0.921
	(King et al., 2014)	0.94	0.93	0.54	0.92	0	0	0.923
	(Chittaranjan et al., 2014)	0.94	0.93	0.28	0.95	0	0	0.926
	(Bar and Dershowitz, 2014)	0.95	0.95	0.56	0.94	0.04	0	**0.940**
SPA-EN Surprise	(Shrestha, 2014)	0.80	0.78	0.23	0.81	0	0	0.778
	(Jain and Bhat, 2014)	0.83	0.84	0.22	0.79	0	0	0.811
	(Lin et al., 2014)	0.83	0.86	0.19	0.80	0.03	0	0.816
	(Barman et al., 2014)	0.84	0.85	0.31	0.82	0.03	0	0.823
	(Chittaranjan et al., 2014)	0.94	0.86	0.14	0.83	0	0	0.824
	(King et al., 2014)	0.84	0.85	0.35	0.81	0	0	0.828
	(Bar and Dershowitz, 2014)	0.85	0.87	0.37	0.83	0.03	0	**0.839**

Table 4: Performance results on language identification at the token level. A '-' indicates there were no tokens of this class in the test set. We ranked systems using weighted averaged f-measure (Avg-F). The "*" marks the system by (Elfardy et al., 2014). This system was not considered in the ranking for the shared task as it was developed by co-organizers of the task.

7 Lessons Learned

Among the things we want to improve for future shared tasks is the issue of data loss due to removal of tweets or users deleting their accounts. We decided to use Twitter data to have a relevant corpus. However, the trade-off is the lack of rights to distribute the data ourselves. This is not just a burden for the participants. It is an awful waste of resources as the data that was expensive to gather and label is not being used beyond the small group of researchers involved in the creation of the corpus. This will deter us from using Twitter data for future shared tasks, at least until a better solution is identified.

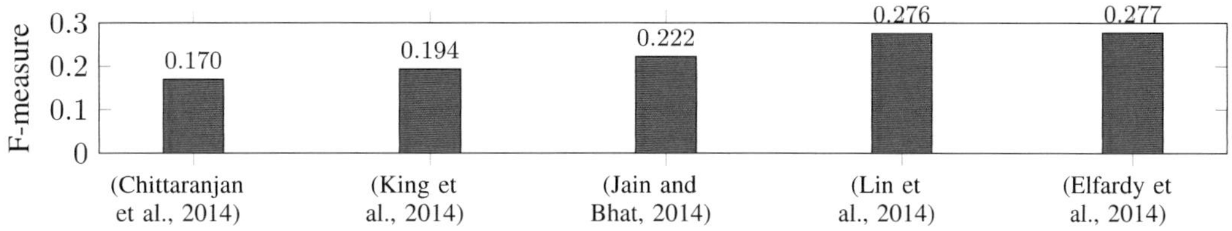

(a) MSA-DA Surprise Genre Results

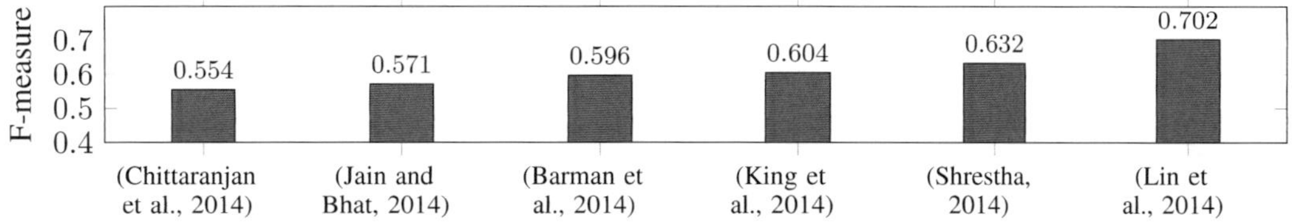

(b) NEP-EN Surprise Genre Results

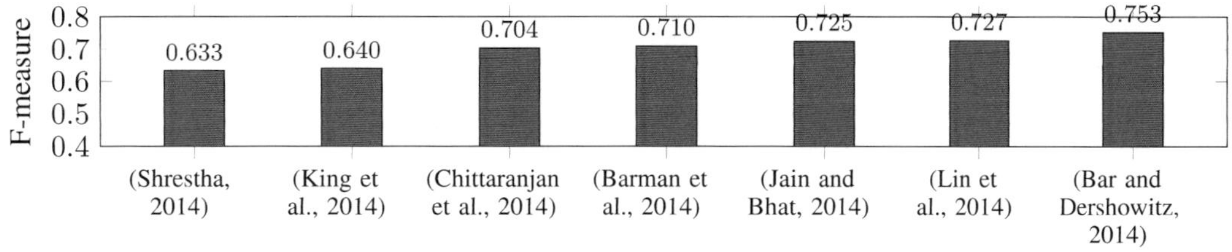

(c) SPA-EN Surprise Genre Results

Figure 2: Prediction results on language identification at the document level for the surprise genre. This is a binary task to distinguish between a monolingual and a code-switched text. We show performance of participating systems using F-measure as the evaluation metric.

Using crowdsourcing for annotating the data is a cheap and easy way for generating resources. But we found out that even when following best practices for quality control, there was a substantial amount of noise in the gold data. We plan to continue working on refining the annotation guidelines and quality control processes to reduce the amount of noise in gold annotations.

8 Conclusion

This is the first shared task on language identification in CS data. Yet, the response was quite positive as we received 42 system runs from seven different teams, plus submissions for MSA-AD from a sub group of the task organizers (Elfardy et al., 2014). The systems presented are overall robust and with interesting differences from one another. Although we did not see a single system ranking in the top places across all language pairs and tasks, we did see systems showing robust performance indicating some level of language independence. But the results are not consistent at the tweet/document level. The language pair that proved to be the most difficult for the task was MSA-DA, where the lexicon baseline system was hard to beat even with an F-measure of 47.1%.

This shared task showed that language identification in code-switched data is still an open problem that warrants further investigation. Perhaps in the near future we will see systems that embed some form of linguistic theory about CS and maybe that would result in more accurate predictions.

Our goal is to support new research addressing CS data. Discussions about the challenge for the next shared task are already underway. One possibility might be parsing. We plan to investigate the challenges in parsing CS data and we will start by exploring the hardships in manually annotating CS with syntactic information. We would also like to explore the possibility of classifying CS points according to their socio-pragmatic role.

Acknowledgments

We would like to thank all shared task participants. We also thank Brian Hester and Mohamed Elbadrashiny for their invaluable support in the development of the gold standard data and analysis of results. We also thank the in-lab annotators and the CrowdFlower contributors. This work was partly funded by NSF under awards 1205475 and 1205556.

References

Kfir Bar and Nachum Dershowitz. 2014. Tel Aviv University system description for the code-switching workshop shared task. In *Proceedings of the First Workshop on Computational Approaches to Code-Switching*, Doha, Qatar, October. ACL.

Utsab Barman, Joachim Wagner, Grzegorz Chrupala, and Jennifer Foster. 2014. DCU-UVT: Word-level language classification with code-mixed data. In *Proceedings of the First Workshop on Computational Approaches to Code-Switching*, Doha, Qatar, October. ACL.

Gokul Chittaranjan, Yogarshi Vyas, Kalika Bali, and Monojit Choudhury. 2014. A framework to label code-mixed sentences in social media. In *Proceedings of the First Workshop on Computational Approaches to Code-Switching*, Doha, Qatar, October. ACL.

Heba Elfardy, Mohamed Al-Badrashiny, and Mona Diab. 2014. AIDA: Identifying code switching in informal Arabic text. In *Proceedings of the First Workshop on Computational Approaches to Code-Switching*, Doha, Qatar, October. ACL.

Naman Jain and Riyaz Ahmad Bhat. 2014. Language identification in codeswitching scenario. In *Proceedings of the First Workshop on Computational Approaches to Code-Switching*, Doha, Qatar, October. ACL.

A. Joshi. 1982. Processing of sentences with intrasentential code-switching. In Ján Horecký, editor, *COLING-82*, pages 145–150, Prague, July.

Ben King and Steven Abney. 2013. Labeling the languages of words in mixed-language documents using weakly supervised methods. In *Proceedings of the 2013 Conference of the North American Chapter of the Association for Computational Linguistics: Human Language Technologies*, pages 1110–1119, Atlanta, Georgia, June. Association for Computational Linguistics.

Levi King, Eric Baucom, Tim Gilmanov, Sandra Kübler, Dan Whyatt, Wolfgang Maier, and Paul Rodrigues. 2014. The IUCL+ system: Word-level language identification via extended Markov models. In *Proceedings of the First Workshop on Computational Approaches to Code-Switching*, Doha, Qatar, October. ACL.

Ying Li, Yue Yu, and Pascale Fung. 2012. A Mandarin-English code-switching corpus. In Nicoletta Calzolari, Khalid Choukri, Thierry Declerck, Mehmet Uğur Doğan, Bente Maegaard, Joseph Mariani, Jan Odijk, and Stelios Piperidis, editors, *Proceedings of the Eighth International Conference on Language Resources and Evaluation (LREC-2012)*, pages 2515–2519, Istanbul, Turkey, May. European Language Resources Association (ELRA). ACL Anthology Identifier: L12-1573.

Constantine Lignos and Mitch Marcus. 2013. Toward web-scale analysis of codeswitching. In *87th Annual Meeting of the Linguistic Society of America*.

Chu-Cheng Lin, Waleed Ammar, Chris Dyer, and Lori Levin. 2014. The CMU submission for the shared task on language identification in code-switched data. In *Proceedings of the First Workshop on Computational Approaches to Code-Switching*, Doha, Qatar, October. ACL.

D.C. Lyu, T.P. Tan, E. Chng, and H. Li. 2010. SEAME: a Mandarin-English code-switching speech corpus in South-East Asia. In *INTERSPEECH*, volume 10, pages 1986–1989.

Dong Nguyen and A. Seza Doğruöz. 2013. Word level language identification in online multilingual communication. In *Proceedings of the 2013 Conference on Empirical Methods in Natural Language Processing*, pages 857–862, Seattle, Washington, USA, October. Association for Computational Linguistics.

Prajwol Shrestha. 2014. An incremental approach for language identification in codeswitched text. In *Proceedings of the First Workshop on Computational Approaches to Code-Switching*, Doha, Qatar, October. ACL.

Anil Kumar Singh and Jagadeesh Gorla. 2007. Identification of languages and encodings in a multilingual document. In *Proceedings of ACL-SIGWAC's Web As Corpus3*, Belgium.

Omar F. Zaidan and Chris Callison-Burch. 2011. The Arabic online commentary dataset: An annotated dataset of informal Arabic with high dialectal content. In *Proceedings of the 49th Annual Meeting of the Association for Computational Linguistics: Human Language Technologies: Short Papers - Volume 2*, HLT '11, pages 37–41, Stroudsburg, PA, USA. Association for Computational Linguistics.

Word-level Language Identification using CRF: Code-switching Shared Task Report of MSR India System

Gokul Chittaranjan
Microsoft Research India
t-gochit@microsoft.com

Yogarshi Vyas *
University of Maryland
yogarshi@cs.umd.edu

Kalika Bali **Monojit Choudhury**
Microsoft Research India
{kalikab, monojitc}@microsoft.com

Abstract

We describe a CRF based system for word-level language identification of code-mixed text. Our method uses lexical, contextual, character n-gram, and special character features, and therefore, can easily be replicated across languages. Its performance is benchmarked against the test sets provided by the shared task on code-mixing (Solorio et al., 2014) for four language pairs, namely, English-Spanish (En-Es), English-Nepali (En-Ne), English-Mandarin (En-Cn), and Standard Arabic-Arabic (Ar-Ar) Dialects. The experimental results show a consistent performance across the language pairs.

1 Introduction

Code-mixing and code-switching in conversations has been an extensively studied topic for several years; it has been analyzed from structural, psycholinguistic, and sociolinguistic perspectives (Muysken, 2001; Poplack, 2004; Senaratne, 2009; Boztepe, 2005). Although bilingualism is very common in many countries, it has seldom been studied in detail in computer-mediated-communication, and more particularly in social media. A large portion of related work (Androutsopoulos, 2013; Paolillo, 2011; Dabrowska, 2013; Halim and Maros, 2014), does not explicitly deal with computational modeling of this phenomena. Therefore, identifying code-mixing in social media conversations and the web is a very relevant topic today. It has garnered interest recently, in the context of basic NLP tasks (Solorio and Liu, 2008b; Solorio and Liu, 2008a), IR (Roy et al., 2013) and social media analysis (Lignos and Marcus, 2013). It should also be noted that the identification of languages due to code-switching is different from identifying multiple languages in documents (Nguyen and Dogruz, 2013), as the different languages contained in a single document might not necessarily be due to instances of code switching.

In this paper, we present a system built with off-the-shelf tools that utilize several character and word-level features to solve the EMNLP Code-Switching shared task (Solorio et al., 2014) of labeling a sequence of words with six tags viz. *lang1*, *lang2*, *mixed*, *ne*, *ambiguous*, and *others*. Here, *lang1* and *lang2* refer to the two languages that are mixed in the text, which could be English-Spanish, English-Nepali, English-Mandarin or Standard Arabic-dialectal Arabic. *mixed* refers to tokens with morphemes from both, *lang1* and *lang2*, *ne* are named entities, a word whose label cannot be determined with certainty in the given context is labeled *ambiguous*, and everything else is tagged *other* (Smileys, punctuations, etc.).

The report is organized as follows. In Sec. 2, we present an overview of the system and detail out the features. Sec. 3 describes the training experiments to fine tune the system. The shared task results on test data provided by the organizers is reported and discussed in Sec. 4. In Sec. 5 we conclude with some pointers to future work.

2 System overview

The task can be viewed as a sequence labeling problem, where, like POS tagging, each token in a sentence needs to be labeled with one of the 6 tags. Conditional Random Fields (CRF) are a reasonable choice for such sequence labeling tasks (Lafferty et al., 2001); previous work (King and Abney, 2013) has shown that it provides good performance for the language identification task as well. Therefore, in our work, we explored various token level and contextual features to build an optimal CRF using the provided training data. The features

**The author contributed to this work during his internship at Microsoft Research India

Proceedings of The First Workshop on Computational Approaches to Code Switching, pages 73–79,
October 25, 2014, Doha, Qatar. ©2014 Association for Computational Linguistics

Lang.	Given Ids		Available		Available (%)	
	Train	Test	Train	Test	Train	Test
Es	11,400	3,014	11,400	1,672	100%	54.5%
Ne	9,999	3,018	9,296	2,874	93%	95.2%
Cn	999	316	995	313	99.6%	99.1%
Ar	5,839	2,363	5,839	2,363	100%	100%
Ar 2	-	1,777	-	1,777	-	100%

Table 2: Number of tweets retrieved for the various datasets.

Source	Language	For
instance_types_en.nt.bz2[1]	English	NE
instance_types_es.nt.bz2[1]	Spanish	NE
eng_wikipedia_2010_1M-text.tar.gz[2]	English	FW
spa_wikipedia_2011_1M-text.tar.gz[2]	Spanish	FW

Table 3: External resources used in the task. [1] http://wiki.dbpedia.org/Download, [2] http://corpora.uni-leipzig.de/download.html; NE:Named entities, FW:Word frequency list

used can be broadly grouped as described below:

Capitalization Features: They capture if letter(s) in a token has been capitalized or not. The reason for using this feature is that in several languages, capital Roman letters are used to denote proper nouns which could correspond to named entities. This feature is meaningful only for languages which make case distinction (e.g., Roman, Greek and Cyrillic scripts).

Contextual Features: They constitute the current and surrounding tokens and the length of the current token. Code-switching points are context sensitive and depend on various structural restrictions (Muysken, 2001; Poplack, 1980).

Special Character Features: They capture the existence of special characters and numbers in the token. Tweets contain various entities like hashtags, mentions, links, smileys, etc., which are signaled by #, @ and other special characters.

Lexicon Features: These features indicate the existence of a token in lexicons. Common words in a language and named entities can be curated into finite, manageable lexicons and were therefore used for cases where such data was available.

Character n-gram features: Following King and Abney (2013), we also used charagter n-grams for n=1 to 5. However, instead of directly using the n-grams as features in the CRF, we trained two binary *maximum entropy* classifiers to identify words of *lang1* and *lang2*. The classifiers returned the probability that a word is of *lang1* (or *lang2*), which were then binned into 10 equal buckets and used as features.

The features are listed in Table 1.

3 Experiments

3.1 Data extraction and pre-processing

The ruby script provided by the shared task organizers was used to retrieve tweets for each of the language pairs. Tweets that could not be downloaded either because they were deleted or protected were excluded from the training set. Table 2 shows the number of tweets that we were able to retrieve for the released datasets. Further, we found a few rare cases of tokenization errors, as evident from the occurrence of spaces within tokens. These were not removed from the training set and instead, the spaces in these tokens were replaced by an underscore.

3.2 Feature extraction and labeling

Named entities for English and Spanish were obtained from DBPedia instance types, namely, *Agent*, *Award*, *Device*, *Holiday*, *Language*, *MeansOfTransportation*, *Name*, *PersonFunction*, *Place*, and *Work*. Frequency lists for these languages were obtained from the Leipzig Copora Collection(Quasthoff et al., 2006); words containing special characters and numbers were removed from the list. The files used are listed in table 3. The *character n-gram* classifiers were implemented using the MaxEnt classifier provided in MALLET (McCallum, 2002). The classifiers were trained on 6,000 positive examples randomly sampled from the training set and negative examples sampled from both, the training set and from word lists of multiple languages from (Quasthoff et al., 2006); the number of examples used for each of these classifiers is given in Table 4.

We used CRF++ (Kudo, 2014) for labeling the tweets. For all language pairs, CRF++ was run under its default settings.

3.3 Model selection

For each language pair, we experimented with various feature combinations using 3-fold cross validation on the released training sets. Table 5 reports the token-level labeling accuracies for the various models, based on which the optimal feature sets for each language pairs were chosen. These optimal features are reported in Table 1, and the corresponding performance for 3-fold cross validation in Table 5. The final runs submitted for the

ID	Feature Description	Type	Features used in the final submission (Optimal set)			
			En-Es	En-Ne	En-Cn	Ar-Ar
Capitalization Features						
CAP1	Is first letter capitalized?	True/False	✓	✓	✓	NA
CAP2	Is any character capitalized?	True/False	✓	✓	✓	NA
CAP3	Are all characters capitalized?	True/False	✓	✓	✓	NA
Contextual Features						
CON1	Current Token	String	✓	✓	✓	✓
CON2	Previous 3 and next 3 tokens	Array (Strings)	✓	✓	✓	
CON3	Word length	String	✓	✓	✓	✓
Special Character Features						
CHR0	Is English alphabet word?	True/False			✓	NA
CHR1	Contains @ in locations 2-end	True/False	✓	✓	✓	✓
CHR2	Contains # in locations 2-end	True/False	✓	✓	✓	✓
CHR3	Contains ' in locations 2-end	True/False	✓	✓	✓	✓
CHR4	Contains / in locations 2-end	True/False	✓	✓	✓	✓
CHR5	Contains number in locations 2-end	True/False	✓	✓	✓	✓
CHR6	Contains punctuation in locations 2-end	True/False	✓	✓	✓	✓
CHR7	Starts with @	True/False	✓	✓	✓	✓
CHR8	Starts with #	True/False	✓	✓	✓	✓
CHR9	Starts with '	True/False	✓	✓	✓	✓
CHR10	Starts with /	True/False	✓	✓	✓	✓
CHR11	Starts with number	True/False	✓	✓	✓	✓
CHR12	Starts with punctuation	True/False	✓	✓	✓	✓
CHR13	Token is a number?	True/False	✓	✓	✓	✓
CHR14	Token is a punctuation?	True/False	✓	✓	✓	✓
CHR15	Token contains a number?	True/False	✓	✓	✓	✓
Lexicon Features						
LEX1	In lang1 dictionary of most frequent words?	True/False	✓	✓	✓	NA
LEX2	In lang2 dictionary of most frequent words?	True/False		✓	NA	NA
LEX3	Is NE?	True/False	✓	✓	NA	NA
LEX4	Is Acronym	True/False	✓	✓	NA	NA
Character n-gram Features						
CNG0	Output of two MaxEnt classifiers that classify lang1 vs. others and lang2 vs. others. This gives 2 probability values binned into 10 bns, two from each classifier, for the two classes.	Array (binned probability)	✓	✓	NA	NA
CRF Feature Type			U	U	U	B

Table 1: A description of features used. NA refers to features that were either not applicable to the language pair or were not available. B/U implies that the CRF has/does not have access to the features of the previous token.

Classifier	Languages used (And # words)
English-Spanish Language Pair	
Spanish vs Others	[es (6000)], [en (4000), fr (500), hi (500), it (500), po (500)]
English vs Others	[en (6000)], [es (4000), fr (500), hi (500), it (500), po (500)]
English-Nepali Language Pair	
Nepali vs Others	[ne (6000)], [en (3500), fr (500), hi (500), it (500), po (500)]
English vs Others	[en (6000)], [ne (3500), fr (500), hi (500), it (500), po (500)]
Standard Arabic vs. Arabic Dialects	
Std vs. Dialect	[lang1 (9000)], [lang2 (3256)]

Table 4: Data to train *character n-gram* classifiers.

shared task, including those for the surprise test sets, use the corresponding optimal feature sets for each language pair.

Feature	**Context**	**Language Pair**				
		En-Es	**En-Ne†**	**En-Cn**	**Ar-Ar**	**Ar-Ar (2)**
Development Set						
All	B	92.8	94.3	93.1	85.5	-
- CON2	B	93.8	95.6	94.9	81.2	-
- CHR*	B	92.3	93.5	91.0	85.3	-
- CAP*	B	92.7	94.2	90.1	-	-
- CON2	U	93.0	94.3	93.1	85.6	-
- CNG0	B	92.7	94.2	-	-	-
- LEX*	B	92.7	94.1	-	-	-
Optimal	-	95.0	95.6	95.0	85.5	-
Results on Test data for the optimal feature sets						
Regular		85.0	95.2	90.4	90.1	53.6
Surprise		91.8	80.8	-	65.0	-

Table 5: The overall token labeling accuracies (in %) for all language pairs on the training and test datasets. "-" indicates the removal of the given feature. '*" is used to indicate a group of features. Refer tab. 1) for the feature Ids and the **optimal** set. *B* and *U* stand for bigram and unigram respectively, where the former refers to the case when the CRF had access to features of the current and previous tokens, and the latter to the case where the CRF had access only to the features of the current token. †: Lexical resources available for *En* only.

4 Results and Observations

4.1 Overall token labeling accuracy

The overall token labeling accuracies for the regular and surpise test sets (wherever applicable) and a second set of dialectal and standard Arabic are reported in the last two rows of Table 5. The same table also reports the results of the 3-fold cross validation on the training datasets. Several important observations can be made from these accuracy values.

Firstly, accuracies observed during the training phase was quite high ($\sim$ 95%) and exactly similar for En-Es, En-Ne and En-Cn data; but for Ar-Ar dataset our method could achieve only up to 85% accuracy. We believe that this is due to unavailability of any of the lexicon features, which in turn was because we did not have access to any lexicon for dialectal Arabic. While complete set of lexical features were not available for En-Cn as well, we did have English lexicon; also, we noticed that in the En-Cn dataset, almost always the En words were written in Roman script and the Cn words were written in the Chinese script. Hence, in this case, script itself is a very effective feature for classification, which has been indirectly modeled by the CHR0 feature. On the other hand, in the Ar-Ar datasets, both the dialects are written using the same script (Arabic). Further, we found that using the CNG0 feature that is obtained by training a character n-gram classifier for the language pairs resulted in the drop of performance. Since we are not familiar with arabic scripts, we are not sure how effective the character n-gram based features are in differentiating between the standard and the dialectal Arabic. Based on our experiment with CNG0, we hypothesize that the dialects may not show a drastic difference in their character n-gram distributions and therefore may not contribute to the performance of our system.

Secondly, we observe that effectiveness of the different feature sets vary across language pairs. Using all the features of the previous words (context = B) seems to hurt the performance, though just looking at the previous 3 and next 3 tokens was useful. On the other hand, in Ar-Ar the reverse has been observed. Apart from lexicons, character n-grams seems to be a very useful feature in En-Es classification. As discussed above, CHR* features are effective for En-Cn because, among other things, one of these features also captures whether the word is in Roman script. For En-Ne, we do not see any particular feature or sets of features that strongly influence the classification.

The overall token labeling accuracy of the shared task runs, at least in some cases, differ quite significantly from our 3-fold cross validation results. On the regular test sets, the results for En-Ne is very similar to, and En-Cn and Ar-Ar are within expected range of the training set results. However, we observe a 10% drop in En-Es. We observe an even bigger drop in the accuracy of the second Ar-Ar test set. We will discuss the possible reason for this in the next subsection. The accuracies on the surprise sets do not show any specific trend. While for En-Es the accuracy is higher by 5% for the surprise set than the regular set, En-Ne and Ar-Ar show the reverse, and a more expected trend. The rather drastic drops in the accuracy for these two pairs on the surprise sets makes error analysis and comparative analysis of the training, test and surprise datasets imperative.

4.2 Error Analysis

Table 6 reports the F-scores for the six labels, i.e., *classes*, and also an overall tweet/post level accuracy. The latter is defined as the percentage of input units (which could be either a tweet or a post or just a sentence depending on the dataset) that are correctly identified as either code-mixed or monolingual; an input unit is considered code-mixed if there is at least one word labeled as *lang1* and one as *lang2*.

For all the language pairs other than Arabic, the F-score for NE is much lower than that for *lang1* and *lang2*. Thus, the performance of the system can be significantly improved by identifying NEs better. Currently, we have used lexicons for only English and Spanish. This information was not available for the other languages, namely, Nepali, Mandarin, and Arabic. The problem of NE detection is further compounded by the informal nature of sentences, because of which they may not always be capitalized or spelt properly. Better detection of NEs in code-mixed and informal text is an interesting research challenge that we plan to tackle in the future.

Note that the *ambiguous* and *mixed* classes can be ignored because their combined occurrence is less than 0.5% in all the datasets, and hence they have practically no effect on the final labeling accuracy. In fact, their rarity (especially in the training set) is also the reason behind the very poor F-scores for these classes. In En-Cn, we also observe a low F-score for *other*.

In the Ar-Ar training data as well as the test set, there are fewer words of *lang2*, i.e., dialectal Arabic. Since our system was trained primarily on the context and word features (and not lexicon or character n-grams), there was not enough examples in the training set for *lang2* to learn a reliable model for identifying *lang2*. Moreover, due to the distributional skew, the system learnt to label the tokens as *lang1* with very high probability. The high accuracy in the Ar-Ar original test set is because 81.5% of the tokens were indeed of type *lang1* in the test data while only 0.26% were labeled as *lang2*. This is also reflected by the fact that though the F-score for *lang2* in Ar-Ar test set is 0.158, the overall accuracy is still 90.1% because F-score for *lang1* is 94.2%.

As shown in Table 7, the distribution of the classes in the second Ar-Ar test set and the surprise set is much less skewed and thus, very different from that of the training and original test sets. In fact, words of *lang2* occur more frequently in these sets than those of *lang1*. This difference in class distributions, we believe, is the primary reason behind the poorer performance of the system on some of the Ar-Ar test sets.

We also observe a significant drop in accuracy for En-Ne surprise data, as compared to the accuracy on the regular En-Ne test and training data. We suspect that it could be either due to the difference in the class distribution or the genre/style of the two datasets, or both. An analysis of the surprise test set reveals that a good fraction of the data consist of long song titles or part of the lyrics of various Nepali songs. Many of these words were labeled as *lang2* (i.e., Nepali) by our system, but were actually labeled as NEs in the gold annotations[1] While song titles can certainly be considered as NEs, it is very difficult to identify them without appropriate resources. It should however be noted that the En-Ne surprise set has only 1087 tokens, which is too small to base any strong claims or conclusions on.

[1]Confirmed by the shared task organizers over email communication.

Language Pair			F-measure (Token-level)				Accuracy of
	Ambiguous	lang1	lang2	mixed	NE	Other	Comment/Post
En-Es	0.000	0.856	0.879	0.000	0.156	0.856	82.1
En-Ne	-	0.948	0.969	0.000	0.454	0.972	95.3
En-Cn	-	0.980	0.762	0.000	0.664	0.344	81.8
Ar-Ar	0.000	0.942	0.158	-	0.577	0.911	94.7
Ar-Ar (2)	0.015	0.587	0.505	0.000	0.424	0.438	71.4
En-Es Surprise	0.000	0.845	0.864	0.000	0.148	0.837	81.5
En-Ne Surprise	-	0.785	0.874	-	0.370	0.808	71.6
Ar-Ar Surprise	0.000	0.563	0.698	0.000	0.332	0.966	84.8

Table 6: Class-wise F-scores and comment/post level accuracy of the submitted runs.

Dataset			Percentage of			
	Amb.	lang1	lang2	mixed	NE	Other
Training	0.89	66.36	13.60	0.01	11.83	7.30
Test-1	0.02	81.54	0.26	0.00	10.97	7.21
Test-2	0.37	32.04	45.34	0.01	13.24	9.01
Surprise	0.91	22.36	57.67	0.03	9.13	9.90

Table 7: Distribution (in %) of the classes in the training and the three test sets for Ar-Ar.

5 Conclusion

In this paper, we have described a CRF based word labeling system for word-level language identification of code-mixed text. The system relies on annotated data for supervised training and also lexicons of the languages, if available. Character n-grams of the words were also used in a MaxEnt classifier to detect the language of a word. This feature has been found to be useful for some language pairs. Since none of the techniques or concepts used here is language specific, we believe that this approach is applicable for word labeling for code-mixed text between any two (or more) languages as long as annotated data is available.

This is demonstrated by the fact that the system performs more or less consistently with accuracies ranging from 80% - 95% across four language pairs (except for the case of Ar-Ar second test set and the surprise set which is due to stark distributional differences between the training and test sets). NE detection is one of the most challenging problems, improving which will definitely improve the overall performance of our system. It will be interesting to explore semi-supervised and unsupervised techniques for solving this task because creating annotated datasets is expensive and effort-intensive.

References

Jannis Androutsopoulos. 2013. Code-switching in computer-mediated communication. In *Pragmatics of Computer-mediated Communication*, pages 667–694. Berlin/Boston: de Gruyter Mouton.

Erman Boztepe. 2005. Issues in code-switching: competing theories and models. *Teachers College, Columbia University Working Papers in TESOL & Applied Linguistics*, 3.2.

Marta Dabrowska. 2013. Functions of code-switching in polish and hindi facebook users' post. *Studia Linguistica Universitatis Lagellonicae Cracoviensis*, 130:63–84.

Nur Syazwani Halim and Marlyana Maros. 2014. The functions of code-switching in facebook interactions. In *Proceedings of the International Conference on Knowledge-Innovation-Excellence: Synergy in Language Research and Practice; Social and Behavioural Sciences*, volume 118, pages 126–133.

Ben King and Steven Abney. 2013. Labeling the languages of words in mixed-language documents using weakly supervised methods. In *Proceedings of NAACL-HLT*, pages 1110–1119.

Taku Kudo. 2014. Crf++: Yet another crf toolkit. `http://crfpp.googlecode.com/svn/trunk/doc/index.html?source=navbar#links`, Retrieved 11.09.2014.

John Lafferty, Andrew McCallum, and Fernando CN Pereira. 2001. Conditional random fields: Probabilistic models for segmenting and labeling sequence data. In *Proceedings of the International Conference on Machine Learning (ICML)*, pages 282–289.

Constantine Lignos and Mitch Marcus. 2013. Toward web-scale analysis of codeswitching. In *87th Annual Meeting of the Linguistic Society of America*.

Andrew Kachites McCallum. 2002. Mallet: A machine learning for language toolkit. `http://mallet.cs.umass.edu`.

Pieter Muysken. 2001. The study of code-mixing. In *Bilingual Speech: A typology of Code-Mixing*. Cambridge University Press.

Dong Nguyen and A. Seza Dogruz. 2013. Word level language identification in online multilingual communication. In *Proceedings of the 2013 Conference on Empirical Methods in natural Language Processing*, pages 857–862.

John C. Paolillo. 2011. Conversational codeswitching on usenet and internet relay chat. *Language@Internet*, 8.

Shana Poplack. 1980. Sometimes i'll start a sentence in Spanish y termino en espanol: Toward a typology of code-switching. *Linguistics*, 18:581–618.

Shana Poplack. 2004. Code-switching. In U. Ammon, N. Dittmar, K.K. Mattheier, and P. Turdgill, editors, *Soziolinguistik. An international handbook of the science of language*. Walter de Gruyter.

U. Quasthoff, M. Richter, and C. Biemann. 2006. Corpus portal for search in monolingual corpora. In *Proceedings of the fifth International Conference on Language Resource and Evaluation*, pages 1799–1802.

Rishiraj Saha Roy, Monojit Choudhury, Prasenjit Majumder, and Komal Agarwal. 2013. Overview and datasets of fire 2013 track on transliterated search. In *Proceedings of the FIRE 2013 Shared Task on Transliterated Search*.

Chamindi Dilkushi Senaratne, 2009. *Sinhala-English code-mixing in Sri Lanka: A sociolinguistic study*, chapter Code-mixing as a research topic. LOT Publications.

Thamar Solorio and Yang Liu. 2008a. Learning to predict code-switching points. In *Proceedings of the Empirical Methods on Natural Language Processing (EMNLP)*, pages 973–981.

Thamar Solorio and Yang Liu. 2008b. Part-of-speech tagging for English-Spanish code-switched text. In *Proceedings of the Empirical Methods on Natural Language Processing (EMNLP)*, pages 1051–1060.

Thamar Solorio, Elizabeth Blair, Suraj Maharjan, Steve Bethard, Mona Diab, Mahmoud Gonheim, Abdelati Hawwari, Fahad AlGhamdi, Julia Hirshberg, Alison Chang, and Pascale Fung. 2014. Overview for the first shared task on language identifiation in code-switched data. In *Proceedings of the First Workshop on Computational Approaches to Code-Switching. Conferencfe on Empirical Methods in Natural Language Processing*.

The CMU Submission for the Shared Task on Language Identification in Code-Switched Data

Chu-Cheng Lin **Waleed Ammar** **Lori Levin** **Chris Dyer**
Language Technologies Institute
Carnegie Mellon University
Pittsburgh, PA, 15213, USA
{chuchenl,wammar,lsl,cdyer}@cs.cmu.edu

Abstract

We describe the CMU submission for the 2014 shared task on language identification in code-switched data. We participated in all four language pairs: Spanish–English, Mandarin–English, Nepali–English, and Modern Standard Arabic–Arabic dialects. After describing our CRF-based baseline system, we discuss three extensions for learning from unlabeled data: semi-supervised learning, word embeddings, and word lists.

1 Introduction

Code switching (CS) occurs when a multilingual speaker uses more than one language in the same conversation or discourse. Automatic idenefication of the points at which code switching occurs is important for two reasons: (1) to help sociolinguists analyze the frequency, circumstances and motivations related to code switching (Gumperz, 1982), and (2) to automatically determine which language-specific NLP models to use for analyzing segments of text or speech.

CS is pervasive in social media due to its informal nature (Lui and Baldwin, 2014). The first workshop on computational approaches to code switching in EMNLP 2014 organized a shared task (Solorio et al., 2014) on identifying code switching, providing training data of multilingual tweets with token-level language-ID annotations. See §2 for a detailed description of the shared task. This short paper documents our submission in the shared task.

We note that constructing a CS data set that is annotated at the token level requires remarkable manual effort. However, collecting raw tweets is easy and fast. We propose leveraging both labeled and unlabeled data in a unified framework; *conditional random field autoencoders* (Ammar et al., 2014). The CRF autoencoder framework consists of an encoding model and a reconstruction model. The encoding model is a linear-chain conditional random field (CRF) (Lafferty et al., 2001) which generates a sequence of labels, conditional on a token sequence. Importantly, the parameters of the encoding model can be interpreted in the same way a CRF model would. This is in contrary to generative model parameters which explain both the observation sequence and the label sequence. The reconstruction model, on the other hand, independently generates the tokens conditional on the corresponding labels. Both labeled and unlabeled data can be efficiently used to fit parameters of this model, minimizing regularized log loss. See §4.1 for more details.

After modeling unlabeled token sequences, we explore two other ways of leveraging unlabeled data: *word embeddings* and *word lists*. The word embeddings we use capture monolingual distributional similarities and therefore may be indicative of a language (see §4.2). A word list, on the other hand, is a collection of words which have been manually or automatically constructed and share some property (see §4.3). For example, we extract the set of surface forms in monolingual corpora.

In §5, we describe the experiments and discuss results. According to the results, modeling unlabeled data using CRF autoencoders did not improve prediction accuracy. Nevertheless, more experiments need to be run before we can conclude this setting. On the positive side, word embeddings and word lists have been shown to improve CS prediction accuracy, provided they have decent coverage of tokens in the test set.

2 Task Description

The shared task training data consists of code–switched tweets with token-level annotations. The data is organized in four language pairs: English–Spanish (En-Es), English–Nepali (En-

Proceedings of The First Workshop on Computational Approaches to Code Switching, pages 80–86,
October 25, 2014, Doha, Qatar. ©2014 Association for Computational Linguistics

Ne), Mandarin–English (Zh-En) and Modern Standard Arabic–Arabic dialects (MSA-ARZ). Table 1 shows the size of the data sets provided for the shared task in each language pair.

For each tweet in the data set, the user ID, tweet ID, and a list of tokens' start offset and end offset are provided. Each token is annotated with one of the following labels: `lang1`, `lang2`, `ne` (i.e., named entities), `mixed` (i.e., mixed parts of lang1 and lang2), `ambiguous` (i.e., cannot be identified given context), and `other`.

Two test sets were used to evaluate each submission for the shared task in each language pair. The first test set consists of Tweets, similar to the training set. The second test set consists of token sequences from a surprise genre. Since participants were not given the test sets, we only report results on a Twitter test set (a subset of the data provided for shared task participants). Statistics of our train/test data splits are given in Table 5.

lang. pair	split	tweets	tokens	users
En–Ne	all	9,993	146,053	18
	train	7,504	109,040	12
	test	2,489	37,013	6
En–Es	all	11,400	140,738	9
	train	7,399	101,451	6
	test	4,001	39,287	3
Zh–En	all	994	17,408	995
	train	662	11,677	663
	test	332	5,731	332
MSA–ARZ	all	5,862	119,775	7
	train	4,800	95,352	6
	test	1,062	24,423	1

Table 1: Total number of tweets, tokens, and Twitter user IDs for each language pair. For each language pair, the first line represents all data provided to shared task participants. The second and third lines represent our train/test data split for the experiments reported in this paper. Since Twitter users are allowed to delete their tweets, the number of tweets and tokens reported in the third and fourth columns may be less than the number of tweets and tokens originally annotated by the shared task organizers.

3 Baseline System

We model token-level language ID as a sequence of labels using a linear-chain conditional random field (CRF) (Lafferty et al., 2001) described in §3.1 with the features in §3.2.

3.1 Model

A linear-chain CRF models the conditional probability of a label sequence $\mathbf{y}$ given a token sequence $\mathbf{x}$ and given extra context ϕ, as follows:

$$p(\mathbf{y} \mid \mathbf{x}, \phi) = \frac{\exp \lambda^\top \sum_{i=1}^{|\mathbf{x}|} \mathbf{f}(\mathbf{x}, y_i, y_{i-1}, \phi)}{\sum_{\mathbf{y}'} \exp \lambda^\top \sum_{i=1}^{|\mathbf{x}|} \mathbf{f}(\mathbf{x}, y'_i, y'_{i-1}, \phi)}$$

where $\boldsymbol{\lambda}$ is a vector of feature weights, and $\mathbf{f}$ is a vector of local feature functions. We use ϕ to explicitly represent context information necessary to compute the feature functions described below.

In a linear-chain structure, y_i only depends on observed variables $\mathbf{x}$, ϕ and the neighboring labels y_{i-1} and y_{i+1}. Therefore, we can use dynamic programming to do inference in run time that is quadratic in the number of unique labels and linear in the sequence length. We use L-BFGS to learn the feature weights $\boldsymbol{\lambda}$, maximizing the L_2-regularized log-likelihood of labeled examples $\mathcal{L}$:

$$\ell\ell_{\text{supervised}}(\boldsymbol{\lambda}) = c_{L_2}||\boldsymbol{\lambda}||_2^2 + \sum_{\langle \mathbf{x},\mathbf{y}\rangle \in \mathcal{L}} \log p(\mathbf{y} \mid \mathbf{x}, \phi)$$

After training the model, we use again use dynamic programming to find the most likely label sequence, for each token sequence in the test set.

3.2 Features

We use the following features in the baseline system:

- character n-grams (loweredcased tri- and quad-grams)
- prefixes and suffixes of lengths 1, 2, 3 and 4
- unicode page of the first character[1]
- case (first-character-uppercased vs. all-characters-uppercased vs. all-characters-alphanumeric)
- tweet-level language ID predictions from two off-the-shelf language identifiers: `cld2`[2] and `ldig`[3]

[1] `http://www.unicode.org/charts/`
[2] `https://code.google.com/p/cld2/`
[3] `https://github.com/shuyo/ldig`

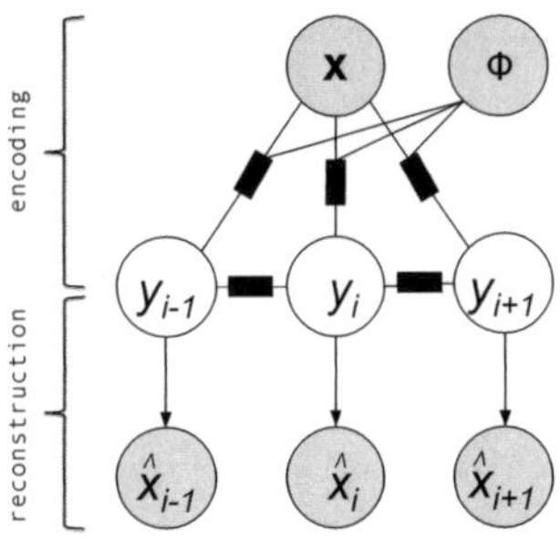

Figure 1: A diagram of the CRF autoencoder

4 Using Unlabeled Data

In §3, we learn the parameters of the CRF model parameters in a standard fully supervised fashion, using labeled examples in the training set. Here, we attempt to use unlabeled examples to improve our system's performance in three ways: modeling unlabeled token sequences in the CRF autoencoder framework, word embeddings, and word lists.

4.1 CRF Autoencoders

A CRF autoencoder (Ammar et al., 2014) consists of an input layer, an output layer, and a hidden layer. Both input and output layer represent the observed token sequence. The hidden layer represents the label sequence. Fig. 1 illustrates the model dependencies for sequence labeling problems with a first-order Markov assumption. Conditional on an observation sequence $\mathbf{x}$ and side information ϕ, a traditional linear-chain CRF model is used to generate the label sequence $\mathbf{y}$. The model then generates $\hat{\mathbf{x}}$ which represents a reconstruction of the original observation sequence. Elements of this reconstruction (i.e., $\hat{x}_i$) are then independently generated conditional on the corresponding label y_i using simple categorical distributions.

The parametric form of the model is given by:

$$p(\mathbf{y}, \hat{\mathbf{x}} \mid \mathbf{x}, \phi) = \prod_{i=1}^{|\mathbf{x}|} \theta_{\hat{x}_i|y_i} \times \frac{\exp \lambda^\top \sum_{i=1}^{|\mathbf{x}|} \mathbf{f}(\mathbf{x}, y_{i-1}, y_i, i, \phi)}{\sum_{\mathbf{y}'} \exp \lambda^\top \sum_{i=1}^{|\mathbf{x}|} \mathbf{f}(\mathbf{x}, y'_{i-1}, y'_i, i, \phi)}$$

where $\boldsymbol{\lambda}$ is a vector of CRF feature weights, $\mathbf{f}$ is a vector of local feature functions (we use the same features described in §3.2), and $\theta_{\hat{x}_i|y_i}$ are categorical distribution parameters of the reconstruction model representing $p(\hat{x}_i \mid y_i)$.

We can think of a label sequence as a low-cardinality lossy compression of the corresponding token sequence. CRF autoencoders explicitly model this intuition by creating an information bottleneck where label sequences are required to regenerate the same token sequence despite their limited capacity. Therefore, when only unlabeled examples $\mathcal{U}$ are available, we train CRF autoencoders by maximizing the regularized likelihood of generating reconstructions $\hat{\mathbf{x}}$, conditional on $\mathbf{x}$, marginalizing values of label sequences $\mathbf{y}$:

$$\ell\ell_{\text{unsupervised}}(\boldsymbol{\lambda}, \boldsymbol{\theta}) = c_{L_2}||\boldsymbol{\lambda}||_2^2 + R_{\text{Dirichlet}}(\boldsymbol{\theta}, \alpha) + \sum_{\langle \mathbf{x}, \hat{\mathbf{x}} \rangle \in \mathcal{U}} \log \sum_{\mathbf{y}:|\mathbf{y}|=|\mathbf{x}|} p(\boldsymbol{y}, \hat{\boldsymbol{x}} \mid \boldsymbol{x})$$

where $R_{\text{Dirichlet}}$ is a regularizer based on a variational approximation of a symmetric Dirichlet prior with concentration parameter α for the reconstruction parameters $\boldsymbol{\theta}$.

Having access to labeled examples, it is easy to modify this objective to learn from both labeled and unlabeled examples as follows:

$$\begin{aligned}\ell\ell_{\text{semi}}(\boldsymbol{\lambda}, \boldsymbol{\theta}) = c_{L_2}||\boldsymbol{\lambda}||_2^2 + R_{\text{Dirichlet}}(\boldsymbol{\theta}, \alpha) + \\ c_{\text{unlabeled}} \times \sum_{\langle \mathbf{x}, \hat{\mathbf{x}} \rangle \in \mathcal{U}} \log \sum_{\mathbf{y}:|\mathbf{y}|=|\mathbf{x}|} p(\boldsymbol{y}, \hat{\boldsymbol{x}} \mid \boldsymbol{x}) + \\ c_{\text{labeled}} \times \sum_{\langle \mathbf{x}, \mathbf{y} \rangle \in \mathcal{L}} \log p(\boldsymbol{y} \mid \boldsymbol{x})\end{aligned}$$

We use block coordinate descent to optimize this objective. First, we use c_{em} iterations of the expectation maximization algorithm to optimize the $\boldsymbol{\theta}$-block while the $\boldsymbol{\lambda}$-block is fixed, then we optimize the $\boldsymbol{\lambda}$-block with c_{lbfgs} iterations of L-BFGS (Liu et al., 1989) while the $\boldsymbol{\theta}$-block is fixed.[4]

4.2 Unsupervised Word Embeddings

For many NLP tasks, using unsupervised word representations as features improves accuracy (Turian et al., 2010). We use `word2vec` (Mikolov et al., 2013) to train 100–dimensional word embeddings from a large Twitter corpus of about 20 million tweets extracted from the live stream, in multiple languages. We define an additional feature function

[4] An open source efficient c++ implementation of our method can be found at `https://github.com/ldmt-muri/alignment-with-openfst`

in the CRF autoencoder model §4.1 for each of the 100 dimensions, conjoined with the label y_i. The feature value is the corresponding dimension for x_i. A binary feature indicating the absence of word embeddings is fired for out-of-vocabulary words (i.e., words for which we do not have word embeddings). The token-level coverage of the word embeddings for each of the languages or dialects used in the training data is reported in Table 2.

4.3 Word List Features

While some words are ambiguous, many words frequently occur in only one of the two languages being considered. An easy way to identify the label of such unambiguous words is to check whether they belong to the vocabulary of either language. Moreover, named entity recognizers typically rely on gazetteers of named entities to improve their performance. We generalize the notion of using monolingual vocabularies and gazetteers of named entities to general word lists. Using K word lists $\{l_1, \ldots, l_K\}$, when a token x_i is labeled with y_i, we fire a binary feature that conjoins $\langle y_i, \delta(x_i \in l_1), \ldots, \delta(x_i \in l_K)\rangle$, where δ is an indicator boolean function. We use the following word lists:

- Hindi and Nepali Wikipedia article titles
- multilingual named entities from the JRC dataset[5] and CoNLL 2003 shared task
- word types in monolingual corpora in MSA, ARZ, En and Es.
- set difference between the following pairs of word lists: MSA-ARZ, ARZ-MSA, En-Es, Es-En.

Transliteration from Devanagari The Nepali–English tweets in the dataset are romanized. This renders our Nepali word lists, which are based on the Devanagari script, useless. Therefore, we transliterate the Hindi and Nepali named entities lists using a deterministic phonetic mapping. We romanize the Devanagari words using the IAST scheme.[6] We then drop all accent marks on the characters to make them fit into the 7–bit ASCII range.

[5]http://datahub.io/dataset/jrc-names

[6]http://en.wikipedia.org/wiki/International_Alphabet_of_Sanskrit_Transliteration

language	embeddings coverage	word lists coverage
ARZ	30.7%	68.8%
En	73.5%	55.7%
MSA	26.6%	76.8%
Ne	14.5%	77.0%
Es	62.9%	78.0%
Zh	16.0%	0.7%

Table 2: The type-level coverage of annotated data according to word embeddings (second column) and according to word lists (third column), per language.

5 Experiments

We compare the performance of five models for each language pair, which correspond to the five lines in Table 3. The first model, "CRF" is the baseline model described in §3. The second "CRF + $\mathfrak{U}_{\text{test}}$" and the third "CRF + $\mathfrak{U}_{\text{all}}$" are CRF autoencoder models (see §4.1) with two sets of unlabeled data: (1) $\mathfrak{U}_{\text{test}}$ which only includes the test set,[7] and (2) $\mathfrak{U}_{\text{all}}$ which includes the test set as well as *all* tweets by the set of users who contributed any tweets in $\mathfrak{L}$. The fourth model "CRF + $\mathfrak{U}_{\text{all}}$ + emb." is a CRF autoencoder which uses word embedding features (see §4.2), as well as the features described in §3.2. Finally, the fifth model "CRF + $\mathfrak{U}_{\text{all}}$ + emb. + lists" further adds word list features (see §4.3). In all but the "CRF" model, we adopt a transductive learning setup.

Since the CRF baseline is used as the encoding part of the CRF autoencoder model, we use the supervisedly-trained CRF parameters to initialize the CRF autoencoder models. The categorical distributions of the reconstruction model are initialized with discrete uniforms. We set the weight of the labeled data log-likelihood $c_{\text{labeled}} = 0.5$, the weight of the unlabeled data log-likelihood $c_{\text{unlabeled}} = 0.5$, the L_2 regularization strength $c_{L_2} = 0.3$, the concentration parameter of the Dirichlet prior $\alpha = 0.1$, the number of L-BFGS iterations $c_{\text{LBFGS}} = 4$, and the number of EM iterations $c_{EM} = 4$.[8] We stop training after 50 iterations of block coordinate descent.

[7]$\mathfrak{U}_{\text{test}}$ is potentially useful when the test set belongs to a different domain than the labeled examples, which is often referred to as "domain adaptation". However we were unable to test this hypothesis since all the CS annotations we had access to are from Twitter.

[8]Hyper-parameters c_{L_2} and α were tuned using cross-validation. The remaining hyper-parameters were not tuned.

config	En–Ne	MSA–ARZ	En–Es	Zh–En
CRF	95.2%	80.5%	94.6%	94.9%
$+\mathcal{T}_{test}$	95.2%	80.6%	94.6%	94.9%
$+\mathcal{T}_{all}$	95.2%	80.7%	94.6%	94.9%
+emb.	95.3%	81.3%	95.1%	95.0%
+lists	97.0%	81.2%	96.7%	95.3%

Table 3: Token level accuracy results for each of the four language pairs.

label	predicted MSA	predicted ARZ
true MSA	93.9%	5.3%
true ARZ	32.1%	65.2%

Table 4: Confusion between MSA and ARZ in the Baseline configuration.

Results. The CRF baseline results are reported in the first line in Table 3. For three language pairs, the overall token-level accuracy ranges between 94.6% and 95.2%. In the fourth language pair, MSA-ARZ, the baseline accuracy is 80.5% which indicates the relative difficulty of this task.

The second and third lines in Table 3 show the results when we use CRF autoencoders with the unlabeled test set ($\mathcal{U}_{test}$), and with all unlabeled tweets ($\mathcal{U}_{all}$), respectively. While semi-supervised learning did not hurt accuracy on any of the languages, it only resulted in a tiny increase in accuracy for the Arabic dialects task.

The fourth line in Table 3 extends the CRF autoencoder model (third line) by adding unsupervised word embedding features. This results in an improvement of 0.6% for MSA-ARZ, 0.5% for En-Es, 0.1% for En-Ne and Zh-En.

The fifth line builds on the fourth line by adding word list features. This results in an improvement of 1.7% in En-Ne, 1.6% in En-Es, 0.4% in Zh-En, and degradation of 0.1% in MSA-ARZ.

Analysis and Discussion The baseline performance in the MSA-ARZ task is considerably lower than those of the other tasks. Table 4 illustrates how the baseline model confuses lang1 and lang2 in the MSA-ARZ task. While the baseline system correctly labels 93.9% of MSA tokens, it only correctly labels 65.2% of ARZ tokens.

Although the reported semi-supervised results did not significantly improve on the CRF baseline, more work needs to be done in order to conclude these results:

lang. pair	$\|\mathcal{U}_{test}\|$	$\|\mathcal{U}_{all}\|$	$\|\mathcal{L}\|$
En–Ne	2489	6230	7504
MSA–ARZ	1062	2520	4800
Zh–En	332	332	663
En–Es	4001	7177	7399

Table 5: Number of tweets in $\mathcal{L}$, $\mathcal{U}_{test}$ and $\mathcal{U}_{all}$ used for semi-supervised learning of CRF autoencoders models.

- Use an out-of-domain test set where some adaptation to the test set is more promising.
- Vary the number of labeled examples $|\mathcal{L}|$ and the number of unlabeled examples $|\mathcal{U}|$. Table 5 gives the number of labeled and unlabeled examples used for training the model. It is possible that semi-supervised learning would have been more useful with a smaller $|\mathcal{L}|$ and a larger $|\mathcal{U}|$.
- Tune $c_{labeled}$ and $c_{unlabeled}$.
- Split the parameters $\boldsymbol{\lambda}$ into two subsets: $\boldsymbol{\lambda}_{labeled}$ and $\boldsymbol{\lambda}_{unlabeled}$; where $\boldsymbol{\lambda}_{labeled}$ are the parameters which have a non-zero value for any input $\mathbf{x}$ in $\mathcal{L}$ and $\boldsymbol{\lambda}_{unlabeled}$ are the remaining parameters in $\boldsymbol{\lambda}$ which only have non-zero values with unlabeled examples but not with the labeled examples.
- Use a richer reconstruction model.
- Reconstruct a transformation of the token sequences instead of their surface forms.
- Train a token-level language ID model trained on a large number of languages, as opposed to disambiguating only two languages at a time.

Word embeddings improve the results for all language pairs, but the largest improvement is in MSA-ARZ and En-Es. Looking into the word embeddings coverage of those languages (i.e., MSA, ARZ, Es, En in Table 2), we find that they are better covered than the other languages (Ne, Zh). We conclude that further improvements on En-Ne and Zh-En may be expected if they are better represented in the corpus used to learn word embeddings.

As for the word lists, the largest improvement we get is the romanized word lists of Nepali, which have a 77.0% coverage and improve the accuracy by 1.7%. This shows that our transliterated word lists not only cover a lot of tokens, and are also useful for language ID. The Spanish

Config	`lang1`	`lang2`	`ne`
+lists	84.1%	76.5%	73.7%
-lists	84.2%	77.1%	71.5%

Table 6: F–Measures of two Arabic configurations. `lang1` is MSA. `lang2` is ARZ.

word lists also have a wide coverage, improving the overall accuracy by 1.6%. The overall accuracy of the Arabic dialects slightly degrades with the addition of the word lists. Closer inspection in table 6 reveals that it improves the F–Measure of the named entities at the expense of both MSA (lang1) and ARZ (lang2).

6 Related Work

Previous work on identifying languages in a multilingual document includes (Singh and Gorla, 2007; King and Abney, 2013; Lui et al., 2014). Their goal is generally more about identifying the languages that appear in the document than intra–sentential CS points.

Previous work on computational models of code–switching include formalism (Joshi, 1982) and language models that encode syntactic constraints from theories of code–switching, such as (Li and Fung, 2013; Li and Fung, 2014). These require the existence of a parser for the languages under consideration. Other work on prediction of code–switching points, such as (Elfardy et al., 2013; Nguyen and Dogruoz, 2013) and ours, do not depend upon such NLP infrastructure. Both of the aforementioned use basic character–level features and dictionaries on sequence models.

7 Conclusion

We have shown that a simple CRF baseline with a handful of feature templates obtains strong results for this task. We discussed three methods to improve over the supervised baseline using unlabeled data: (1) modeling unlabeleld data using CRF autoencoders, (2) using pre-trained word embeddings, and (3) using word list features.

We show that adding word embedding features and word lists features is useful when they have good coverage of words in a data set. While modest improvements are observed due to modeling unlabeled data with CRF autoenocders, we identified possible directions to gain further improvements.

While bilingual disambiguation was a good first step for identifying code switching, we suggest a reformulation of the task such that each label can take on one of many languages.

Acknowledgments

We thank Brendan O'Connor who helped assemble the Twitter dataset. We also thank the workshop organizers for their hard work, and the reviewers for their comments. This work was sponsored by the U.S. Army Research Laboratory and the U.S. Army Research Office under contract/grant number W911NF-10-1-0533. The statements made herein are solely the responsibility of the authors.

References

Waleed Ammar, Chris Dyer, and Noah A. Smith. 2014. Conditional random field autoencoders for unsupervised structured prediction. In *Proc. of NIPS*.

Heba Elfardy, Mohamed Al-Badrashiny, and Mona Diab. 2013. Code switch point detection in arabic. In *Natural Language Processing and Information Systems*, pages 412–416. Springer.

John J. Gumperz. 1982. *Discourse Strategies*. Studies in Interactional Sociolinguistics. Cambridge University Press.

Aravind K. Joshi. 1982. Processing of sentences with intra-sentential code-switching. In *Proceedings of the 9th Conference on Computational Linguistics - Volume 1*, COLING '82, pages 145–150, Czechoslovakia. Academia Praha.

Ben King and Steven Abney. 2013. Labeling the languages of words in mixed-language documents using weakly supervised methods. Proceedings of the 2013 Conference of the North American Chapter of the Association for Computational Linguistics: Human Language Technologies, pages 1110–1119. Association for Computational Linguistics.

John Lafferty, Andrew McCallum, and Fernando Pereira. 2001. Conditional random fields: Probabilistic models for segmenting and labeling sequence data. In *Proc. of ICML*.

Ying Li and Pascale Fung. 2013. Improved mixed language speech recognition using asymmetric acoustic model and language model with code-switch inversion constraints. In *Acoustics, Speech and Signal Processing (ICASSP), 2013 IEEE International Conference on*, pages 7368–7372, May.

Ying Li and Pascale Fung. 2014. Code switch language modeling with functional head constraint. In *Acoustics, Speech and Signal Processing (ICASSP), 2014 IEEE International Conference on*, pages 4913–4917, May.

D. C. Liu, J. Nocedal, and C. Dong. 1989. On the limited memory bfgs method for large scale optimization. *Mathematical Programming*.

Marco Lui and Timothy Baldwin. 2014. Accurate language identification of twitter messages. In *Proceedings of the 5th Workshop on Language Analysis for Social Media (LASM)*, pages 17–25, Gothenburg, Sweden, April. Association for Computational Linguistics.

Marco Lui, Han Jey Lau, and Timothy Baldwin. 2014. Automatic detection and language identification of multilingual documents. *Transactions of the Association of Computational Linguistics*, 2:27–40.

Tomas Mikolov, Kai Chen, Greg Corrado, and Jeffrey Dean. 2013. Efficient estimation of word representations in vector space. In *Proc. of ICLR*.

Dong Nguyen and Seza A. Dogruoz. 2013. Word level language identification in online multilingual communication. Proceedings of the 2013 Conference on Empirical Methods in Natural Language Processing, pages 857–862. Association for Computational Linguistics.

Anil Kumar Singh and Jagadeesh Gorla. 2007. Identification of languages and encodings in a multilingual document. In *Building and Exploring Web Corpora (WAC3-2007): Proceedings of the 3rd Web as Corpus Workshop, Incorporating Cleaneval*, volume 4, page 95.

Thamar Solorio, Elizabeth Blair, Suraj Maharjan, Steve Bethard, Mona Diab, Mahmoud Gonheim, Abdelati Hawwari, Fahad AlGhamdi, Julia Hirshberg, Alison Chang, and Pascale Fung. 2014. Overview for the first shared task on language identification in code-switched data. In *Proceedings of the First Workshop on Computational Approaches to Code-Switching*.

Joseph Turian, Lev Ratinov, and Yoshua Bengio. 2010. Word representations: A simple and general method for semi-supervised learning. In *Proceedings of the 48th Annual Meeting of the Association for Computational Linguistics*, ACL '10, pages 384–394, Stroudsburg, PA, USA. Association for Computational Linguistics.

Language Identification in Code-Switching Scenario

Naman Jain
LTRC, IIIT-H, Hyderabad, India
naman.jain@research.iiit.ac.in

Riyaz Ahmad Bhat
LTRC, IIIT-H, Hyderabad, India
riyaz.bhat@research.iiit.ac.in

Abstract

This paper describes a CRF based token level language identification system entry to *Language Identification in Code-Switched (CS) Data* task of *CodeSwitch 2014*. Our system hinges on using conditional posterior probabilities for the individual codes (words) in code-switched data to solve the language identification task. We also experiment with other linguistically motivated language specific as well as generic features to train the CRF based sequence labeling algorithm achieving reasonable results.

1 Introduction

This paper describes our participation in the *Language Identification in Code-Switched Data* task at *CodeSwitch 2014* (Solorio et al., 2014). The workshop focuses on NLP approaches for the analysis and processing of mixed-language data with a focus on intra sentential code-switching, while the shared task focuses on the identification of the language of each word in a code-switched data, which is a prerequisite for analyzing/processing such data. Code-switching is a sociolinguistics phenomenon, where multilingual speakers switch back and forth between two or more common languages or language-varieties, in the context of a single written or spoken conversation. Natural language analysis of code-switched (henceforth CS) data for various NLP tasks like Parsing, Machine Translation (MT), Automatic Speech Recognition (ASR), Information Retrieval (IR) and Extraction (IE) and Semantic Processing, is more complex than monolingual data. Traditional NLP techniques perform miserably when processing mixed language data. The performance degrades at a rate proportional to the amount and level of code-switching present in the data. Therefore, in order to process such data, a separate language identification component is needed, to first identify the language of individual words.

Language identification in code-switched data can be thought of as a sub-task of a document level language identification task. The latter aims to identify the language a given document is written in (Baldwin and Lui, 2010), while the former addresses the same problem, however at the token level. Although, both the problems have separate goals, they can fundamentally be modeled with a similar set of features and techniques. However, language identification at the word level is more challenging than a typical document level language identification problem. The number of features available at document level is much higher than at word level. The available features for word level identification are word morphology, syllable structure and phonemic (letter) inventory of the language(s). Since these features are related to the structure of a word, letter based n-gram models have been reported to give reasonably accurate and comparable results (Dunning, 1994; Elfardy and Diab, 2012; King and Abney, 2013; Nguyen and Dogruoz, 2014; Lui et al., 2014). In this work, we present a token level language identification system which mainly hinges on the posterior probabilities computed using n-gram based language models.

The rest of the paper is organized as follows: In Section 2, we discuss about the data of the shared task. In Section 3, we discuss the methodology we adapted to address the problem of language identification, in detail. Experiments based on our methodology are discussed in Section 4. In Section 5, we present the results obtained, with a brief discussion. Finally we conclude in Section 6 with some future directions.

Proceedings of The First Workshop on Computational Approaches to Code Switching, pages 87–93,
October 25, 2014, Doha, Qatar.

2 Data

The *Language Identification in the Code-Switched (CS) data* shared task is meant for language identification in 4 language pairs (henceforth LP) namely, *Nepali-English* (N-E), *Spanish-English* (S-E), *Mandarin-English* (M-E) and *Modern Standard Arabic-Arabic dialects* (MSA-A). So as to get familiar with the training and testing data, trial data sets consisting of 20 tweets each, corresponding to all the language-pairs, were first released. Additional test data as "surprise genre" for *S-E, N-E* and *MSA-A* were also released, which comprised of data from Facebook, blogs and Arabic commentaries.

2.1 Tag Description

Each word in the training data is classified into one of the 6 different classes which are, **Lang1**, **Lang2**, **Mixed**, **Other**, **Ambiguous** and **NE**. "Lang1" and "Lang2" tags correspond to words specific to the languages in an LP. "Mixed" words are those words that are partially in both the languages. "Ambiguous" words are the ones that could belong to either of the language. All gibberish and unintelligible words and words that do not belong to any of the languages fall under "Other" category. "Named Entities" (NE) comprise of proper names that refer to people, places, organizations, locations, movie titles and song titles etc.

2.2 Data Format and Data Crawling

Due to Twitter policies, distributing the data directly is not possible in the shared task and thus the trial, training and testing data are provided as char offsets with label information along with tweetID[1] and userID[2]. We use *twitter*[3] python script to crawl the tweets and our own python script to further tokenize and synchronize the tags in the data.

Since the data for "surprise genre" comes from different social media sources, the ID format varies from file to file but all the other details are kept as is. In addition to the details, the tokens referenced by the offsets are provided unlike Twitter data. (1) and (2) below, show the format of tweets in train and test data respectively, while (3) shows a typical tweet in the surprise genre data.

(1) *TweetID UserID startIndex endIndex Tag*

(2) *TweetID UserID startIndex endIndex*

(3) *SocialMediaID UserID startIndex endIndex Word*

2.3 Data Statistics

The CS data is divided into two types of tweets (henceforth posts)[4] namely, Code-switched posts and Monolingual posts. Table 1 shows the original number of posts that are released for the shared task for all LPs, along with their tag counts. Due to the dynamic nature of social media, the posts can be either deleted or updated and thus different participants would have crawled different number of posts. Thus, to come up with a comparable platform for all the teams, the intersection of data from all the users is used as final testing data to report the results. Table 1 shows the number of tweets or posts in testing data that are finally used for the evaluation.

3 Methodology

We divided the language identification task into a pipeline of 3 sub-tasks namely *Pre-Processing*, *Language Modeling*, and *Sequence labeling using CRF*[5]. The pipeline is followed for all the LPs with some LP specific variations in selecting the most relevant features to boost the results.

3.1 Pre-Processing

In the pre-processing stage, we crawl the tweets from Twitter given their offsets in the training data and then tokenize and synchronize the words with their tags as mentioned in Section 2.2. For each LP we separate out the tokens into six classes to use the data for Language Modeling and also to manually analyze the language specific properties to be used as features further in sequence labeling . While synchronizing the words in a tweet with their tags, we observed that some offsets do not match with the words and this would lead to mismatch of labels with tokens and thus degrade the quality of training data.

To filter out the incorrect instances from the training data, we frame pattern matching rules which are specific to the languages present. But this filtering is done only for the words present in

[1] Each tweet on Twitter has a unique tweetID

[2] Each user on Twitter carries a userID

[3] http://emnlp2014.org/workshops/CodeSwitch/scripts/twitter.zip

[4] In case of twitter data, we have tweets but in case of surprise genre data we have posts

[5] Conditional Random Field

	Language Pairs	# Tweets		# Tokens					
		CodeSwitched	Monolingual	Ambiguous	Lang1	Lang2	Mixed	NE	Other
Train	MSA-A dialects	774	5,065	1,066	79,134	16,291	15	14,112	8,699
Train	Mandarin-English	521	478	0	12,114	2,431	12	1,847	1,025
Train	Nepali-English	7,203	2,790	126	45,483	60,697	117	3982	35,651
Train	Spanish-English	3,063	8,337	344	77,107	33,099	51	2,918	27,227
Test	MSA-A dialects I	32	2,300	11	44,314	141	0	5,939	3,902
Test	Mandarin-English	247	66	0	4,703	881	1	254	442
Test	Nepali-English	2,665	209	0	12,286	17,216	60	1,071	9,635
Test	Spanish-English	471	1,155	43	7,040	5,549	12	464	4,311
Test	MSA-A dialects II	293	1,484	119	10,459	14,800	2	4,321	2,940
Surprise	MSA-A dialects	-	-	110	2,687	6,930	3	1,097	1,190
Surprise	Nepali-English	20	82	0	173	699	0	127	88
Surprise	Spanish-English	22	27	1	636	306	1	38	120

Table 1: Data Statistics

'Lang1' and 'Lang2' classes. There are two reasons to consider these labels. First, 'Lang1' and 'Lang2' classes hold maximum share of words in any LP as shown in Table 1, and thus have a higher impact on the overall accuracy of the language identification system. In addition to the above, these categories correspond to the focus point of the shared task. Second, for 'Ambiguous', 'NE' and 'Other' categories, it is difficult to find the patterns according to their definitions. Although rules can be framed for 'Mixed' category, since their count is too less as compared to the other categories (Table 1), it is of no use to train a separate language model with very less number of instances.

For Mandarin and Arabic data sets, any word present in Roman script is excluded from the data. Similarly for English and Nepali, if any word contains characters other than Roman or numeral they are excluded from the data. In addition to the rule for English and Nepali, the additional alphabets in Spanish are also included in the set of Roman and numeral entries. Table 2 shows the number of words that remained in each of the languages/dialects, after the preprocessing.

One of the bonus points in the shared task is that 3 out of 4 LPs share 'English' as their second language. In order to increase the training size for English, we merged all the English words into a single file and thus reduced the number of language models to be trained from 8 to 6, one for each language (or dialect).

Language	Data Size	Average Token Length
Arabic	10,380	8.14
English	105,014	3.83
Mandarin	12,874	4.99
MSA	53,953	8.93
Nepali	35,620	4.26
Spanish	32,737	3.96

Table 2: Data Statistics after Filtering

3.2 Language Modeling

In this stage, we train separate smoothed n-gram based language models for each language in an LP. We compute the conditional probability for each word using these language models, which is then used as a feature, among others for sequence labeling to finally predict the tags.

3.2.1 N-gram Language Models

Given a word w, we compute the conditional probability corresponding to k[6] classes c_1, c_2, ... , c_k as:

$$p(c_i|w) = p(w|c_i) * p(c_i) \quad (1)$$

The prior distribution $p(c)$ of a class is estimated from the respective training sets shown in Table 2. Each training set is used to train a separate letter-based language model to estimate the probability of word w. The language model $p(w)$ is implemented as an n-gram model using the IRSTLM-Toolkit (Federico et al., 2008) with Kneser-Ney smoothing. The language model is

[6] In our case value of k is 2 as there are 2 languages in an LP

defined as:

$$p(w) = \prod_{i=1}^{n} p(l_i|l_{i-k}^{i-1}) \quad (2)$$

where l is a letter and k is a parameter indicating the amount of context used (e.g., $k=4$ means 5-gram model).

3.3 CRF based Sequence Labeling

After Language Modeling, we use CRF-based (Conditional Random Fields (Lafferty et al., 2001)) sequence labeling to predict the labels of words in their surrounding context. The CRF algorithm predicts the class of a word in its surrounding context taking into account other features not explicitly represented in its structure.

3.3.1 Feature Set

In order to train CRF models, we define a feature set which is a hybrid combination of three subtypes of features namely, Language Model Features (LMF), Language Specific Features (LSF) and Morphological Features (MF).

LMF: This sub-feature set consists of posterior probability scores calculated using language models for each language in an LP. Although we trained language models only for 'Lang1' and 'Lang2' classes, we computed the probability scores for all the words belonging to any of the categories.

LSF: Each language carries some specific traits that could assist in language identification. In this sub-feature set we exploited some of the language specific features exclusively based on the description of the tags provided. The common features for all the LPs are *HAS_NUM* (Numeral is present in the word), *HAS_PUNC* (Punctuation is present in the word), *IS_NUM* (Word is a numeral), *IS_PUNC* (word is a punctuation or a collection of punctuations), *STARTS_NUM* (word starts with a numeral) and *STARTS_PUNC* (word starts with a punctuation). All these features are used to generate variations to distinguish 'Other' class from rest of the classes during prediction.

Two features exclusively used for the English sharing LPs are *HAS_CAPITAL* (capital letters are present in the word) and *IS_ENGLISH* (word belongs to English or not). *HAS_CAPITAL* is used to capture the capitalization property of the English writing system. This feature is expected to help in the identification of 'NEs'. *IS_ENGLISH* is used to indicate whether a word is an valid English word or not, based on its presence in English dictionaries. We used dictionaries available in *PyEnchant*[7].

For the *M-E* LP, we are using 'TYPE'[8] as a feature with possible values as ENGLISH, MANDARIN, NUM, PUNC and OTHER. If all the characters in the word are English alphabets ENGLISH is taken as the value and Mandarin otherwise. Similar checks are used for NUM and PUNC types. But if no case is satisfied, OTHER is taken as the value.

We observed that the above features did not contribute much to distinguish between any of the tags in case of the *MSA-A* LP. Since this pair consists of two different dialects of a language rather than two different languages, the posterior probabilities would be close to each other as compared to other LPs. Thus we use the difference of these probabilities as a feature in order to discriminate ambiguous words or NEs that are spelled similarly.

MF: This sub-feature set comprises of the morphological features corresponding to a word. We automatically extracted these features using a python script. The first feature of this set is a binary length variable (MORE/LESS) depending on the length of the word with threshold value 4. The other 8 features capture the prefix and suffix properties of a word, 4 for each type. In prefix type, 4, 3, 2 and 1 characters, if present, are taken from the beginning of a word as 4 features. Similarly for the suffix type, 1, 2, 3 and 4 characters, again if present, are taken from the end of a word as 4 features. In both the cases if any value is missing, it is kept as NULL (LL). (4) below, shows a typical example from English data with the MF sub-feature set for the word 'one', where F1 represents the value of binary length variable, F2-F5 and F6-F9 represent the prefix and suffix features respectively.

(4)

one	Less	LL	one	on	o	LL	one	ne	e
Word	**F1**	**F2**	**F3**	**F4**	**F5**	**F6**	**F7**	**F8**	**F9**

3.3.2 Context Window

Along with the above mentioned features, we chose an optimal context template to train the CRF

[7]PyEnchant is a spell checking library in Python (http://pythonhosted.org/pyenchant/)

[8]Since it captures the properties of IS_NUM and IS_PUNC, these features are not used again

models. We selected the window size to be 5, with 2 words before and after the target word. Furnishing the training, testing and surprise genre data with the features discussed in 3.3.1, we trained 4 CRF models on training data using feature templates based on the context decided. These models are used to finally predict the tags on the testing and surprise genre data.

4 Experiments

The pipeline mentioned in Section 3 was used for the language identification task for all the LPs. We carried out a series of experiments with preprocessing to clean the training data and also to synchronize the testing data. We also did some post-processing to handle language and tag specific cases.

In order to generate language model scores, we trained 6 language models (one for each language/dialect) on the filtered-out training data as mentioned in Table 2. We experimented with different values of n-gram to select the optimal value based on the F1-measure. Table 3 shows the optimal order of n-gram, selected corresponding to the highest value of *F1-score*. Using the optimal value of n-gram, language models have been trained and then posterior probabilities have been calculated using equation (1).

Finally, we trained separate CRF models for each LP, using the *CRF++*[9] tool kit based on the features described in Section 3.3.1 and the feature template in Section 3.3.2. To empirically find the relevance of features we also performed leave-one out experiments so as to decide the optimal features for the language identification task (more details in Section 4.1). Then, using these CRF models, tags were predicted on the testing and surprise genre datasets.

Language-Pair	N-gram
MSA-A	5
M-E	5
N-E	6
S-E	5

Table 3: Optimal Value of N-gram

4.1 Feature Ranking

We expect that some features would be more important than others and would impact the task of language identification irrespective of the language pair. In order to identify such optimal features for the language identification task, we rank them based on their information gain scores.

4.1.1 Information Gain

We used information gain to score features according to their expected usefulness for the task at hand. Information gain is an information theoretic concept that measures the amount of knowledge that is gained about a given class by having access to a particular feature. If f is the occurrence an individual feature and $\bar{f}$ the non-occurrence of a feature, information gain can be measured by the following formula:

$$G(x) = P(f)\sum P(y|f)logP(y|f) + P(\bar{f})\sum logP(y|\bar{f})logP(y|\bar{f}) \quad (3)$$

For each language pair, the importance of feature types are represented by the following order:

- **MSA-A dialects:** token > word morphology > posterior probabilities > others
- **Mandarin-English:** token > posterior probabilities > word morphology > language type > others
- **Nepali-English:** token > posterior probabilities > word morphology > dictionary > others
- **Spanish-English:** token > posterior probabilities > word morphology > others > dictionary

Apart from MSA-A dialects, top 3 features suggested by information gain are token and its surrounding context, posterior probabilities and word morphology. For Arabic dialects word morphology is more important than posterior probabilities. It could be due to the fact that Arabic dialects share a similar phonetic inventory and thus have similar posterior probabilities. However, they differ significantly in their morphological structure (Zaidan and Callison-Burch, 2013).

We also carried out leave-one-out experiments over all the features to ascertain their impact on the classification performance. The results of these experiments are shown in Table (5). Accuracies are averaged over 5-fold cross-validation.

[9] http://crfpp.googlecode.com/svn/trunk/doc/index.html?source=navbar

	Language Pairs	Ambiguous			Lang1			Lang2			Mixed			NE			Other			Overall Accuracy
		R	P	F1	R	P	F1	R	P	F1	R	P	F1	R	P	F1	R	P	F1	
Test	**MSA-A I**	0.00	0.00	0.00	0.92	0.95	0.94	0.40	0.03	0.06	-	-	-	0.70	0.77	0.73	0.90	0.85	0.87	0.90
Test	**M-E**	-	-	-	0.98	0.98	0.98	0.67	0.66	0.67	0.00	1.00	0.00	0.84	0.38	0.53	0.22	0.71	0.33	0.88
Test	**N-E**	-	-	-	0.95	0.93	0.94	0.98	0.96	0.97	0.00	1.00	0.00	0.39	0.79	0.52	0.94	0.96	0.95	0.95
Test	**S-E**	0.00	1.00	0.00	0.88	0.81	0.84	0.83	0.90	0.86	0.00	1.00	0.00	0.16	0.40	0.23	0.83	0.80	0.82	0.83
Test	**MSA-A II**	0.00	0.00	0.00	0.91	0.47	0.62	0.36	0.84	0.51	0.00	1.00	0.00	0.59	0.80	0.68	0.80	0.71	0.75	0.60
Surprise	**MSA-A**	0.00	0.00	0.00	0.94	0.38	0.54	0.46	0.93	0.61	0.00	1.00	0.00	0.52	0.78	0.62	0.96	0.96	0.96	0.62
Surprise	**N-E**	-	-	-	0.92	0.76	0.84	0.95	0.89	0.91	-	-	-	0.35	0.92	0.50	0.85	0.89	0.87	0.86
Surprise	**S-E**	0.00	1.00	0.00	0.86	0.81	0.83	0.82	0.87	0.85	0.00	1.00	0.00	0.15	0.40	0.22	0.82	0.78	0.80	0.94

(Token Level spans Ambiguous through Other.)

Table 4: Token Level Results

Left Out Feature	MSA-A	M-E	N-E	S-E
Context	76.32	94.07	93.97	92.30
Morphology	79.29	93.67	93.98	93.51
Probability	79.24	89.16	93.86	93.28
Dictionary	-	87.75	93.73	92.99
Language Type	-	87.97	-	-
Others	78.80	83.84	92.10	92.20
All Features	79.37	95.11	94.52	93.54

Table 5: Leave-one-out Experiments

	Language Pairs	Tweet Level			
		Accuracy	Recall	Precision	F-score
Test	**MSA-A I**	0.605	0.719	0.025	0.048
Test	**M-E**	0.751	0.814	0.863	0.838
Test	**N-E**	0.948	0.979	0.966	0.972
Test	**S-E**	0.835	0.773	0.692	0.730
Test	**MSA-A II**	0.469	0.823	0.213	0.338
Surprise	**MSA-A**	0.457	0.833	0.128	0.222
Surprise	**N-E**	0.735	0.900	0.419	0.571
Surprise	**S-E**	0.830	0.765	0.689	0.725

Table 6: Comment/Post/Tweet Level Results

5 Results and Discussion

Each language identification system is evaluated against two data tracks namely, 'Testing' and 'Surprise Genre' data as mentioned in Section 2. Surprise genre data of Mandarin-English LP was not provided, so no results are available. All the results are provided on two levels, comment/post/tweet and token level. Tables 4 and 6 show results of our language identification system on both the levels respectively.

In case of Tweets, systems are evaluated using the following measures: *Accuracy*, *Recall*, *Precision* and *F-Score*. However at token level, systems are evaluated separately for each tag in an LP using *Recall*, *Precision* and *F1-Score* as the measures. Table 4 shows that the results for 'Ambiguous' and 'Mixed' categories are either missing (due to absence of tokens in that category), or have 0.00 F1-Score. One obvious reason could be the sparsity of data for these categories.

6 Conclusion and Future Work

In this paper, we have described a CRF based token level language identification system that uses a set of naive easily computable features guaranteeing reasonable accuracies over multiple language pairs. Our analysis showed that the most important feature is the word structure which in our system is captured by n-gram posterior probabilities and word morphology. Our analysis of Arabic dialects shows that word morphology plays an important role in the identification of mixed codes of closely related languages.

7 Acknowledgement

We would like to thank Himani Chaudhry for her valuable comments and suggestions that helped us to improve the quality of the paper.

References

Timothy Baldwin and Marco Lui. 2010. Language identification: The long and the short of the matter. In *Human Language Technologies: The 2010 Annual Conference of the North American Chapter of the Association for Computational Linguistics*, pages 229–237. Association for Computational Linguistics.

Ted Dunning. 1994. *Statistical identification of language*. Computing Research Laboratory, New Mexico State University.

Heba Elfardy and Mona T Diab. 2012. Token level identification of linguistic code switching. In *COLING (Posters)*, pages 287–296.

Marcello Federico, Nicola Bertoldi, and Mauro Cettolo. 2008. Irstlm: an open source toolkit for handling large scale language models. In *Interspeech*, pages 1618–1621.

Ben King and Steven P Abney. 2013. Labeling the languages of words in mixed-language documents using weakly supervised methods. In *HLT-NAACL*, pages 1110–1119.

John Lafferty, Andrew McCallum, and Fernando CN Pereira. 2001. Conditional random fields: Probabilistic models for segmenting and labeling sequence data. In *Proceedings of the International Conference on Machine Learning*, pages 282–289.

Marco Lui, Jey Han Lau, and Timothy Baldwin. 2014. Automatic detection and language identification of multilingual documents. volume 2, pages 27–40.

Dong Nguyen and A Seza Dogruoz. 2014. Word level language identification in online multilingual communication. In *Proceedings of the 2013 Conference on Empirical Methods in Natural Language Processing*.

Thamar Solorio, Elizabeth Blair, Suraj Maharjan, Steve Bethard, Mona Diab, Mahmoud Gonheim, Abdelati Hawwari, Fahad AlGhamdi, Julia Hirshberg, Alison Chang, and Pascale Fung. 2014. Overview for the first shared task on language identification in code-switched data. In *Proceedings of the First Workshop on Computational Approaches to Code-Switching. EMNLP 2014, Conference on Empirical Methods in Natural Language Processing, Octobe, 2014, Doha, Qatar*.

Omar F Zaidan and Chris Callison-Burch. 2013. Arabic dialect identification. *Computational Linguistics*, 40(1):171–202.

AIDA: Identifying Code Switching in Informal Arabic Text

Heba Elfardy
Department of Computer Science
Columbia University
New York, NY
heba@cs.columbia.edu

Mohamed Al-Badrashiny, Mona Diab
Department of Computer Science
The George Washington University
Washington, DC
{badrashiny, mtdiab}@gwu.edu

Abstract

In this paper, we present the latest version of our system for identifying linguistic code switching in Arabic text. The system relies on Language Models and a tool for morphological analysis and disambiguation for Arabic to identify the class of each word in a given sentence. We evaluate the performance of our system on the test datasets of the shared task at the EMNLP workshop on Computational Approaches to Code Switching (Solorio et al., 2014). The system yields an average token-level $F_{\beta=1}$ score of 93.6%, 77.7% and 80.1%, on the first, second, and surprise-genre test-sets, respectively, and a tweet-level $F_{\beta=1}$ score of 4.4%, 36% and 27.7%, on the same test-sets.

1 Introduction

Most languages exist in some standard form while also being associated with informal regional varieties. Some languages exist in a state of diglossia (Ferguson, 1959). Arabic is one of those languages comprising a standard form known as Modern Standard Arabic (MSA), that is used in education, formal settings, and official scripts; and dialectal variants (DA) corresponding to the native tongue of Arabic speakers. While these variants have no standard orthography, they are commonly used and have become pervasive across web-forums, blogs, social networks, TV shows, and normal daily conversations. Arabic dialects may be divided into five main groups: Egyptian (including Libyan and Sudanese), Levantine (including Lebanese, Syrian, Palestinian and Jordanian), Gulf, Iraqi and Moroccan. Sub-dialectal variants also exist within each dialect (Habash, 2010). Speakers of a specific Arabic Dialect typically code switch between their dialect and MSA, and less frequently between different dialects, both inter and intra-sententially. The identification and classification of these dialects in diglossic text can enhance semantic predictability.

In this paper we modify an existing system AIDA (Elfardy and Diab, 2012b), (Elfardy et al., 2013) that identifies code switching between MSA and Egyptian DA (EDA). We apply the modified system to the datasets used for evaluating systems participating at the EMNLP Workshop on Computational Approaches to Linguistic Code Switching.[1]

2 Related Work

Dialect Identification in Arabic is crucial for almost all NLP tasks, and has recently gained interest among Arabic NLP researchers. One of the early works is that of (Biadsy et al., 2009) where the authors present a system that identifies dialectal words in speech through acoustic signals. Zaidan and Callison-Burch (2011) crawled a large dataset of MSA-DA news commentaries and annotated part of the dataset for sentence-level dialectalness employing Amazon Mechanical Turk. Cotterell and Callison-Burch (2014) extended the previous work by handling more dialects. In (Cotterell et al., 2014), the same authors collect and annotate on Amazon Mechanical Turk a large set of tweets and user commentaries pertaining to five Arabic dialects. Bouamor et al. (2014) select a set of 2,000 Egyptian Arabic sentences and have them translated into four other Arabic dialects to present the first multidialectal Arabic parallel corpus.

Eskander et al. (2014) present a system for handling Arabic written in Roman script *"Arabizi"*. Using decision trees; the system identifies whether each word in the given text is a foreign word or not and further divides non foreign words into four

[1]Another group in our lab was responsible for the organization of the task, hence we did not officially participate in the task.

Proceedings of The First Workshop on Computational Approaches to Code Switching, pages 94–101,
October 25, 2014, Doha, Qatar.

classes: Arabic, Named Entity, punctuation, and sound.

In the context of machine-translation, Salloum and Habash (2011) tackle the problem of DA to English Machine Translation (MT) by pivoting through MSA. The authors present a system that uses DA to MSA transfer rules before applying state of the art MSA to English MT system to produce an English translation. In (Elfardy and Diab, 2012a), we present a set of guidelines for token-level identification of DA while in (Elfardy and Diab, 2012b), (Elfardy et al., 2013) we tackle the problem of token-level dialect-identification by casting it as a code-switching problem. Elfardy and Diab (2013) presents our solution for the sentence-level dialect identification problem.

3 Shared Task Description

The shared task for "Language Identification in Code-Switched Data" (Solorio et al., 2014) aims at allowing participants to perform word-level language identification in code-switched Spanish-English, MSA-DA, Chinese-English and Nepalese-English data. In this work, we only focus on MSA-DA data. The dataset has six tags:

1. **lang1**: corresponds to an MSA word, ex. الراهن, AlrAhn [2] meaning "the current";
2. **lang2**: corresponds to a DA word, ex. ازيك, ezyk meaning "how are you";
3. **mixed**: corresponds to a word with mixed morphology, ex. المألوشون, Alm>lw$wn meaning "the ones that were excluded or rejected";
4. **other**: corresponds to punctuation, numbers and words having punctuation or numbers attached to them;
5. **ambig**: corresponds to a word where the class cannot be determined given the current context, could either be lang1 or lang2; ex. the phrase كله تمام, klh tmAm meaning "all is well" is ambiguous if enough context is not present since it can be used in both MSA and EDA.
6. **NE**: corresponds to a named-entity, ex. مصر, mSr meaning "Egypt".

[2] We use Buckwalter transliteration scheme http://www.qamus.org/transliteration.htm

4 Approach

We use a variant of the system that was presented in (Elfardy et al., 2013) to identify the tag of each word in a given Arabic sentence. The original approach relies on language models and a morphological analyzer to assign tags to words in an input sentence. In this new variant, we use MADAMIRA (Pasha et al., 2014); a tool for morphological analysis and disambiguation for Arabic. The advantage of using MADAMIRA over using a morphological analyzer is that MADAMIRA performs contextual disambiguation of the analyses produced by the morphological analyzer, hence reducing the possible options for analyses per word. Figures 1 illustrates the pipeline of the proposed system.

4.1 Preprocessing

We experiment with two preprocessing techniques:

1. **Basic**: In this scheme, we only perform a basic clean-up of the text by separating punctuation and numbers from words, normalizing word-lengthening effects, and replacing all punctuation, URLs, numbers and non-Arabic words with *PUNC*, *URL*, *NUM*, and *LAT* keywords, respectively
2. **Tokenized**: In this scheme, in addition to basic preprocessing, we use MADAMIRA toolkit to tokenize clitics and affixes by applying the D3-tokenization scheme (Habash and Sadat, 2006). For example, the word بجد, *bjd*which means "with seriousness" becomes "ب+ جد", "b+ jd" after tokenization.

4.2 Language Model

The '*Language Model*' (LM) module uses the preprocessed training data to build a 5-gram LM. All tokens in a given sentence in the training data are tagged with either *lang1* or *lang2* as described in Section 5. The prior probabilities of each *lang1* and *lang2* words are calculated based on their frequency in the training corpus. SRILM toolkit (Stolcke, 2002) and the tagged corpora are then used to build the LM.[3] If *tokenized* preprocessing scheme is used, then the built LM is tokenized where all tokens corresponding to a certain word are assigned the same tag corresponding to the tag

[3] A full description of the approach is presented in (Elfardy and Diab, 2012b).

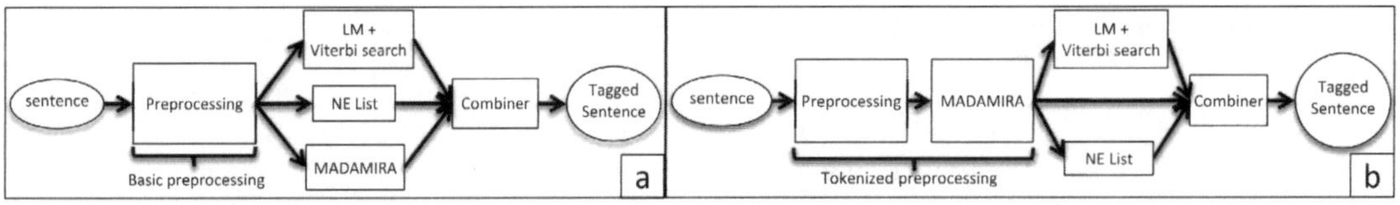

Figure 1: AIDA pipeline. **a)** The pipeline with the basic preprocessing scheme. **b)** The pipeline with the tokenized preprocessing scheme.

of the original word. For example, if بجد, *bjd* is tagged as *lang2*, both "+ب", b+ and "جد", jd get tagged as *lang2*.

For any new untagged sentence, the '*Language Model*' module uses the already built LM and the prior probabilities via Viterbi search to find the best sequence of tags for the given sentence. If there is an out-of-vocabulary word in the input sentence, the '*Language Model*' leaves it untagged.

4.3 MADAMIRA

Using *MADAMIRA*, each word in a given untagged sentence is tokenized, lemmatized, and POS-tagged. Moreover, the MSA and English glosses for each morpheme of the given word are provided. Since *MADAMIRA* uses two possible underlying morphological analyzers CALIMA (Habash et al., 2012) and SAMA (Maamouri et al., 2010), as part of the output, *MADAMIRA* indicates which of them is used to retrieve the glosses.

4.4 Named Entities List

We use the ANERGazet (Benajiba et al., 2007) to identify named-entities. ANERGazet consists of the following Gazetteers:

- **Locations:** 1,545 entries corresponding to names of continents, countries, cities, etc. (ex. المغرب, *Almgrb*) which means "Morocco";
- **People:** 2,100 entries corresponding to names of people. (ex. فهد, fhd);
- **Organizations:** 318 entries corresponding to names of Organizations such as companies and football teams. (ex. تشلسي, *t$lsy* meaning "Chelsea"

4.5 Combiner

Each word in the input sentence can get different tags from each module. Thus, the '*Combiner*' module uses all of these decisions and the following set of rules to assign the final tag to each word in the input sentence.

1. If the word contains any numbers or punctuation, it is assigned *other* tag;
2. Else if the word is present in any of the gazetteers or if MADAMIRA assigns it *noun_prop* POS tag, the word is tagged as *NE*;
3. Else if the word is (or all of its morphemes in the tokenized scheme are) identified by the LM as either *lang1* or *lang2*, the word is assigned the corresponding tag;
4. Else if the word's morphemes are assigned different tags, the word is assigned the *mixed* tag;
5. Else if the LM does not tag the word (i.e. the word is considered an out of vocabulary word by the LM) and:
   - If MADAMIRA retrieved the glosses from SAMA, the word is assigned a *lang1* tag;
   - Else if MADAMIRA outputs that the glosses were retrieved from CALIMA, then the word is assigned a *lang2* tag
   - Else if the word is still untagged (i.e. non-analyzable), the word is assigned *lang2* tag.

5 Experiments and Results

5.1 Training Phase

The training data that is used to build our LM consists of two main sources:

1. **Shared-task's training data (*STT*)**: 119,326 words collected from Twitter. They are manually annotated on the token-level. We split this corpus into:
   (a) **Training-set; (*STT-Tr*)**; 107,398 tweets representing 90% of *STT* and used for training the system

(b) **Development-set; (*STT-Dev*)**: 11,928 words representing 10% of *STT* and used for tuning the system.

2. **Web-log training data (*WLT*)**: 8 million words. Half of which comes from *lang1* corpora while the other half is from *lang2* corpora. The data is weakly labeled where all tokens in the sentence/comment are assigned the same tag according to the dialect of the forum (MSA or EDA) it was crawled from.

During the development phase, we use *STT-Tr* and *WLT* to train our system. We run several experiments to test the different setups and evaluate the performance of each of these setups on *STT-Dev*. Once we find the optimal configuration, we then use it to retrain the system using all of *STT-Tr*, *STT-Dev*, and *WLT*.

Since the size of *STT* is very small compared to *WLT* (0.1% of *WLT* size), the existence of six different tags in this corpus can add noise to the already weakly labeled *WLT* data. Thus, to make *STT* consistent with *WLT*, we changed the labels of *STT* as follows:

- If the number of *lang1* tokens in the tweet exceeds the number of *lang2* tokens; we assign all tokens in the tweet *lang1* tag.
- Otherwise, all tokens in the tweet are assigned *lang2* tag.

All tokens in *STT* tagged as *NE* have been used to enrich our named entity list.

5.2 Development Phase

Two different setups are tested using *WLT* and *STT-Tr*:

- **Surface form setup**; uses the basic preprocessing pipeline described earlier on both the input data and on the training data used to build the LM
- **Tokenized form setup**: uses the tokenized preprocessing pipeline described earlier on both the input data and the training data used to build the LM.

As mentioned earlier, since the size of *STT-Tr* is much smaller than that of *WLT*, this causes both datasets to be statistically incomparable. We tried increasing the weights assigned by the LM to *STT-Tr* by duplicating *STT-Tr*. We experimented with one, four, and eight copies of *STT-Tr* for each of the basic and tokenized experimental setups.

The shared task evaluation script has been used to evaluate each setup. The evaluation script produces two main sets of metrics. The first metric yields the accuracy, precision, recall, and $F_{\beta=1}$ score for code switching classification on the tweet-level, while the second set of metrics uses evaluates performance of each tag on the token-level. In this paper, we add an extra metric corresponding to the weighted average of the tag on the token level $F_{\beta=1}$ score in order to rank our overall performance against other participating groups in the task.

Tables 1 and 2 summarize our results for both Surface Form and Tokenized Form setups on *STT-Dev*. In all experiments, the Tokenized Form setup outperforms the Surface Form setup.

As shown in Table 2, the system that yields the best weighted-average token-level $F_{\beta=1}$ score (77.6%) on the development-set is **Tokenized-2**. Throughout the rest of the paper, we will use the system's name "**AIDA**"; to refer to this best configuration (Tokenized-2).

	Accuracy	Precision	Recall	$F_{\beta=1}$
Tokenized-1	51.5%	43.7%	97.4%	60.3%
Tokenized-2	52.5%	44.2%	97.4%	60.8%
Tokenized-8	54.2%	45.1%	96.9%	**61.6%**
Surface-1	45.4%	40.9%	99.5%	57.9%
Surface-2	45.8%	41.1%	99.5%	58.1%
Surface-8	46.5%	41.4%	99.5%	58.5%

Table 1: Results on *STT-Dev* using the tweet-level evaluation. (-1, -2, and -8) correspond to the number of copies of *STT-Tr* that were added to *WLT*

5.3 Testing Phase

Three blind test sets have been used for the evaluation:

- *Test1*: 54,732 words of 2,363 tweets collected from some unseen users in the training set;
- *Test2*: Another 32,641 words of 1,777 tweets collected from other unseen users in the training set;
- *Surprise*: 12,017 words of 1,222 sentences from collected from Arabic commentaries.

Table 3 shows the distribution of each test set over the different tags

	ambig	lang1	lang2	mixed	NE	other	Avg-$F_{\beta=1}$
Tokenized-1	0.0%	79.5%	71.5%	0.0%	83.6%	98.9%	77.5%
Tokenized-2	0.0%	79.6%	71.6%	0.0%	83.6%	98.9%	**77.6%**
Tokenized-8	0.0%	79.5%	71.4%	0.0%	83.6%	98.9%	77.5%
Surface-1	0.0%	76.0%	65.4%	0.0%	83.6%	98.9%	73.5%
Surface-2	0.0%	76.1%	65.6%	0.0%	83.6%	98.9%	73.7%
Surface-8	0.0%	76.2%	65.5%	0.0%	83.6%	98.9%	73.7%

Table 2: Results on *STT-Dev* using the token-level evaluation. (-1, -2, and -8) correspond to the number of copies of *STT-Tr* that were added to *WLT*

	ambig	lang1	lang2	mixed	NE	other
Test1	0.0%	81.5%	0.3%	0.0%	10.9%	7.3%
Test2	0.4%	32.0%	45.3%	0.0%	13.2%	9.0%
Surprise	0.9%	22.4%	57.7%	0.0%	9.1%	9.9%

Table 3: Test sets tag distributions

Tables 4, 5, and 6 show the tweet-level evaluation on the three test sets. While tables 7, 8, and 9 show the token-level evaluation on the same test sets. The tables compare the results of our best setup against the other systems that participated in the task[4].

To make the comparison easier, we have calculated the overall weighted $F_{\beta=1}$ score for all systems using the three test sets together.

Table 10 shows the $F_{\beta=1}$ score of each system averaged over all three test-sets. Our system outperforms all other systems in the token-level evaluation and comes in the second place after CMU in the tweet-level classification.

	Accuracy	Precision	Recall	$F_{\beta=1}$
AIDA	45.2%	2.3%	93.8%	4.4%
CMU	86.1%	5.2%	53.1%	9.5%
A3-107	60.5%	2.5%	71.9%	4.8%
IUCL	97.4%	11.1%	12.5%	11.8%
MSR-IN	94.7%	9.7%	34.4%	**15.2%**

Table 4: Tweet-level evaluation on *Test1* set.

	Accuracy	Precision	Recall	$F_{\beta=1}$
AIDA	44.0%	22.2%	95.6%	36.0%
CMU	66.2%	29.2%	73.4%	**41.7%**
A3-107	46.9%	21.3%	82.3%	33.8%
IUCL	76.6%	27.1%	24.9%	26.0%
MSR-IN	71.4%	18.3%	21.2%	19.6%

Table 5: Tweet-level evaluation on *Test2* set.

[4]The results of the other groups have been obtained from the workshop website. We use *"MSR-IN"* to refer to *"MSR-India"*

	Accuracy	Precision	Recall	$F_{\beta=1}$
AIDA	55.6%	16.3%	91.2%	**27.7%**
CMU	79.8%	20.7%	41.2%	27.6%
A3-107	45.7%	12.8%	83.3%	22.2%
IUCL	87.7%	25.0%	15.8%	19.4%
MSR-IN	84.8%	17.3%	16.7%	17.0%

Table 6: Tweet-level evaluation on *Surprise* set.

	ambig	lang1	lang2	mixed	NE	other	Avg-$F_{\beta=1}$
AIDA	0.0%	94.5%	5.6%	0.0%	85.0%	99.4%	**93.6%**
CMU	0.0%	94.4%	9.0%	0.0%	74.0%	98.1%	92.2%
A3-107	0.0%	93.8%	5.7%	0.0%	73.4%	87.4%	90.9%
IUCL	0.0%	88.2%	14.2%	0.0%	0.6%	0.6%	72.0%
MSR-IN	0.0%	94.2%	15.8%	0.0%	57.7%	91.1%	89.8%

Table 7: Token-level evaluation on *Test1* set.

6 Error Analysis

Tables 11, 12, and 13 show the confusion matrices of our best setup for all six tags over the three test sets. The rows represent the gold-labels while the columns represent the classes generated by our system. For example, row 4-column 2 corresponds to the percentage of words that have *lang1* (i.e. MSA) gold-label and were incorrectly classified as *ambig*. The diagonal of each matrix corresponds to the correctly classified instances. All cells of each matrix add-up to 100%. In all three tables, it's clear that the highest confusability is between *lang1* and *lang2* classes. In Test-set1, since the majority of words (81.5%) have a *lang1* gold-label and a very tiny percentage (0.3%) has

	ambig	lang1	lang2	mixed	NE	other	Avg-$F_{\beta=1}$
AIDA	0.0%	73.4%	73.2%	1.0%	91.8%	98.1%	77.7%
CMU	0.0%	76.3%	81.3%	0.0%	73.4%	98.4%	**79.9%**
A3-107	0.0%	62.0%	49.4%	0.0%	67.5%	75.0%	58.0%
IUCL	0.0%	59.0%	59.3%	0.0%	13.1%	1.7%	47.7%
MSR-IN	1.5%	58.7%	50.5%	0.0%	42.4%	43.8%	51.3%

Table 8: Token-level evaluation on *Test2* set.

	ambig	lang1	lang2	mixed	NE	other	Avg-$F_{\beta=1}$
AIDA	0.0%	66.6%	81.9%	0.0%	87.9%	99.9%	**80.1%**
CMU	0.0%	68.0%	82.1%	0.0%	61.2%	97.5%	77.8%
A3-107	0.0%	53.8%	61.3%	0.0%	62.3%	96.1%	62.6%
IUCL	0.0%	48.8%	60.9%	0.0%	5.5%	2.0%	46.7%
MSR-IN	0.0%	56.3%	69.8%	0.0%	33.2%	96.6%	65.4%

Table 9: Token-level evaluation on *Surprise* set.

	Tweet Avg-$F_{\beta=1}$	Token Avg-$F_{\beta=1}$
AIDA	20.2%	**86.8%**
CMU	**24.3%**	86.4%
A3-107	18.4%	76.6%
IUCL	18.2%	61.0%
MSR-IN	17.1%	74.2%

Table 10: Overall tweet-level and token-level $F_{\beta=1}$ scores. (Averaged over the three test-sets)

a *lang2* gold-label, the percentage of words that have a gold label of *lang1* and get classified as *lang2* is much larger than in the other two test-sets and much larger than the opposite-case where the ones having a gold-label of *lang2* get classified as *lang1*.

Table 14 shows examples of the words that were misclassified by AIDA. All of the shown examples are quite challenging. In example 1, the misclassified named-entity refers to the name of a TV show but the word also means *"clearly"* which is a *"lang1"* word. Similarly in example 2, the named-entity can mean *"stable"* which is again a *"lang1"* word. Another misclassification is that in example 3, where a mixed-morphology *"mixed"* word meaning *"those who were excluded/rejected"* is misclassified as being a *"lang2"* word. When we looked at why this happened, we found that the word wasn't tokenized by MADAMIRA. Our approach only assigns *"mixed"* tag if after tokenization, different morphemes of the word get different tags. Since in this example the word wasn't tokenized, it could not get the "*mixed*" tag. However, *"lang2"* tag (assigned by AIDA) is the second most appropriate tag since the main morpheme of the word is dialectal/lang2. An example of a *"mixed"* word that was correctly classified by AIDA is حتؤدي, Ht&dy meaning *"will lead to"* where the main morpheme تؤدي, t&dy "lead to" is *"lang1"* and the clitic ح, H "will" is *"lang2"*.

Examples 4 and 5 show instances of the confusability between "*lang1*" and "*lang2*" classes. Both words in these two examples can belong to either one of "*lang1*" and "*lang2*" classes depending on the context.

One interesting observation is that AIDA, outperforms all other systems tagging named-entities. This suggests the robustness of the NER approach used by AIDA.

The performance on the other tags varies across the three test-sets.

	AIDA (Predicted)					
	ambig	**lang1**	**lang2**	**mixed**	**NE**	**other**
ambig	0.0%	0.0%	0.0%	0.0%	0.0%	0.0%
lang1	0.0%	74.4%	5.7%	0.0%	1.3%	0.0%
lang2	0.0%	0.1%	0.2%	0.0%	0.0%	0.0%
mixed	0.0%	0.0%	0.0%	0.0%	0.0%	0.0%
NE	0.0%	1.5%	0.3%	0.0%	9.1%	0.1%
other	0.0%	0.0%	0.0%	0.0%	0.0%	7.3%

Table 11: The token-level confusion matrix for the best performing setup on *Test1* set.

	AIDA (Predicted)					
	ambig	**lang1**	**lang2**	**mixed**	**NE**	**other**
ambig	0.0%	0.3%	0.1%	0.0%	0.0%	0.0%
lang1	0.0%	28.8%	2.8%	0.1%	0.2%	0.1%
lang2	0.0%	16.4%	28.3%	0.5%	0.2%	0.1%
mixed	0.0%	0.0%	0.0%	0.0%	0.0%	0.0%
NE	0.0%	1.0%	0.6%	0.0%	11.5%	0.2%
other	0.0%	0.0%	0.0%	0.0%	0.0%	8.9%

Table 12: The token-level confusion matrix for the best performing setup on *Test2* set.

	AIDA (Predicted)					
	ambig	**lang1**	**lang2**	**mixed**	**NE**	**other**
ambig	0.0%	0.6%	0.3%	0.0%	0.0%	0.0%
lang1	0.0%	19.0%	2.9%	0.0%	0.5%	0.0%
lang2	0.0%	14.5%	42.7%	0.0%	0.5%	0.0%
mixed	0.0%	0.0%	0.0%	0.0%	0.0%	0.0%
NE	0.0%	0.5%	0.6%	0.0%	8.0%	0.0%
other	0.0%	0.0%	0.0%	0.0%	0.0%	9.9%

Table 13: The token-level confusion matrix for the best performing setup on *Surprise* set.

	Sentence	Word	Gold-Label	AIDA-Label
Ex. 1.	Allylp AlEA$rp w AlnSf msA' s>kwn Dyf AlAstA∗ Emrw Allyvy fy brnAmjh bwDwH ElY qnAp AlHyAp اللّيله العاشرة و النصف مساء سأكون ضيف الاستاذ عمرو اللّيثي في برنامجه بوضوح علي قناة الحياة	bwDwH, بوضوح	NE	lang1
Ex. 2.	wlsh mqhwr yA EynY mn **vAbt** bA$A AlbTl wSAlH bA$A slym AllY AvbtwA An nZrthm fykm SH ولسه مقهور يا عينى من **ثابت** باشا البطل وصالح باشا سليم اللّى اثبتوا ان نظرتهم فيكم صح	vAbt, ثابت	NE	lang1
Ex. 3.	Anh tAnY yqwm hykwn mE **Alm>lw$yn** انه تانى يقوم هيكون مع **المألوشين**	Alm>lw$yn, المألوشين	mixed	lang2
Ex. 4.	kfAyh $bEnA mnk AgAnyky Alqdymh jmylh lkn AlAn **lAnTyq** Swtk wlA Swrtk hwynA bqh كفايه شبعنا منك اغانيكي القديمه جميله لكن الان **لانطيق** صوتك ولا صورتك هوينا بقه	lAnTyq, لانطيق	lang1	lang2
Ex. 5.	AlrAbT Ally byqwl >ny Swrt Hlqp mE rAmz jlAl gyr SHyH . dh fyrws ElY Alfys bwk . rjA' AlH∗r الرابط اللّي بيقول أني صورت حلقة مع رامز جلال غير صحيح . ده فيروس على الفيس بوك . رجاء الحذر	Hlqp, حلقة	lang2	lang1

Table 14: Examples of the words that were misclassified by AIDA

7 Conclusion and Future Work

In this work, we adapt a previously proposed system for automatic detection of code switching in informal Arabic text to handle twitter data. We experiment with several setups and report the results on two twitter datasets and a surprise-genre test-set, all of which were generated for the shared task at EMNLP workshop for Computational Approaches to Code Switching. In the future we plan on handling other Arabic dialects such as Levantine, Iraqi and Moroccan Arabic as well as adapting the system to other genres.

8 Acknowledgment

This work has been funded by the NSF CRI Code Switching Project.

We would like to thank Mahmoud Ghoneim for his thorough review of the paper and the data. We also thank the anonymous reviewer for the useful comments.

References

Yassine Benajiba, Paolo Rosso, and Jos Miguel Benedruiz. 2007. Anersys: An arabic named entity recognition system based on maximum entropy. In *In Proceedings of CICLing-2007.*

Fadi Biadsy, Julia Hirschberg, and Nizar Habash. 2009. Spoken arabic dialect identification using phonotactic modeling. In *Proceedings of the Workshop on Computational Approaches to Semitic Languages at the meeting of the European Association for Computational Linguistics (EACL), Athens, Greece.*

Houda Bouamor, Nizar Habash, and Kemal Oflazer. 2014. A multidialectal parallel corpus of arabic. In *Proceedings of LREC.*

Ryan Cotterell and Chris Callison-Burch. 2014. A multi-dialect, multi-genre corpus of informal written arabic. In *Proceedings of the Language Resources and Evaluation Conference (LREC)*.

Ryan Cotterell, Adithya Renduchintala, Naomi Saphra, and Chris Callison-Burch. 2014. An algerian arabic-french code-switched corpus. In *LREC Workshop on Free/Open-Source Arabic Corpora and Corpora Processing Tools*.

Heba Elfardy and Mona Diab. 2012a. Simplified guidelines for the creation of large scale dialectal arabic annotations. In *Proceedings of LREC*.

Heba Elfardy and Mona Diab. 2012b. Token level identification of linguistic code switching. In *Proceedings of COLING, Mumbai, India*.

Heba Elfardy and Mona Diab. 2013. Sentence-Level Dialect Identification in Arabic. In *Proceedings of ACL2013*, Sofia, Bulgaria, August.

Heba Elfardy, Mohamed Al-Badrashiny, and Mona Diab. 2013. Code Switch Point Detection in Arabic. In *Proceedings of the 18th International Conference on Application of Natural Language to Information Systems (NLDB2013)*, MediaCity, UK, June.

Ramy Eskander, Mohamed Al-Badrashiny, Nizar Habash, and Owen Rambow. 2014. Foreign words and the automatic processing of arabic social media text written in roman script. *In Proceedings of the First Workshop on Computational Approaches to Code-Switching. EMNLP 2014, Conference on Empirical Methods in Natural Language Processing, October, 2014, Doha, Qatar*.

Ferguson. 1959. *Diglossia. Word 15. 325340*.

Nizar Habash and Fatiha Sadat. 2006. Arabic preprocessing schemes for statistical machine translation.

Nizar Habash, Ramy Eskander, and AbdelAti Hawwari. 2012. A Morphological Analyzer for Egyptian Arabic. In *NAACL-HLT 2012 Workshop on Computational Morphology and Phonology (SIGMORPHON2012)*, pages 1–9.

Nizar Habash. 2010. Introduction to arabic natural language processing. *Advances in neural information processing systems*.

Mohamed Maamouri, Dave Graff, Basma Bouziri, Sondos Krouna, Ann Bies, and Seth Kulick. 2010. Ldc standard arabic morphological analyzer (sama) version 3.1.

Arfath Pasha, Mohamed Al-Badrashiny, Mona Diab, Ahmed El Kholy, Ramy Eskander, Nizar Habash, Manoj Pooleery, Owen Rambow, and Ryan M. Roth. 2014. MADAMIRA: A Fast, Comprehensive Tool for Morphological Analysis and Disambiguation of Arabic. In *Proceedings of LREC*, Reykjavik, Iceland.

Wael Salloum and Nizar Habash. 2011. Dialectal to standard arabic paraphrasing to improve arabic-english statistical machine translation. In *Proceedings of the First Workshop on Algorithms and Resources for Modelling of Dialects and Language Varieties*. Association for Computational Linguistics.

Thamar Solorio, Elizabeth Blair, Suraj Maharjan, Steve Bethard, Mona Diab, Mahmoud Gonheim, Abdelati Hawwari, Fahad AlGhamdi, Julia Hirshberg, Alison Chang, , and Pascale Fung. 2014. Overview for the first shared task on language identification in code-switched data. In *In Proceedings of the First Workshop on Computational Approaches to Code-Switching. EMNLP 2014, Conference on Empirical Methods in Natural Language Processing, October, 2014, Doha, Qatar*.

Andreas Stolcke. 2002. Srilm an extensible language modeling toolkit. In *Proceedings of ICSLP*.

Omar F Zaidan and Chris Callison-Burch. 2011. The arabic online commentary dataset: an annotated dataset of informal arabic with high dialectal content. In *ACL*.

The IUCL+ System: Word-Level Language Identification via Extended Markov Models

Levi King, Eric Baucom, Timur Gilmanov, Sandra Kübler, Daniel Whyatt
Indiana University
{leviking,eabaucom,timugilm,skuebler,dwhyatt}@indiana.edu

Wolfgang Maier
Universität Düsseldorf
maierw@hhu.de

Paul Rodrigues
University of Maryland
prr@umd.edu

Abstract

We describe the IUCL+ system for the shared task of the First Workshop on Computational Approaches to Code Switching (Solorio et al., 2014), in which participants were challenged to label each word in Twitter texts as a named entity or one of two candidate languages. Our system combines character n-gram probabilities, lexical probabilities, word label transition probabilities and existing named entity recognition tools within a Markov model framework that weights these components and assigns a label. Our approach is language-independent, and we submitted results for all data sets (five test sets and three "surprise" sets, covering four language pairs), earning the highest accuracy score on the tweet level on two language pairs (Mandarin-English, Arabic-dialects 1 & 2) and one of the surprise sets (Arabic-dialects).

1 Introduction

This shared task challenged participants to perform word level analysis on short, potentially bilingual Twitter and blog texts covering four language pairs: Nepali-English, Spanish-English, Mandarin-English and Modern Standard Arabic-Arabic dialects. Training sets ranging from 1,000 to roughly 11,000 tweets were provided for the language pairs, where the content of the tweets was tokenized and labeled with one of six labels. The goal of the task is to accurately replicate this annotation automatically on pre-tokenized texts. With an inventory of six labels, however, the task is more than a simple binary classification task. In general, the most common labels observed in the training data are `lang1` and `lang2`, with `other` (mainly covering punctuation and emoticons) also common. Named entities (`ne`) are also frequent, and accounting for them adds a significant complication to the task. Less common are `mixed` (to account for words that may e.g., apply L1 morphology to an L2 word), and `ambiguous` (to cover a word that could exist in either language, e.g., *no* in the Spanish-English data).

Traditionally, language identification is performed on the document level, i.e., on longer segments of text than what is available in tweets. These methods are based on variants of character n-grams. Seminal work in this area is by Beesley (1988) and Grefenstette (1995). Lui and Baldwin (2014) showed that character n-grams also perform on Twitter messages. One of a few recent approaches working on individual words is by King et al. (2014), who worked on historical data; see also work by Nguyen and Dogruz (2013) and King and Abney (2013).

Our system is an adaptation of a Markov model, which integrates lexical, character n-gram, and label transition probabilities (all trained on the provided data) in addition to the output of pre-existing NER tools. All the information sources are weighted in the Markov model.

One advantage of our approach is that it is language-independent. We use the exact same architecture for all language pairs, and the only difference for the individual language pairs lies in a manual, non-exhaustive search for the best weights. Our results show that the approach works well for the one language pair with different writing systems (Mandarin-English) as well as for the most complex language pair, the Arabic set. In the latter data set, the major difficulty consists in the extreme skewing with an overwhelming dominance of words in Modern Standard Arabic.

2 Method

Our system uses an extension of a Markov model to perform the task of word level language identification. The system consists of three main components, which produce named entity probabilities, emission probabilities and label transition probabilities. The outputs of these three components are weighted and combined inside the extended Markov model (eMM), where the best tag sequence for a given tweet (or sentence) is determined via the Viterbi algorithm.

In the following sections, we will describe these components in more detail.

2.1 Named Entity Recognition

We regard named entity recognition (NER) as a standalone task, independent of language identification. For this reason, NER is performed first in our system. In order to classify named entities in the tweets, we employ two external tools, Stanford-NER and TwitterNLP. Both systems are used in a black box approach,

Proceedings of The First Workshop on Computational Approaches to Code Switching, pages 102–106,
October 25, 2014, Doha, Qatar. ©2014 Association for Computational Linguistics

without any attempt at optimization. I.e., we use the default parameters where applicable.

Stanford NER (Finkel et al., 2005) is a state-of-the-art named entity recognizer based on conditional random fields (CRF), which can easily be trained on custom data.[1] For all of the four language pairs, we train a NER model on a modified version of the training data in which we have kept the label "ne" as our target label, but replaced all others with the label "O". Thus, we create a binary classification problem of distinguishing named entities from all other words. This method is applicable for all data sets.

For the Arabic data, we additionally employ a gazetteer, namely ANERgazet (Benajiba and Rosso, 2008).[2] However, we do not use the three classes (person, location, organization) available in this resource.

The second NER tool used in our system is the TwitterNLP package. [3] This system was designed specifically for Twitter data. It deals with the particular difficulties that Twitter-specific language (due to spelling, etc.) poses to named entity recognition. The system has been shown to be very successful: Ritter et al. (2011, table 6) achieve an improvement of 52% on segmentation F-score in comparison with Stanford NER on hand-annotated Twitter data, which is mainly due to a considerably increased recall.

The drawback of using TwitterNLP for our task is that it was developed for English, and adapting it to other languages would involve a major redesign and adaptation of the system. For this reason, we decided to use it exclusively on the language pairs that include English. An inspection of the training data showed that for all language pairs involving English, a majority of the NEs are written in English and should thus be recognizable by the system.

TwitterNLP is an IOB tagger. Since we do not distinguish between the beginning and the rest of a named entity, we change all corresponding labels to "ne" in the output of the NER system.

In testing mode, the NER tools both label each word in a tweet as either "O" or "ne". We combine the output such that "ne" overrides "O" in case of any disagreements, and pass this information to the eMM. This output is weighted with optimized weights unique to each language pair that were obtained through 10-fold cross validation, as discussed below. Thus, the decisions of the NER systems is not final, but they rather provide evidence that can be overruled by other system components.

2.2 Label Transition Models

The label transition probability component models language switches on the sequence of words. It is also trained on the provided training data. In effect, this component consists of unigram, bigram, and trigram probability models of the sequences of labels found in the training data. Our MM is second order, thus the transition probabilities are linear interpolations of the uni-, bi-, and trigram label transition probabilities that were observed in the training data. We add two beginning-of-sentence buffer labels and one end-of-sentence buffer label to assist in deriving the starting and ending probabilities of each label during the training.

2.3 Emission Probabilities

The emission probability component is comprised of two subcomponents: a lexical probability component and a character n-gram probability component. Both are trained on the provided training data.

Lexical probabilities: The lexical probability component consists of a dictionary for each label containing the words found under that label and their relative frequencies. Each word type and its count of tokens are added to the total for each respective label. After training, the probability of a given label emitting a word (i.e., $P(word|label)$) is derived from these counts. To handle out-of-vocabulary words, we use Chen-Goodman "one-count" smoothing, which approximates the probabilities of unknown words as compared to the occurrence of singletons (Chen and Goodman, 1996).

Character n-gram probabilities: The character-based n-gram model serves mostly as a back-off in case a word is out-of-vocabulary, in which case the lexical probability may not be reliable. However, it also provides important information in the case of mixed words, which may use morphology from one language added to a stem from the other one. In this setting, unigrams are not informative. For this reason, we select longer n-grams, with n ranging between 2 and 5.

Character n-gram probabilities are calculated as follows: For each training set, the words in that training set are sorted into lists according to their labels. In training models for each value of n, $n-1$ buffer characters are added to the beginning and end of each word. For example, in creating a trigram character model for the `lang1` (English) words in the Nepali-English training set, we encounter the word *star*. We first generate the form *$$star##*, then derive the trigrams. The trigrams from all training words are counted and sorted into types, and the counts are converted to relative frequencies.Thus, using four values of n for a data set containing six labels, we obtain 24 character n-gram models for that language pair. Note that because this component operates on individual words, character n-grams never cross a word boundary.

In testing mode, for each word and for each value of n, the component generates a probability that the word occurred under each of the six labels. These values

[1] See `http://nlp.stanford.edu/software/CRF-NER.shtml`.

[2] As available from `http://users.dsic.upv.es/grupos/nle/`.

[3] See `https://github.com/aritter/twitter_nlp`.

are passed to the eMM, which uses manually optimized weights for each value of n to combine the four n-gram scores for each label into a single n-gram score for each label. In cases where an n-gram from the test word was not present in the training data, we use a primitive variant of LaPlace smoothing, which returns a fixed, extremely low non-zero probability for that n-gram.

2.4 The Extended Markov Model

Our approach is basically a trigram Markov model (MM), in which the observations are the words in the tweet (or blog sentence) and the underlying states correspond to the sequence of codeswitching labels (`lang1`, `lang2`, `ne`, `mixed`, `ambiguous`, `other`). The MM, as usual, also uses starting and ending probabilities (in our case, derived from standard training of the label transition model, due to our beginning- and end-of-sentence buffer labels), label/state transition probabilities, and probabilities that the state labels will emit particular observations. The only difference is that we modify the standard HMM emission probabilities. We call this resulting Markov model extended (eMM).

First, for every possible state/label in the sequence, we linearly interpolate "lexical (emission) probabilities" P_{lex} (the standard emission probabilities for HMMs) with character n-gram probabilities P_{char}. That is, we choose $0 \leq \lambda_{lex} \leq 1$ and $0 \leq \lambda_{char} \leq 1$ such that $\lambda_{lex} + \lambda_{char} = 1$. We use them to derive a new emission probability $P_{combined} = \lambda_{lex} \cdot P_{lex} + \lambda_{char} \cdot P_{char}$. This probability represents the likelihood that the given label in the hidden layer will emit the lexical observation, along with its corresponding character n-gram sequence.

Second, only for `ne` labels in the hidden layer, we modify the probabilities that they will emit the observed word *if* that word has been judged by our NER module to be a named entity. Since the NER component exhibits high precision but comparatively low recall, we boost the $P_{combined}(label = \texttt{ne}|word)$ if the observed word is judged to be a named entity, but we do not penalize the regular $P_{combined}$ if not. This boosting is accomplished via linear interpolation and another set of parameters, $0 \leq \lambda_{ne} \leq 1$ and $0 \leq \lambda_{combined} \leq 1$ such that $\lambda_{ne} + \lambda_{combined} = 1$. Given a positive decision from the NER module, the new probability for the `ne` label emitting the observed word is derived as $P_{ne+combined} = \lambda_{ne} \cdot 0.80 + \lambda_{combined} \cdot P_{combined}$, i.e., we simply interpolate the original probability with a high probability. All $lambda$ values, as well as the weights for the character n-gram probabilities, were set via 10-fold cross-validation, discussed below.

2.5 Cross Validation & Optimization

In total, the system uses 11 weights, each of which is optimized for each language pair. In labeling named entities, the output of the NER component is given one weight and the named entity probabilities of the other sources (emission and label transition components) is given another weight, with these weights summing to one. For the label transition component, the uni-, bi- and trigram scores receive weights that sum to one. Likewise, the emission probability component is comprised of the lexical probability and the character n-gram probability, with weights that sum to one. The character n-gram component is itself comprised of the bi-, tri-, four- and five-gram scores, again with weights that sum to one.

For each language pair, these weights were optimized using a 10-fold cross validation script that splits the original training data into a training file and a test file, runs the split files through the system and averages the output. As time did not allow an exhaustive search for optimal weights in this multi-dimensional space, we narrowed the space by first manually optimizing each subset of weights independently, then exploring combinations of weights in the resulting neighborhood.

3 Results

3.1 Main Results

The results presented in this section are the official results provided by the organizers. The evaluation is split into two parts: a tweet level evaluation and a token level evaluation. On the tweet level, the evaluation concentrates on the capability of systems to distinguish monolingual from multilingual tweets. The token level evaluation is concerned with the classification of individual words into the different classes: `lang1`, `lang2`, `ambiguous`, `mixed`, `ne`, and `other`.

Our results for the tweet level evaluation, in comparison to the best or next-best performing system are shown in table 1. They show that our system is capable of discriminating monolingual from multilingual tweets with very high precision. This resulted in the best results in the evaluation with regard to accuracy for Mandarin-English and for both Arabic-dialects settings. We note that for the latter setting, reaching good results is exceedingly difficult without any Arabic resources. This task is traditionally approached by using a morphological analyzer, but we decided to use a knowledge poor approach. This resulted in a rather high accuracy but in low precision and recall, especially for the first Arabic test set, which was extremely skewed, with only 32 out of 2332 tweets displaying codeswitching.

Our results for the token level evaluation, in comparison to the best performing system per language, are shown in table 2. They show that our system surpassed the baseline for both language pairs for which the organizers provided baselines. In terms of accuracy, our system is very close to the best performing system for the pairs Spanish-English and Mandarin English. For the other language pairs, we partially suffer from a weak NER component. This is especially obvious for the Arabic dialect sets. However, this is also a problem that can be easily fixed by using a more com-

lang. pair	system	Acc.	Recall	Precision	F-score
Nep.-Eng.	IUCL+	91.2	95.6	94.9	95.2
	dcu-uvt	95.8	99.4	96.1	97.7
Span.-Eng.	IUCL+	83.8	51.4	87.7	64.8
	TAU	86.8	72.0	80.3	75.9
Man.-Eng.	IUCL+	82.4	94.3	85.0	89.4
	MSR-India	81.8	95.5	83.7	89.2
Arab. dia.	IUCL+	97.4	12.5	11.1	11.8
	MSR-India	94.7	34.4	9.7	15.2
Arab. dia. 2	IUCL+	76.6	24.9	27.1	26.0
	MSR-India	71.4	21.2	18.3	19.6

Table 1: Tweet level results in comparison to the system with (next-)highest accuracy.

			lang1			lang2			mixed			ne		
lang. pair	system	Acc.	R	P	F	R	P	F	R	P	F	R	P	F
Nep.-Eng.	IUCL+	75.2	85.1	89.1	87.1	68.9	97.6	80.8	1.7	100	3.3	55.1	48.7	51.7
	dcu-uvt	96.3	97.9	95.2	96.5	98.8	96.1	97.4	3.3	50.0	6.3	45.6	80.4	58.2
	base	70.0	57.1	76.5	65.4	92.3	62.8	74.7	0.0	100	0.0	0.0	100	0.0
Span.-Eng.	IUCL+	84.4	88.9	82.3	85.5	85.1	89.9	87.4	0.0	100	0.0	30.4	48.5	37.4
	TAU	85.8	90.0	83.0	86.4	86.9	91.4	89.1	0.0	100	0.0	31.3	54.1	39.6
	base	70.3	85.1	67.6	75.4	78.1	72.8	75.4	0.0	100	0.0	0.0	100	0.0
Man.-Eng.	IUCL+	89.5	98.3	97.8	98.1	83.9	66.6	74.2	0.0	100	0.0	70.1	50.3	58.6
	MSR-India	90.4	98.4	97.6	98.0	89.1	66.6	76.2	0.0	100	0.0	67.7	65.2	66.4
Arab. dia.	IUCL+	78.8	96.1	81.6	88.2	34.8	8.9	14.2	–	–	–	3.3	23.4	5.8
	CMU	91.0	92.2	97.0	94.6	57.4	4.9	9.0	–	–	–	77.8	70.6	74.0
Arab. dia. 2	IUCL+	51.9	90.7	43.8	59.0	47.7	78.3	59.3	0.0	0.0	0.0	8.5	28.6	13.1
	CMU	79.8	85.4	69.0	76.3	76.1	87.3	81.3	0.0	100	0.0	68.7	78.8	73.4

Table 2: Token level results in comparison to the system with highest accuracy (results for `ambiguous` and `other` are not reported).

			lang1			lang2			ne		
lang. pair	system	Acc.	R	P	F	R	P	F	R	P	F
Nep.-Eng.	IUCL+	80.5	86.1	78.8	82.3	97.6	80.9	88.5	29.9	80.9	43.7
	JustAnEagerStudent	86.5	91.3	80.2	85.4	93.6	91.1	92.3	39.4	83.3	53.5
Span.-Eng.	IUCL+	91.8	87.4	81.9	84.5	84.5	87.4	85.9	28.5	47.4	35.6
	dcu-uvt	94.4	87.9	80.5	84.0	84.1	86.7	85.4	22.4	55.2	31.9
Arab. dia.	IUCL+	48.9	91.7	33.3	48.8	48.4	81.9	60.9	3.3	17.6	5.5
	CMU	77.5	87.6	55.5	68.0	75.6	89.8	82.1	52.3	73.8	61.2

Table 3: Token level results for the out-of-domain data.

petitive, language dependent system. Another problem constitutes the `mixed` cases, which cannot be reliably annotated.

3.2 Out-Of-Domain Results

The shared task organizers provided "surprise" data, from domains different from the training data. Our results on those data sets are shown in table 3. For space reasons, we concentrate on the token level results only. The results show that our system is very robust with regard to out-of-domain settings. For Nepali-English and Spanish-English, we reach higher results than on the original test sets, and for the Arabic dialects, the results are only slightly lower. These results need further analysis for us to understand how our system performs in such situations.

4 Conclusions

We have presented the IUCL+ system for word level language identification. Our system is based on a Markov model, which integrates different types of information, including the named entity analyses, lexical and character n-gram probabilities as well as transition probabilities. One strength of the system is that it is completely language independent. The results of the shared task have shown that the system generally provides reliable results, and it is fairly robust in an out-of-domain setting.

References

Kenneth R. Beesley. 1988. Language identifier: A computer program for automatic natural-language identification of on-line text. In *Proceedings of the 29th Annual Conference of the American Translators Association*, volume 47, page 54.

Yassine Benajiba and Paolo Rosso. 2008. Arabic named entity recognition using conditional random fields. In *Proceedings of Workshop on HLT & NLP within the Arabic World, LREC 2008*, Marakech, Morroco.

Stanley F. Chen and Joshua Goodman. 1996. An empirical study of smoothing techniques for language modeling. In *Proceedings of the 34th annual meeting on Association for Computational Linguistics*, pages 310–318.

Jenny Rose Finkel, Trond Grenager, and Christopher Manning. 2005. Incorporating non-local information into information extraction systems by gibbs sampling. In *Proceedings of the 43rd Annual Meeting of the Association for Computational Linguistics (ACL'05)*, pages 363–370.

Gregory Grefenstette. 1995. Comparing two language identification schemes. In *Proceedings of the Third International Conference on Statistical Analysis of Textual Data (JADT)*, volume 2.

Ben King and Steven Abney. 2013. Labeling the languages of words in mixed-language documents using weakly supervised methods. In *Proceedings of the 2013 Conference of the North American Chapter of the Association for Computational Linguistics: Human Language Technologies*, pages 1110–1119. Association for Computational Linguistics.

Levi King, Sandra Kübler, and Wallace Hooper. 2014. Word-level language identification in The Chymistry of Isaac Newton. *Literary and Linguistic Computing*.

Marco Lui and Timothy Baldwin. 2014. Accurate language identification of Twitter messages. In *Proceedings of the 5th Workshop on Language Analysis for Social Media (LASM)*, pages 17–25, Gothenburg, Sweden.

Dong Nguyen and A. Seza Dogruz. 2013. Word level language identification in online multilingual communication. In *Proceedings of the 2013 Conference on Empirical Methods in Natural Language Processing*, pages 857–862.

Alan Ritter, Sam Clark, Mausam, and Oren Etzioni. 2011. Named entity recognition in tweets: An experimental study. In *Proceedings of the 2011 Conference on Empirical Methods in Natural Language Processing*, pages 1524–1534, Edinburgh, Scotland, UK., July. Association for Computational Linguistics.

Thamar Solorio, Elizabeth Blair, Suraj Maharjan, Steve Bethard, Mona Diab, Mahmoud Gonheim, Abdelati Hawwari, Julia Hirshberg, Alison Chang, and Pascale Fung. 2014. Overview for the first shared task on language identification in code-switched data. In *Proceedings of the First Workshop on Computational Approaches to Code-Switching*. EMNLP 2014, Conference on Empirical Methods in Natural Language Processing, Doha, Qatar.

Mixed-Language and Code-Switching in the Canadian Hansard

Marine Carpuat
Multilingual Text Processing
National Research Council
Ottawa, ON K1A0R6, Canada
Marine.Carpuat@nrc.gc.ca

Abstract

While there has been lots of interest in code-switching in informal text such as tweets and online content, we ask whether code-switching occurs in the proceedings of multilingual institutions. We focus on the Canadian Hansard, and automatically detect mixed language segments based on simple corpus-based rules and an existing word-level language tagger.

Manual evaluation shows that the performance of automatic detection varies significantly depending on the primary language. While 95% precision can be achieved when the original language is French, common words generate many false positives which hurt precision in English. Furthermore, we found that code-switching does occur within the mixed languages examples detected in the Canadian Hansard, and it might be used differently by French and English speakers.

This analysis suggests that parallel corpora such as the Hansard can provide interesting test beds for studying multilingual practices, including code-switching and its translation, and encourages us to collect more gold annotations to improve the characterization and detection of mixed language and code-switching in parallel corpora.

1 Introduction

What can we learn from language choice patterns observed within multilingual organizations? While this question has been addressed, for instance, by conducting fieldwork in European Union institutions (Wodak et al., 2012), we aim to use natural language processing tools to study language choice directly from text, leveraging the publicly available proceedings of multilingual institutions, which are already widely used for machine translation. Early work on statistical approaches to machine translation (Brown et al., 1990) was made possible by the availability of the bilingual Canadian Hansard in electronic form[1]. Today, translated texts from the Hong Kong Legislative Council, the United Nations, the European Union are routinely used to build machine translation systems for many languages in addition to English and French (Wu, 1994; Koehn, 2005; Eisele and Chen, 2010, inter alia), and to port linguistic annotation from resource-rich to resource-poor languages (Yarowsky et al., 2001; Das and Petrov, 2011, among many others).

As a first step, we focus on detecting code-switching between English and French in the Canadian Hansard corpus, drawn from the proceedings of the Canadian House of Commons. Code-switching occurs when a speaker alternates between the two languages in the context of a single conversation. Since interactions at the House of Commons are public and formal, we suspect that code-switching does not occur as frequently in the Hansard corpus as in other recently studied datasets. For instance, Solorio and Liu (2008) used transcriptions of spoken language conversation, while others focused on informal written genres, such as microblogs and other types of online content (Elfardy et al., 2013; Cotterell et al., 2014). At the same time, the House of Commons is a "bilingual operation where French-speaking and English-speaking staff work together at every level" (Hicks, 2007), so it is not unreasonable to assume that code-switching should occur. In addition, according to the "Canadian Candidate Survey", in 2004, the percentage of candidates for the House of Commons who considered themselves bilingual ranged from 34% in the Conservative

[1] See http://cs.jhu.edu/~post/bitext/ for a historical perspective

Proceedings of The First Workshop on Computational Approaches to Code Switching, pages 107–115,
October 25, 2014, Doha, Qatar.

party to 86% in the Bloc Québecois. The study also shows that candidates have a wide range of attitudes towards bilingualism and the importance of language to their sense of identity (Hicks, 2007). This suggests that code-switching, and more generally language choice, might reveal an interesting range of multilingual practices in the Hansard.

In this paper, we adopt a straightforward strategy to detect mixed language in the Canadian Hansard, using (1) constraints based on the parallel nature of the corpus and (2) a state-of-the-art language detection technique (King and Abney, 2013). Based on this automatic annotation, we conduct a detailed analysis of results to address the following questions:

- How hard is it to detect mixed language in the Canadian Hansard? What are the challenges raised by the Hansard domain for state-of-the-art models?
- Within these mixed language occurrences, does code-switching occur? What kind of patterns emerge from the code-switched text collected?

After introducing the Canadian Hansard corpus (Section 2), we describe our strategy for automatically detecting mixed language use (Section 3). We will see that it is a challenging task: precision varies varies significantly depending on the primary language, and recall is much lower than precision for both languages. Finally, we will focus on the patterns of mixed language use (Section 4): they suggest that code-switching does occur within the mixed language examples detected in the Canadian Hansard, and that it might be used differently by French and English speakers.

2 The Canadian Hansard Corpus

According to Canada's Constitution, "either the English or French language may be used by any person in the debates of the Houses of the Parliament."[2] As a result, speaker interventions can be in French or English, and a single speaker can in principle switch between the two languages.

Our corpus consists of manual transcriptions and translations of meetings of Canada's House of Commons and its committees from 2001 to 2009. Discussions cover a wide variety of topics, and speaking styles range from prepared speeches by a single speaker to more interactive discussions. The part of the corpus drawn from meetings of the House of Commons, is often also called *Hansard*, while *committees* refers to the transcriptions of committee meetings.

This corpus is well-suited to the study of multilingual interactions and their translation for two main reasons. First, the transcriptions are annotated with the original language for each intervention. Second, the translations are high quality direct translations between French and English. In contrast, a French-English sentence pair in the European Parliament corpus (Koehn, 2005) could have been generated from an original sentence in German that was translated into English, and then in turn from English into French. Direct translation eliminates the propagation of "translationese" effects (Volansky et al., 2013), and avoids losing track of code-switching examples by translation into a second or third language.

One potential drawback of working with transcribed text is that the transcription process might remove pauses, repetitions and other disfluencies. However, it is unclear whether this affects mixed language utterances differently than single language ones.

2.1 Corpus Structure and Processing

The raw corpus consists of one file per meeting. The file starts with a header containing meta information about the meeting (event name, type, time and date, etc.), followed by a sequence of "fragments". Each "fragment" corresponds to a short segment of transcribed speech by a single speaker, usually several paragraphs. Fragments are the unit of text that translators work on, so the original language of the fragment is tagged in the corpus, as it determines whether the content should be translated into French or into English. We use the original language tagged as a gold label to define the primary language of the speaker in our study of code-switching.

The raw data was processed using the standard procedure for machine translation data. Processing steps included sentence segmentation and sentence alignment within each fragment, as well as tokenization of French and English. This process yields a total of 8,194,055 parallel sentences. We exclude subsets reserved for the evaluation of machine translation systems, and work with the re-

[2] *Constitution Act*, 1867, formerly the *British North America Act*, 1867, "Appendices", *Revised Statuses of Canada* (RS 1985), s.133.

Data origin	# English segments	# French segments
Committees	4,316,239	915,354
Hansard	2,189,792	738,967
Total	6,506,031	1,654,321

Table 1: Language use by segment

Data origin	# English speakers	# French speakers	# Bilingual speakers
Committees	8787	888	3496
Hansard	198	61	327
Total	8985	949	3823

Table 2: Language use by speaker

maining 8,160,352 parallel segments.[3]

2.2 Corpus-level Language Patterns

English is used more frequently than French: it accounts for 80% of segments, as can be seen in Table 1. The French to English ratio is significantly higher in the Hansard than in the Committees section of the corpus. But how often are both languages used in a single meeting? We use the "DocumentTitle" tags marked in the metadata in order to segment our corpus into meetings. Both French and English segments are found in the resulting 4740 meetings in the committees subcorpus and 927 meetings in the Hansard subcorpus.

How many speakers are bilingual? Table 2 describes language use per speaker per subcorpus. Here, we define a speaker as bilingual if their name is associated with both French and English fragments. Note that this method might overestimate the number of biilingual speakers, as it does not allow us to distinguish between two different individuals with the same name. Overall 22% of speakers are bilingual. The percentage of bilingual speakers in the Hansard (56%) is more than twice that in the Committees (26.5%), reflecting the fact that Hansard speakers are primarily Members of Parliament and Ministers, while speakers that address the Committees represent a much wider sample of Canadian society.

[3]The raw and processed versions of the corpus are both available on request.

3 Automatic Detection of Mixed Language

3.1 Task Definition

We aim to detect code-switching between English and French only. While we found anecdotal evidence of other languages such as Spanish and Italian in the corpus[4], these occurrences seem extremely rare and detecting them is beyond the scope of this study.

We define mixed-language segments as segments which contain words in the language other than their "original language". Recall that the original language is the manually assigned language of the fragment which the segment is part of (Section 2). We want to automatically (1) detect mixed-language segments, and (2) label the French and English words that compose them, in order to enable further processing. These two goals can be accomplished simultaneously by a word-level language tagger.

In a second stage, the automatically detected mixed language segments are used to manually study code-switching, since our mixed language tagger does not yet distinguish between code-switching and other types of mixed language (e.g., borrowings).

3.2 Challenges

When the identity of the languages mixed is known, the state-of-the-art approach to word-level language identification is the weakly supervised approach proposed by King and Abney (2013). They frame the task as a sequence labeling problem with monolingual text samples for training data. A Conditional Random Field (CRF) trained with generalized expectation criteria performs best, when evaluated on a corpus comprising 30 languages, including many low resources languages such as Azerbaijani or Ojibwa.

In our case, there are only two high-resource languages involved, which could make the language detection task easier. However, the Hansard domain also presents many challenges: English and French are closely related languages and share many words; the Hansard corpus contains many occurrences of proper names from various origins which can confuse the language detector; the corpus is very large and unbalanced as we expect the vast majority of segments to be monolingual.

[4]e.g., "merci beaucoup, thank you very much, grazie mille"

To address these challenges, we settled on a two pass approach: (1) select sentences that are likely to contain mixed language, and (2) apply CRF-based word-level language tagging to the selected sentences.

3.3 Method: Candidate Sentence Selection

We select candidates for mixed language tagging using two complementary sources of information:

- frequent words in each language: a mixed-language segment is likely to contain words that are known to be frequent in the second language. For instance, if a segment produced by a French speaker contains the string "of", which is frequent in English, then it is likely to be a mixed language utterance.
- parallel nature of corpus: if a French speaker uses English in a predominantly French segment, the English words used are likely to be found verbatim in the English translation. As a result, overlap[5] between a segment and its translation can signal mixed language.

We devise a straightforward strategy for selecting segments for word-level language tagging:

1. identify the top 1000 most frequent words on each side of the parallel Hansard corpus.
2. exclude words that occur both in the French and English list (e.g., the string "on" can be both an English preposition and a French pronoun)
3. select originally French sentences where (a) at least one word from the English list occurs, and (b) at least two words from the French sentence overlap with the English translation
4. select originally English sentences in the same manner.

3.4 Method: Word-level Language Tagging

The selected segments are then tagged using the CRF-based model proposed by King and Abney (2013). It requires samples of a few thousand words of French and English for training. How can we select samples of English and French that are strictly monolingual?

We solve this problem by leveraging the parallel nature of our corpus again: We assume that a segment is strictly monolingual if there is no overlap in vocabulary between a segment and its translation. Using this approach, we randomly select a sample of 1000 monolingual French segments and 1000 monolingual English segments. This yields about 21k/4k word tokens/types for English, and 24k/4.6k for French. Using these samples, we apply the CRF approach on each candidate sentence selected during the previous step. For the low resource languages used by King and Abney (2013), the training samples were much smaller (in the order of hundreds of words per language), and learning curves suggest that the accuracy reaches a plateau very quickly. However, we decide to use larger samples since they are very easy to construct in our large data setting.

[5]Except for numbers, punctuation marks and acronyms.

fr mixed in en	gold pos.	gold neg.	total
predicted pos.	21	8	29
predicted neg.	1	109	110
total	22	117	139

Table 4: Confusion matrix for detecting segments containing French words when English is the original language. It yields a Precision of 95.4% and a Recall of 72.4%

en mixed in fr	gold pos.	gold neg.	total
predicted pos.	3	1	4
predicted neg.	13	105	118
total	16	106	122

Table 5: Confusion matrix for detecting segments containing English words when French is the original language. It yields a Precision of 75% and a Recall of 18.75%

3.5 Evaluation

At this stage, we do not have any gold annotation for code-switching or word-level language identification on the Hansard corpus. We therefore ask a bilingual human annotator to evaluate the precision of the approach for detecting mixed language segments on a small sample of 100 segments for each original language. The annotator tagged each example with the following information: (1) does the segment actually contain mixed language? (2) are the language boundaries correctly detected? (3) what does the second language express? (e.g., organization name, idiomatic expression, quote, etc. The annotator was not given predefined categories) . Table 3 provides annotation examples.

Tagged Lang.	**[FR** Et le premier ministre nous répond que] **[EN** a farmer is a farmer a Canadian is a Canadian] **[FR** d' un bout à l' autre du Canada]
Gold Lang.	**[FR** Et le premier ministre nous répond que] **[EN** a farmer is a farmer a Canadian is a Canadian] **[FR** d' un bout à l' autre du Canada]
Evaluation	Mixed-language segment? **yes** Are boundaries correct? **yes** What is the L2 content? **quote**
Tagged Lang.	**[FR** Autrement] **[EN** dit they are getting out of the closet] **[FR** parce que cela leur donne le droit d avoir deux enfants]
Gold Lang.	**[FR** Autrement dit] **[EN** they are getting out of the closet] **[FR** parce que cela leur donne le droit d avoir deux enfants]
Evaluation	Mixed-language segment? **yes** Are boundaries correct? **no** What is the L2 content? **idiom**

Table 3: Example of manual evaluation: the human annotator answers three questions for each tagged example, based on their knowledge of what the gold language tags should be.

2-step	*committees*		*Hansard*	
detection	en	fr	en	fr
Selection	62,069	13,278	42,180	13,558
Tagger	7,713	317	3,993	164

Table 6: Number of mixed-language segments detected by each automatic tagging stage, as described in Section 3.

Based on this gold standard, we can first evaluate the performance of the segment-level mixed language detector (Task (1) as defined in Section 3.1). Confusion matrices for English and French sentences are given in Tables 5 and 4 respectively. The gold label counts confirm that the classes are very unbalanced, as expected.

The comparison of the predictions with the gold labels yields quite different results for the two languages. On English sentences, the mixed language tagger achieves a high precision (95.4%) at a reasonable level of recall (72.4%) , which is encouraging. However, on French sentences, the mixed language tagger achieves a slightly lower precision (75%) with an extremely low recall (18.75%). These scores are computed based on a very small number of positive predictions by the tagger (4 only) on the sample of 100+ sentences. Nevertheless, these results suggest that, while we might miss positive examples due to the low recall, the precision of the mixed language detector is sufficiently high to warrant a more detailed study of the examples of mixed language detected.

lang	corpus	detection precision	segmentation precision
en	committees	72.6%	44.4%
	Hansard	45.9%	28.6%
fr	committees	98.4%	67.7%
	Hansard	96.8%	75.4%

Table 7: Evaluation of positive predictions: precision of mixed language detection at the segment level, and precision of the language segmentation (binary judgment on accuracy of predicted language boundaries for each segment.)

4 Patterns of Mixed Language Use

Discovering patterns of mixed language use, including code-switching, requires a large sample of mixed language segments. Since the gold standard constructed for the above evaluation (Section 3) only provides few positive examples, we ask the human annotator to apply the annotation procedure illustrated in Table 3 to a sample of positive predictions: French segments where the tagger found English words, and vice versa.

The number of positive examples detected can be found in Table 6. Only a small percentage of the original corpus is tagged as positive, but given that our corpus is quite large, we already have more than 10,000 examples to learn from.

The human annotator annotated a random sample of 60+ examples for each original language and corpus partition. The resulting precision

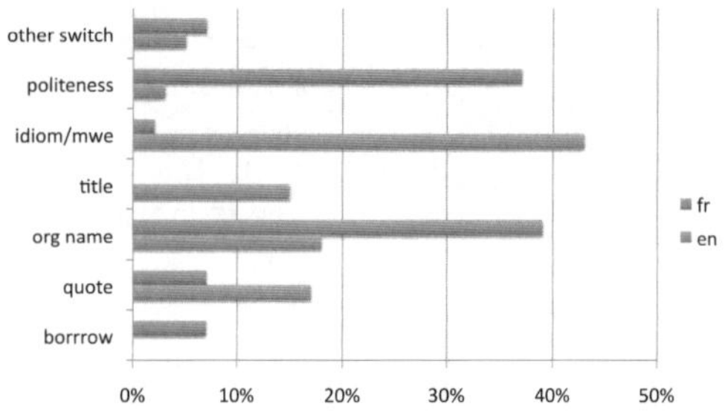

Figure 1: Categories of mixed language use observed depending on the original language of the segment, in the *committees* data

scores, both for mixed language detection at the segment level, and for accurately tagging words with French and English, are given in Table 7. For segment level detection, the precision is much higher on French than on English, as observed previously. On English data, the annotation reveals that most false positives are due to frequent words that occur both in languages (e.g., "province","Premier","plus"), and are incorrectly tagged as French in our English segment. The boundaries of French and English segments are correctly detected for up to 75% of French segments, but only for 44% at best in English segments. More work is therefore needed to accurately tag languages at the word-level. Some of the second language words are usually detected, but the boundaries are often wrong, especially at code-switching points.

In addition to correctness, the annotator was asked to identify the kind of information conveyed by the second language, and they came up with categories that reflected the patterns that emerged from the examples. Examples of these categories are given for each language in Table 8, and the percentage of examples observed per category for each language are plotted in Figure 1.

While many correctly detected mixed language segments are due to borrowings, use of organization names or titles in the other language, we do find examples of code switching such as:

- quotes
- multiword expressions or idioms,
- politeness formulas and formality.

The distribution of code-switching across these categories is very different for French and English as original languages. Multiword expressions and idioms account for more than 40% of English use in French segments, while there are no examples of French idioms in English segments. Conversely, while politeness formulas in French account for more than 30% of correctly detected mixed language use in English segments, there are only fewer than 5% such instances in French. This might suggest that French speakers who code-switch are more proficient in English than English speakers in French, or that code-switching is used for different purposes by English and French speakers in the Hansard context.

While more analysis is definitely needed to better understand code-switching patterns and their use, we have established that code-switching occurs in the Hansard corpus, and that it might be used differently by French and English speakers.

In the parallel corpus, different types of mixed language are handled differently by human translators, which suggests that machine translation of code-switched data requires specific strategies: while English idioms, quotes or named entities in a French segment might be directly copied to the output when translating into English, other categories should be handled diffferently. For instance, mixed language that discusses translation of terms might require to *avoid translating* the original French terms in order not to lose the original meaning in translation. When English is used in politeness, the reference translations often perform a *normalization* of titles and capitalization. In that case, copying the English segments in the French sentence to the MT output would produce translations that are understandable, but would not match the conventions used in the reference.

5 Related Work

To the best of our knowledge, this is the first study of mixed language and code-switching in the Canadian Hansard parallel corpus, a very large parallel corpus commonly used to build generic machine translation systems.

Previous work at the intersection of *machine translation* and *mixed languages* has focused on specific application scenarios: word translation disambiguation for mixed language queries (Fung et al., 1999), or building applications to help second language learners, such as translating of short L1 phrases in sentences that are predominantly

	Use of English in primarily French segments
Quote	**[FR** C' est écrit] "**[EN** will have full access] " **[FR** Vous avez dit et je vous cite] " **[EN** we do not have to change the definition of marriage to protect equality rights] "
Translation	**[FR** On parle en anglais de] **[EN** carrots and sticks] **[FR** Milliard correspond à] **[EN** billion] **[FR** en anglais]
Politeness	**[FR** Nous accueillons ce matin M Brulé M Baines M McDougall et M Mann] **[EN** Welcome to all of you] **[EN** Thank you Mr Chair] **[FR** Merci beaucoup]
Idioms/MWEs	**[FR** Le contraire ne m avait jamais été dit] **[EN** by the way] **[FR** Oui en français] **[EN** as well]
Title	**[FR** Je cite l auteur israélien Simha Flapan dans l ouvrage] **[EN** The Birth of Israel] **[FR** Des courts métrages présents dans la compétition officielle] **[EN** The stone of folly] **[FR** a nettement été le film préféré du public]
Organization	**[FR** La] **[EN** Western Canadian Wheat Growers Association] **[FR** est une association de producteurs] **[FR** M Thomas Axworthy l ancien président du] **[EN** Centre for the Study of Democracy] **[FR** s y trouvait aussi]
Other	**[FR** Alors en ce moment le comité est maître de sa propre procédure pour étudier cette question importante] **[EN** this breach of its own privileges which appears to have taken place] **[FR** Merci aux collègues] **[EN** who gave me this opportunity]
	Use of French in primarily English segments
Quote	**[EN** The great French philosopher Blaise Pascal spoke of the essence of human life as a gamble] **[FR** un pari] **[EN** and so it is in political life] **[EN** You mentioned] **[FR** les fusions] **[EN** but I gather that] **[FR** les défusions] **[EN** is now the order of the day in Quebec]
Translation	**[EN** The French text had a small error in that it used the word] **[FR** aux] **[EN** where the word] **[Fr** des] **[EN** should have been used] **[EN** Mr Speaker to teach is to open doors to a better world in French] **[FR** enseigner ouvre les portes vers un monde meilleur]
Politeness	**[EN** Thank you Mr Chairman] **[FR** monsieur le président] **[EN** honourable members] **[FR** mesdames et messieurs] **[EN** On this important traditional Chinese holiday] **[FR** bonne année à toute la communauté canadienne] **[EN** I wish all Canadians health happiness and prosperity in the year of the ox]
Idioms/MWEs	**[EN** We were the first ones to start to ask about it and we are following] **[FR** à la lettre] **[EN** as we say in French **[EN** So that s just to]**[FR** entrer en matière]
Borrowing	**[EN** We think it fundamentally adjusts the loss of culture and language which was the] **[FR** raison d'être] **[EN** of the residential school program] **[EN** Everything is a] **[FR** fait accompli]
Organization	**[EN** That s a fair question and I d like to thank Mr Blaney for participating in the] **[FR** Forum socioéconomique des Premières Nations] **[EN** If the **[EN** Bloc Québécois] **[EN** brings forward a witness you may want to go to them first]
Other	**[EN** The same committee rejected an amendment] **[FR** proposé par le Bloc québécois proposé par moi pour le NPD] **[EN** This is not the current government] **[FR** C est la même chose] **[EN** it doesn t matter which one is in power]

Table 8: Examples of mixed language segments

L2[6] (van Gompel and van den Bosch, 2014), or on detecting code-mixing to let an email translation system handle words created on the fly by bilingual English-Spanish speakers (Manandise and Gdaniec, 2011). While code-switched data is traditionally viewed as noise when training machine translation systems, Huang and Yates (2014) showed that appropriately detecting code-switching can help inform word alignment and improve machine translation quality.

There has been renewed interest on the study of mixed language recently, focusing on detecting code-switching points (Solorio and Liu, 2008; Elfardy et al., 2013) and more generally detecting mixed language documents. Lui et al. (2014) use a generative mixture model reminiscent of Latent Dirichlet Allocation to detect mixed language documents and the languages inside them. Unlike the CRF-based approach of King and Abney (2013), the languages involved do not need to be known ahead of time. In contrast with all these approaches, we work with parallel data with unbalanced original languages.

6 Conclusion

We investigated whether code-switching occurs in the Canadian Hansard parallel corpus.

We automatically detected mixed language segments using a two-step approach: (1) candidate sentence selection based on frequent words in each language and overlap between the two side of the parallel corpus, and (2) tag each word in the segment as French or English using the CRF-based approach of King and Abney (2013).

Manual evaluation showed that automatic detection can be done with high precision when the original language is French, but common words generate many false positives which hurt precision in English. More research is needed to improve recall, which is lower than precision in both languages, and particularly low when the original language is French. Further analysis reveals that code-switching does occur within the mixed language examples detected in the Canadian Hansard, and suggests that it is used differently by French and English speakers.

While much work is still needed to construct larger evaluation suites with gold annotations, and improving the detection and tagging of mixed language sentences, this work suggests that the proceedings of multilingual organizations such as the Canadian Hansard can provide interesting test beds for (1) corpus-based study of language choice and code-switching, which can complement the direct observation of meetings, as conducted by Wodak et al. (2012), and (2) investigating the interactions of code-switching and machine translation. Furthermore, it would be interesting to study how code-switching in the Hansard differs from code-switching in more informal settings.

[6] http://alt.qcri.org/semeval2014/task5/

References

Peter Brown, John Cocke, Stephen Della Pietra, Vincent Della Pietra, Frederik Jelinek, John Lafferty, Robert Mercer, and Paul Rossin. 1990. A statistical approach to machine translation. *Computational Linguistics*, 16:79–85.

Ryan Cotterell, Adithya Renduchintala, Naomi Saphra, and Chris Callison-Burch. 2014. An Algerian Arabic-French code-switched corpus. In *Workshop on Free/Open-Source Arabic Corpora and Corpora Processing Tools*. May.

Dipanjan Das and Slav Petrov. 2011. Unsupervised part-of-speech tagging with bilingual graph-based projections. In *Proceedings of the 49th Annual Meeting of the Association for Computational Linguistics: Human Language Technologies - Volume 1*, HLT '11, pages 600–609, Stroudsburg, PA, USA.

Andreas Eisele and Yu Chen. 2010. MultiUN: A multilingual corpus from United Nation documents. In *Proceedings of the Seventh conference on International Language Resources and Evaluation*, pages 2868–2872, 5.

Heba Elfardy, Mohamed Al-Badrashiny, and Mona Diab. 2013. Code switch point detection in Arabic. In *Natural Language Processing and Information Systems*, pages 412–416. Springer.

Pascale Fung, Xiaohu Liu, and Chi Shun Cheung. 1999. Mixed Language Query Disambiguation. In *Proceedings of ACL'99*, Maryland, June.

Bruce Hicks. 2007. Bilingualism and the Canadian house of commons 20 years after B and B. In *Parliamentary Pespectives*. Canadian Study of Parliament Group.

Fei Huang and Alexander Yates. 2014. Improving word alignment using linguistic code switching data. In *Proceedings of the 14th Conference of the European Chapter of the Association for Computational Linguistics*, pages 1–9, Gothenburg, Sweden, April.

Ben King and Steven Abney. 2013. Labeling the languages of words in mixed-language documents using weakly supervised methods. In *Proceedings of the 2013 Conference of the North American Chapter of the Association for Computational Linguistics: Human Language Technologies*, pages 1110–1119, Atlanta, Georgia, June.

Philipp Koehn. 2005. Europarl: A parallel corpus for statistical machine translation. In *Machine Translation Summit X*, Phuket, Thailand, September.

Marco Lui, Jey Han Lau, and Timothy Baldwin. 2014. Automatic detection and language identification of multilingual documents. *Transactions of the Association for Computational Linguistics*.

Esmé Manandise and Claudia Gdaniec. 2011. Morphology to the rescue redux: Resolving borrowings and code-mixing in machine translation. *Systems and Frameworks for Computational Morphology*, pages 86–97.

Thamar Solorio and Yang Liu. 2008. Learning to predict code-switching points. In *Proceedings of the 2008 Conference on Empirical Methods in Natural Language Processing*, pages 973–981, Honolulu, Hawaii, October.

Maarten van Gompel and Antal van den Bosch. 2014. Translation assistance by translation of L1 fragments in an L2 context. In *Proceedings of the 52nd Annual Meeting of the Association for Computational Linguistics (Volume 1: Long Papers)*, pages 871–880, Baltimore, Maryland, June.

Vered Volansky, Noam Ordan, and Shuly Wintner. 2013. On the features of translationese. *Literary and Linguistic Computing*.

Ruth Wodak, Michal Krzyzanowski, and Bernhard Forchtner. 2012. The interplay of language ideologies and contextual clues in multilingual interactions: Language choice and code-switching in European Union institutions. *Language in Society*, 41:157–186.

Dekai Wu. 1994. Aligning a parallel English-Chinese corpus statistically with lexical criteria. In *Proceedings of the 32Nd Annual Meeting on Association for Computational Linguistics*, ACL '94, pages 80–87, Stroudsburg, PA, USA.

David Yarowsky, Grace Ngai, and Richard Wicentowski. 2001. Inducing multilingual text analysis tools via robust projection across aligned corpora. In *Proceedings of the First International Conference on Human Language Technology Research*, HLT '01, pages 1–8, Stroudsburg, PA, USA.

"I am borrowing *ya* mixing ?"
An Analysis of English-Hindi Code Mixing in Facebook

Kalika Bali **Jatin Sharma** **Monojit Choudhury**
Microsoft Research Lab India
{kalikab,jatin.sharma,monojitc}@microsoft.com

Yogarshi Vyas*
University of Maryland
yogarshi@cs.umd.edu

Abstract

Code-Mixing is a frequently observed phenomenon in social media content generated by multi-lingual users. The processing of such data for linguistic analysis as well as computational modelling is challenging due to the linguistic complexity resulting from the nature of the mixing as well as the presence of non-standard variations in spellings and grammar, and transliteration. Our analysis shows the extent of Code-Mixing in English-Hindi data. The classification of Code-Mixed words based on frequency and linguistic typology underline the fact that while there are easily identifiable cases of borrowing and mixing at the two ends, a large majority of the words form a continuum in the middle, emphasizing the need to handle these at different levels for automatic processing of the data.

1 Introduction

The past decade has seen an explosion of Computer Mediated Communication (CMC) worldwide (Herring 2003). CMC provides users with multiple options, both asynchronous and synchronous, like email, chat, and more recently, social media like Facebook and Twitter (Isharayanti et al 2009, Paolillo 2011). This form of communication raises interesting questions on language use across these media. Language use in CMC lies somewhere in between spoken and written forms of a language, and tend to use simple shorter constructions, contractions, and phrasal repetitions typical of speech (Dannett and Herring 2007) Such conversations, especially in social-media are also multi-party and multilingual, with switching between, and mixing of two or more languages, the choice of language-use being highly influenced by the speakers and their communicative goals (Crystal 2001).

Code-Switching and Code-Mixing are stable and well-studied linguistic phenomena of multilingual speech communities. **Code-Switching** is "*juxtaposition within the same speech exchange of passages of speech belonging to two different grammatical systems or sub-systems*" (Gumperz 1982), and **Code-Mixing** refers to *the embedding of linguistic units such as phrases, words and morphemes of one language into an utterance of another language* (Myers-Scotton 1993, 2002). Thus, Code-Switching is usually *inter-sentences* while Code-Mixing (CM) is an *intra-sentential* phenomenon. Linguists believe that there exists a *continuum* in the manner in which a lexical item transfers from one to another of two languages in contact (Myers-Scotton 2002, Thomason 2003). Example (1) below illustrates the phenomenon of Code-Switching, while (2) shows Code-Mixing.

(1) I was going for a movie yesterday. *raaste men mujhe Sudha mil gayi.*
Gloss: [I was going for a movie yesterday.] way in I Sudha meet went
Translation: I was going for a movie yesterday; I met Sudha on the way.

[1] This work was done during the author's internship at Microsoft Research Lab India.

Proceedings of The First Workshop on Computational Approaches to Code Switching, pages 116–126,
October 25, 2014, Doha, Qatar.

(2) *Main kal* movie *dekhne jaa rahi thi* and *raaste me* I met *Sudha*.
Gloss: I yesterday [movie] to-see go Continuous-marker was [and] way in [I met] Sudha.
Translation: I was going for a movie yesterday and on the way I met Sudha.

The main view held by linguists being that a lexical item goes from being used as a foreign word to a valid loanword indistinguishable from the native vocabulary by virtue of repeated use and adoption of morpho-syntactic features of the recipient language (Auer 1984). However, in the case of single words, most scholars agree that it is difficult to determine whether or not a word is a "bona fide loanword/borrowing" or an instance of nonce borrowing[2] or CM (Alex 2008, Bentahila and Davies, 1991, Field 2002, Myers-Scotton 2002, Winford 2003). In this study, we only consider Code-mixing examples, i.e., intra-sentential embedding of a language in another language.
Processing such language data is challenging from the perspective of linguistic understanding vis-à-vis discourse and conversational analysis, as well as computational modelling and applications to Machine Translation, Information Retrieval and Natural Interfaces. Especially, in the case of social-media content where there are added complications due to contractions, non-standard spellings, and ungrammatical constructions as well as mixing of scripts. Many languages that use non-Roman scripts, like Hindi, Bangla, Chinese, Arabic etc., are often represented using Roman transliterations (Virga and Khudanpur 2003, Sowmya et al 2010). This poses additional challenges of accurately identifying and separating the two languages. Further, it is often difficult to disambiguate a borrowing as a valid native vocabulary from a mixing of a second language when dealing with single words. An understanding of the nature of mixing in such data is one of the first steps towards processing this data and hence, making a more natural interaction in CMC a real possibility.

In this paper, we analyze social media content from English-Hindi (En-Hin) bilingual users to better understand CM in such data. We look at the extent of CM in both Hindi embedding in English, as well as English in Hindi. Our analysis of the type of CM in this context based on frequency of use and linguistic typology helps further an understanding of the different kinds of CM employed by users and emphasizes the need to tackle these at different levels.

Facebook Page	No. of likes	No. of posts collected	No. of comments collected
Amitabh Bachchan	12,674,509	5	3364
BBC Hindi	1,876,306	18	240
Narendra Modi	15,150,669	15	2779
Shahrukh Khan	8,699,146	2	600
Total		**40**	**6983**

Table 1: Facebook Data Source

2 Corpus Creation and Annotation

For the creation of corpus for studying En-Hin CM, data from public Facebook pages in which En-Hin bilinguals are highly active was considered appropriate. Hence, we chose the Facebook pages of three Indian public figures, two prominent Bollywood stars viz, Amitabh Bachchan and Shahrukh Khan, and the then-PM-elect Narendra Modi. We also collected data from the BBC Hindi News page. The assumption was that Bollywood, politics and news being three very popular areas of interest for Indians, we would see a lot of activity from the community on these pages. A total of 40 posts from Oct 22- 28, 2013 were manually collected and preference was given to posts having a long (50+) thread of comments. This is because CM and non-standard use of language is more frequent in comments. In the rest of the paper, we shall use the term *posts* to cover both comments and posts. The data was semi-automatically cleaned and formatted, removing user names for privacy. The names of public figures in the posts were retained. The final corpus consisted of 6983

[2] **Nonce-borrowings** are typically borrowings that do not necessarily follow any phonological, morpho-syntactic or sociolinguistic constraints on their assimilation into the host language (Poplack et al 1988). However, it is not clear if this is always a defining feature between established loanwords and nonce-borrowing, the line between them being extremely tenuous (Sankoff et al, 1990)

posts and 113,578 words. Table 1 shows the data source statistics.

While a number of posts were in the Devanagari script, the largest representation was that of Roman script. A small number of posts were found in the script of other Indian languages like Bangla, Telugu etc. Tables 2 (a) and (b) show the distribution of posts and words by script

Facebook Page	Deva-nagari	Roman	Mixed Script	Other Script
Amitabh Bachhcan	73	3168	112	16
BBC Hindi	56	175	27	0
Narendra Modi	77	2633	84	11
Shahrukh Khan	0	578	23	1

Table 2 (a): Script used for Posts

Facebook Page	Deva-nagari	Roman	Other Script	Symbols
Amitabh Bachhcan	2661	38144	439	1768
BBC Hindi	5225	4265	23	160
Narendra Modi	9509	43,804	217	1470
Shahrukh Khan	0	5,514	105	274

Table 2(b): Script used for Words

2.1 Annotation

As a first step towards analysis, it is imperative that an annotation scheme be arrived at that captures the richness, diversity and uniqueness of the data. Any analysis of code-mixed CMC language-use requires inputs at social, contextual, and different linguistic and meta-linguistic levels that operate on various sub-parts of the conversation. This would help label not only the structural linguistics phenomena such as POS tagging, Chunks, Phrases, Semantic Roles etc. but also the various socio-pragmatic contexts (User demographics, Communicative intent, Polarity etc.). However, an initial attempt at such a rich, layered annotation proved the task to be immensely resource intensive. Hence, for the initial analysis the annotation scheme was scaled down to four labels:

Matrix: Myers Scotton's (1993) framework, CM occurs where one language provides the morpho-syntactic frame into which a second language inserts words and phrases. The former is termed as the *Matrix* while the latter is called *Embedding*. Usually, matrix language can be assigned to clauses and sentences.

Following this framework, the annotator was asked to split all posts into contiguous fragments of words such that each fragment has a unique matrix language (En or Hin)

Word Origin: Every embedded word is marked for its origin (En or Hin) depending on whether the source language was English or Hindi. A word from a language other than English or Hindi was marked as Other (Ot). It was assumed that the unmarked words within a matrix language originated in that language. In our data we did not find examples of sub-lexical CM. For example an English word with Hindi inflection like *computeron (कम्प्यूटरों)* were the English word "computer" is inflected by the Hindi plural marker *–on*. However, this can be a possible occurrence in En-Hin CM and needs to be marked as such.

Normalization: Whenever a word in its native script uses a non-standard spelling (including contractions) it is marked with its correct spellings. For transliterations of Hindi in Roman script, the word is marked with the correct spelling in Devanagari script.

POS tagging: Each word is labelled with its POS tag following the Universal Tagset proposed by Petrov et al (2011). This tagset uses 12 high-level tags for main POS classes. While, this tagset is not good at capturing granularity at a deeper level, we chose this because of a) its applicability to both English and Hindi doing away with the need for any mapping of labels between the two languages, and b) the small size of the corpus posed serious doubts on the usefulness of a more granular tagset for any analysis.

The POS tags were decided on the basis of the function of the word in a context rather than a de-contextualized absolute word class. This was done because often in the case of embedded words, the lexical category of the original language is completely lost and it is the function of the word in the matrix language that applies and assumes importance.

Named Entities: Named Entities (NE) are perhaps the most common and amongst the first to form the borrowed or mixed vocabulary in CM. As the Universal Tagset did not have a separate

category for NEs, we chose to label and classify them as people, locations and organizations. It is important to remember that while NEs are perhaps the most frequent “borrowings” the notion of Word Origin in the context of CM is debatable. However, these need to be analyzed and processed separately for any NLP application.
1062 posts consisting of 1071 words were randomly selected and annotated by a linguist who is a native speaker of Hindi and proficient in English. Non-overlapping subsets of the annotations were then reviewed and corrected by two expert linguists.
The two annotated examples from the corpus of En in Hin Matrix and Hin in En Matrix are given below:

```
<s>
      <matrix name="Hindi">
love_NOUN/E affection_NOUN/E le-
kar_VERB/"ले कर"
salose_NOUN=saalon/"सालों से"
sunday_NOUN/E ke_ADP/"के"
din_NOUN/"दिन" chali_VERB/ "चली" aar-
ahi_VERB/"आ रही" divine_ADJ/E param-
para_NOUN/"परंपरा" ko_ADP/"को"
age_NOUN=aage/"आगे" badhha_VERB/"बढ़ा"
rahe_VERB/"रहे" ho_VERB/"हो"
      </matrix>
</s>
```

Translation: The divine tradition that (you) have been carrying forward every Sunday with love and affection.

```
<s>
<matrix name="English">
      sir_NOUN u_PRON=you r_VERB=are
blessed_VERB by_ADP entire_ADJ brah-
mand_NOUN/H"ब्रहमाण्ड"
      </matrix>
</s>
```

Translation: Sir, you are blessed by the entire Universe.

It was observed that a large chunk of data consisted of short posts typically a greeting or a eulogy from a fan of the public figures and were uninteresting from a structural linguistic analysis of CM. Thus, all such posts (consisting of 5 or less words) were deleted from the corpus and the remaining corpus of 381 posts and 4135 words was used for further analysis.

3 An Analysis of Code Mixed Data

The annotated data consists of 398 Hin sentences, 698 En and 6 Ot in a single language. 45 posts show at least one switch in matrix between En and Hin. Thus, at least 4.2% of the data is Code-Switched. It should be noted however that this is matrix switching within an utterance. If we consider Code-Switching at a global level to include switching from one language to another within a conversation thread then all the threads in the data show code-switching as they contain utterances from both English and Hindi.
Looking at the 398 Hindi matrices, we find that 23.7% of them show at least one En embedding as compared to only 7.2% of the En matrices with Hin embedding. In total 17.2% of all posts which consist of nearly a quarter of all words in the data show some amount of CM.
If we look at the number of points in a single matrix where embedding happens, we find that in 86% of the En matrices, Hin embeddings appear only once or twice. En embeddings in Hin matrix is not only twice as more frequent, but can occur more often in a single matrix (more than 3 times in at least 10% of the cases). Table 3 shows the distribution of CM points for both the cases.

# of points	**Hin in En**	**En in Hin**
1	11 (36.66%)	19 (31.15%)
2	15 (50%)	28 (45.9%)
3	2 (6.67%)	2 (3.28%)
4	2 (6.67%)	9 (5.49%)
5	0	2 (3.28%)
6	0	1 (1.64%)
Total	30	61

Table 3: Distribution of CM points

NE Type Person	159
NE Type Location	39
NE Type Organization	35
Total NE	233

Table 4: Distribution of NE by Type

As expected, NEs are common in the corpus and there are a total of 233 NEs in 406 matrices (322 of 4134 words). The distribution of NEs by subclasses is given in Table 4.
Table 5 shows the distribution of the various POS in the entire corpus, as well as for the embedded words. Nouns do form the largest class of words

overall as well as for Hin as well as En embedding. In fact, for Hin in English matrix, there are only two instances of words which are not Nouns. Table 5 shows the distribution of POS for Hin in En matrix, and En in Hin matrix

Looking at these top-level distributions we can observe that though there are some similarities between the patterns of CM for Hin in English and En in Hindi matrices (the high frequency of nouns, for instance), they both exhibit distinct patterns in terms of how often CM occurs as well as in the prevalence of POS other than Nouns. In Section 3.1 and 3.2 we will look at both these L1 embedding in L2 matrix individually in more detail.

POS Tag	Over-all	En in Hin matrix*	Hin in En matrix*
NOUN	1260	77	32
VERB	856	8	
PRON	499	4	
ADP	445	0	
ADJ	302	16	
PRT	241	4	1
DET	141	2	
.	125	NA	
ADV	104	3	
CNJ	98	2	
NUM	46	0	
X	18	0	
Total	4135		

Table 5: POS distribution for the Annotated Corpus.

* Overall distribution is given at token level whereas the embedding En in Hin matrix, and Hin in E matrix are at Unique Word level.

3.1 Hindi words in English matrix

As mentioned above, most of the Hin embedding in En (32 out of 33) matrices are Nouns. The exception is variation of the particle "ji" used as an honorific marker in Hindi. The particle is used to denote respect and occurs in formulaic expression of the kind <(name/address form)> ji as in:

"Amit *ji*, I am your fan and have seen all your movies"

A closer look at the embedded Hin Nouns shows that a large number of them are actually part of multi-word Named Entities which do not fall under the categories defined in the annotation guidelines. Almost all of them also function as regular Nouns or Verbs in Hindi. For example, the word "hunkaar" (a roar) is not an NE, however its use in the following sentence, where it is used to de note the name of a particular rally (event) can be viewed as an NE.

"*hunkar* rally will be held tomorrow"

Similarly, the word "yaatraa" in Hindi means journey whereas its use in the phrase "Kerala *yaatraa*" is specific to a tour of Kerala.

There are some instances of nonce-borrowing or CM where Hindi Nouns are not used as a part of a potential NE or formulaic expressions. For example, in the following sentence:

"…and the party workers (will) come with me without *virodh*"

The Hindi word "virodh" is used instead of the English alternative "protest" or "objection". It can only be assumed that the user did this for sociolinguistic or pragmatic reasons to emphasize or humour.

Kinship terms form another domain of frequent embedding of Hin in En. Hindi has a more complex system of kinship terms where not only are there finer distinctions maintained between maternal and paternal relations but also kinship terms are used to address older (and hence) respectable people. Thus, we find the use of "chacha" (father's younger brother), "bhaiya" (elder brother) as well as "baapu" (father) used frequently in the data as address forms.

3.2 English words in Hindi matrix

There is a far greater use of English words in Hindi matrices both as single words as well as multi-word expressions. A total of 116 unique Hindi words are found embedded in En matrices of which 76 are single word embedding and the rest are a part of 16 multi-word expressions. While Nouns continue to dominate the POS class of the Hindi embedding as well, there is far more variations in the type of CM that seems to be happening in this case.

3.2.1 Single Word Embedding

As in the case of English embedding (3.1) we find a number of Hindi Noun embedding to be of kinship terms, greetings and other address form.

Words like, "sir", "uncle", "hello", "good morning" etc are used frequently to start or end a particular turn.
A fraction of Nouns are genuine borrowings into the language is no Hindi equivalent for that word/concept. Common examples are words like "goal" and "bomb" which may be considered a part of the Hindi vocabulary. What is interesting is that users' variations in spellings these words either in English ("goal", "bomb") or in equivalent Hindi transliteration ("gol", "bam"). This may be taken as an indication that the user is not actively conscious of using an English word. However, there are a fairly large number of Nouns as single words where this is not applicable as in:

"agar aap BJP ke **follower** hain to is **page** ko **like** karen"

(If you are a BJP follower then like this page)

where there are frequently used Hindi equivalents but the user seems to be following certain conventions on Facebook ("page" and "like") or is mixing for other purposes ("follower")

Single adjectives are not as common and when used are mostly intensifiers such as "very" or "best" etc. There are some instances of adjectives as nonce-borrowings such as in the following example:

"...**divine** paramparaa ko aage..."
(...(taking the) divine tradition forward...)

Single verb embedding of En words are always of the form V + *kar* in the data. The verb *karnaa* ("to do") in Hindi is used to form conjunctives in Hindi. Thus, we have a number of Hindi phrases of the type: *kaam karnaa* " work to do" (to work), and a closer look at the English Verbs embedded in Hindi shows that most of these are actually in their nominalized form, such as " **driving** karnaa", or as a V + V conjunct such as "**admit** karnaa".
There are fewer instances of other POS classes, however, one interesting case is the use of conjuncts like "but" and "and" to join two Hindi clauses as in:

"main to gayi thi **but** wo wahaan nahi thaa"
(I had gone but he wasn't there)

3.2.2 Multi Word Embedding

Multi word expressions in English used in a Hindi matrix range from standard formulaic expressions to clause or phrase insertion. Other than standard greetings, these formulaic (or frozen) expression may work as Named Entities or Nominal compounds as in the case of "Film star", "Cricket player", "Health minister", "Educational Institutes" and "Participation Certificate". There are also other expressions that border on formulaic in English but which nevertheless have an ambiguous status within Hindi, such as, "love and affection". Another example of such a case of MW embedding is:

"**Befitting reply** to mere papa ne maaraa"

(my father gave a befitting reply)

Here, while "befitting reply" is not really a formulaic expression in Hindi, the user is clearly using it as such with the use of the emphatic *to* and the use of the verb *maaraa* ("hit") instead of *diyaa* ("gave")

Clause or phrase level mixing, though less frequent can also be found in the data. For example,

"**Those who support the opposition** kabhi Muzaffarnagar aa kar dekho"

(Those who support the opposition should come to Muzaffarnagar and see (for themselves))

This is a classic case of CM where both the phrases retain the grammatical structure of the language concerned.

As can be seen from the analysis of the annotated corpus above, Code-Mixing if understood as the insertion of words from a language into the grammatical structure of another, can show a wide variation in its structural linguistic manifestation.

4 Borrowing *ya* Mixing?

In linguistic literature on "other language embedding" there has been a long-standing debate on what is true Code-mixing, what is nonce-word borrowing, and what are "loanwords" that are integrated into the native vocabulary and grammatical structure (Bentahila and Davies, 1991, Field 2002, Myers-Scotton 2002, Winford 2003, Poplack and Dion 2012). Many linguists believe that loan-words start out as a CM or Nonce-borrowing but by repeated use and diffusion across the language they gradually convert to native vocabulary and acquire the characteristics of the "borrowing" language (see Alex (2008) for a discussion). Normally, they look at spoken forms to see phonological convergence and inflections for morpho-syntactic convergence. However, as pointed out by Poplack and Dion (2012) the problem with this is that in many cases a native "accent" might be mistaken for phonological convergence, and a morpho-syntactic marking might not be readily visible. For example, most Hindi speakers of English would pronounce an English alveolar /d/ as a retroflex because an alveolar plosive is not a part of the Hindi phonology. However, this does not imply that the said English word has become a part of the native vocabulary. Similarly, if we look at the two sentences:

"sab artists ko bulayaa hai"
(all artists have been called),

and

"sab artist kal aayenge"
(all artists will come tomorrow)

In the first sentence the English inflection –s on the word artist marks it as plural but in the second case, the plural is marked on the Hindi Verb. Does this imply that in the first case it is CM and in the second a case of borrowing given that both the forms and the structures are equally acceptable and common in Hindi?

Many studies (Mysken 2000, Gardner-Chloros. 2009, Poplack and Dion 2012 etc.) thus point out that it is not easy to decide these categories especially for single words without looking at diachronic data and the inherent fuzziness of the distinction itself. In general, it is believed that there exists a sort of continuum between CM and loan vocabulary where the edges might be clearly distinguishable but it is difficult to disambiguate the vast majority in the middle especially for single words.

As we have seen in the preceding Section CM of Hin in English matrix mainly follows a very distinct pattern of using NEs (and functional NEs) and formulaic expressions. However, in the case of En in Hindi CM, there is a far wider variation and it could be difficult in many instances to decide by just looking at the data whether a certain embedding is a borrowing or CM.

One way to make a distinction between a borrowing and CM could be to look at the diffusion of the word in the native language. Borrowed words often appear in monolingual usage long before dictionaries and lexicons adopt them as native vocabulary. Thus, to judge the diffusion of an English word one would have to look at the frequency of its use in suitable monolingual context such as news wire data, chat logs or telephone conversations.

For a further analysis of En embedding in Hin matrix in our data, we decided to check their frequency based diffusion in a monolingual new corpus of Hindi. For this purpose we took a corpus of 51,277,891words from *Dainik Jagaran* (http://www.jagran.com/), a popular daily newspaper in Hindi, and created a frequency count of the 230,116 unique words in it. News corpora are a reasonable choice for monolingual frequencies as code-mixing is relatively rare and frowned upon in news unless it refers to a named entity or is a part of a direct quote. We then mapped common Hindi equivalents of all the English words used in the corpora. Finally, we checked the frequency of both the English embedding as well as their corresponding Hindi equivalents. As mentioned before, a number of English words do not have Hindi equivalents and for these words we expect the English words themselves to have a high frequency count in the corpus.

An analysis of the results thus obtained shows that the English words do indeed fall into two distinct buckets at the edges. Thus, for words such as "party" (as in "political party"), "vote", "team" we find that not only are the word counts quite high (over 67K for "party" and over 18k for "vote" and "team") but the counts for the equivalent Hindi forms are relatively low. Similarly, words like "affection", "driving", "easily" etc. were not found in the corpus, while their Hindi equivalents had relatively medium to high counts. However, there is a large number of words in the middle where both the English and the Hindi equivalents have a comparative count or the difference is not significant. For these words it is difficult to decide whether they ought to be classified as borrowing or CM.

Let us denote the frequency of an En word as f_e and that of its Hin synonym as f_h. Let δ be an arbitrary margin > 0. The aforementioned intuition about the nature of CM and borrowing can be formalized as follows:

- If for a given word $\log(f_h/f_e) > \delta$, we call it CM

- If for a given word $\log(f_h/f_e) < -\delta$, we call it a *borrowing*.
- If $-\delta \leq \log(f_h/f_e) \leq \delta$, it is not possible to decide between the two cases, and hence we call the word *ambiguous*.

Figure 1 shows the scatter plot of the frequency of all the En words that occur within Hin matrix (119 in total) in the Dainik Jagaran data (x-axis) against the frequency of its Hindi synonym (y-axis) in the same corpus. Since frequency follows Zipfs law, the axes are in log-scale. The words, which are represented by dots in Figure 1, are scattered all over the plot without any discernable pattern. This indicates that there are no distinct classes of words that can be called borrowings or mixing; rather, it is a continuum. If we assume δ to be 1, an arbitrary value, we can divide the plot into three zones using the three rules proposed above. These zones, bounded by the blue lines are shown in Figure 1: Mixing – words that are code-mixed (top-left triangle), borrowings (bottom-right triangle) and ambiguous (the narrow zone running diagonally between the two with a width of 2δ.

However, we observe that some En words which has very high frequency in our corpus (e.g., *vote*, *party*, *team*), are classified as *ambiguous* because their Hin synonyms have a comparable high frequency as well. To a native speaker of Hindi, these words are clearly borrowings and used even in formal Hin text. In fact, it seems reasonable to declare an En word as a *borrowing* solely on the basis of its very high frequency in the monolingual corpus. We could choose another arbitrary threshold $\alpha = 1000$, such that a word is declared as a borrowing if the following two conditions are satisfied:

- $-\delta \leq \log(f_h/f_e) \leq \delta$
- $f_e > \alpha$

Note that the choice of α should also depend on the size of the corpus. Table 6 reports the number of CM in the data with and without applying the large frequency rule. We see that the number of CM words is the highest followed by ambiguous words. This clearly indicates that CM is a very common phenomenon on social media. Appendix A lists all the En words and their classes.

Using arbitrary thresholds, δ and α, to classify the words into three distinct set is a convenient tool to deal with code-mixing; but it ignores the fact that in reality it is not possible to classify words into a few distinct categories. There is always a continuum between borrowing and mixing. Figure 1 shows a more appropriate gradient based visualization of the space. Words falling on the darker regions of this plot are more likely to be borrowing. The gradients reflect the two equations discussed above. The darkness linearly increases with $\log(f_e)$ and decreases with $\log(f_h/f_e)$. The overall darkness is a simple linear combination of these two independent factors. Note that this formulation is only for a visualization purpose, and should not be interpreted as some formal probability or measure of "borrowing-ness" of a word.

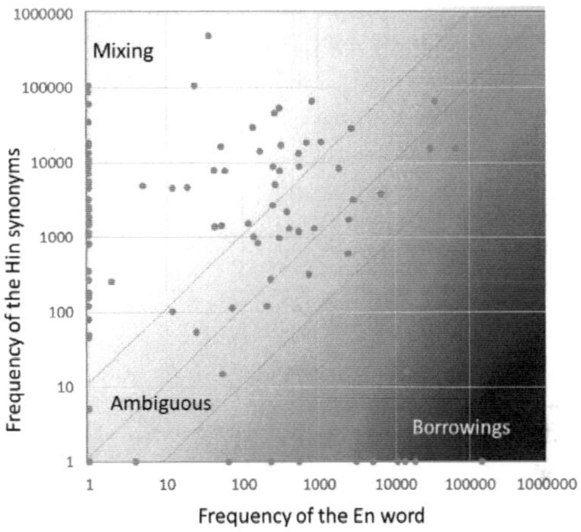

Figure 1: Plot of the frequencies of En words embedded in Hin matrix (x-axis) and their Hin synonyms (y-axis) in the Dainik Jagaran corpus.

	CM	Ambiguous	Borrowing
w/o α-Rule	69	39	11
w/ α-Rule	69	31	19

Table 6: Classification of embedded En words into three classes for $\delta = 1$.

A note on synonym selection: Which synonym(s) of an En word should be considered for CM vs. borrowing analysis is a difficult question. First, a word can have many senses. E.g., the word *party* can mean a political party, a group of people, or a social gathering, and also a verb – to participate in a social gathering. Each of these senses can be translated in, often more than one ways. E.g., *dala* in the sense of political party, *anusThANa* or *dAwata* in the sense of social gathering, etc. To complicate the situation further, these Hindi words can have many senses as well (e.g., the word *dala* can mean a sports team, or a political party or group of people or animals).

Thus, when we compare synonyms without context, we cannot be sure in which sense the words are used and therefore, the frequency counts maybe misleading. A second problem arise with phrase embedding. While an entire phrase can be borrowed, its words may not be (e.g., *clean chit* -Indian version of the English expression "clean sheet"- is a borrowed expression in Hindi, but *clean* is not). However, we had access to only the wordlist and word frequencies, which made it impossible to disentangle such effects. Comparing contexts automatically deciphering word sense is a complex problem in itself. For this work, we used an En to Hin lexicon (http://shabdkosh.raftaar.in/) to find out the synonyms, and for every synonym extracted the frequency from the wordlist, and deemed the highest frequency as the f_h for the word. A more thorough synonym selection using context and phrase level analysis would be an interesting extension of this work.

4.1 Ambiguous Words

The words classified as *ambiguous* pose a problem as we do not know whether these words are in the process of being borrowed, or are working as near-synonym of the Hindi equivalent, or are CMs where the intention of the user is the motivation for the "other language" use.

Poplack and Dion (2012) are of the view that there does not exist a continuum between CM, Nonce-borrowing and loanwords. In their diachronic study on En-French CM, the authors show that the frequency of all three categories remain stable. According to them, a user is always aware whether they are using an "other language" word as a CM (for socio-linguistic purposes) or as a socio-linguistically unmarked borrowing. Our data does not capture diachronic statistics neither does our monolingual corpus is at the scale at which language changes occur. However, we interpret our results to indicate that there is indeed a fuzzy boundary between CM and borrowing. Nevertheless, this distinction may not be readily observable through word classification or even diffusion and/or other structural linguistic features. The notion of "social acceptance" of a particular word in that language community may play a big role.

Further, the perception of a word as either CM, or borrowing could depend on a large number of meta- and extra-linguistic factors that may include including the fluency of the user in English, familiarity with the word, and the pragmatic/discourse/socio-linguistics reasons for using them. Thus, for a true bilingual, fluent in both languages, an adverb like "easily" might be more stable and almost a borrowing, but for someone with less familiarity with English, it might be a mixing. Similarly, whether or not a person is consciously using the English word to make a point can matter. A frequent example of this in our data is the use of swear words and expletives which are often accompanied by a switch in language. These words thus are difficult to disambiguate without more information and data, and an analysis that takes into account the non-structural linguistic motivations.

5 Conclusion

In this paper, we present an analysis of data from Facebook generated by En-Hin bilingual users. Our analysis shows that a significant amount of this data shows Code Mixing in the form of En in Hindi matrix as well as Hin in English matrix. While the embedding of Hindi words in English mostly follows formulaic patterns of Nouns and Particles, the mixing of English in Hindi is clearly happening at different levels, and is of different types. This can range from single words to multiword phrases ranging from frozen expressions to clauses. Considering monolingual corpus frequency counts clearly shows that the words themselves fall into three categories of clear CM, clear Borrowings and Ambiguous where the distinction becomes fuzzy. The problem is amplified because in transliterated text, even the borrowings are mostly in English spellings and sometimes Hindi spellings (goal vs gol), and will be identified as English words. From an NLP perspective, all these have to be handled differently. Some are easier to handle ("party" would be in a Hindi lexicon, for example, and NEs) and some are more difficult for example where Adverbials or clauses are involved.

The insights from this analysis indicate that any future work on CM in social media content would have to involve a deeper analysis at the intersection of structural and discourse linguistics. We plan to continue our work in this area in the future with focus on larger data sets, richer annotations which take into account not only structural linguistics annotation but also discourse and pragmatic level annotations. We believe that an understanding of the interaction between morpho-syntax and discourse, and a deeper look at sociolinguistic context of the interaction in the future will help us to better define and understand this phenomenon and hence, implement suitable NLP techniques for processing such data.

Appendix A

List of English words embedded in Hindi matrix found in our data, classified into three classes for $\delta = 1$ and $\alpha = 1000$.

Code-mixed words: *health, public, army, India, affection, divine, pm, drama, clean, anti, young, follower, page, like, request, easily, Indian, uncle, comment, reply, sun, bomb, means, game, month, spokesperson, actor, I, word, admit, good, afternoon, time, look, please, help, husband, artists, very, sad, but, higher, planning, mad, keep, failure, well, strike, sorry, girlfriend, those, who, support, opposition, and, profile, right, good, men, driving, lady, leader, singer, shift, culture, only, with, befitting, reply*

Ambiguous words: *blast, daily, love, sir, bloody, cheapo, chit, hello, it, football, style, pant, hi, commonwealth, participation, certificates, education, robot, Bollywood, player, big, bee, the, agency, women, line, trolling, ODI, tiger, comedy*

Borrowings: *CBI, goal, rally, match, police, film, cricket, appeal, Italian, fan, best, vote, party, power, minister, team, you, photo, star*

Reference

Beatrice Alex. 2008. *Automatic Detection of English Inclusions in Mixed-lingual Data with an Application to Parsing*, Doctor of Philosophy Thesis, School of Informatics, University of Edinburgh, Edinburgh, UK.

Celso Alvarez-Cáccamo. 2011. "Rethinking conversational code-switching: codes, speech varieties, and contextualization." *Proceedings of the Annual Meeting of the Berkeley Linguistics Society*. Vol. 16.

Peter Auer. 1984. *The Pragmatics of Code-Switching: A Sequential Approach.* Cambridge University Press.

Abdelali Bentahila and Eirlys E. Davies. 1991. "Constraints on code-switching: A look beyond grammar. *Papers for the symposium on code-switching in blingual studies: Theory, significance and perspectives*. Strasbourg: European Science Foundation.

MS Cardenas-Claros and N Isharyanti. 2009. Code-switching and code-mixing in internet chatting: Between yes, ya, and si- a case study. In *The JALT CALL Journal, 5*

David Crystal. 2001. *Language and the Internet.* Cambridge University Press.

B. Danet and S. Herring. 2007. *The Multilingual Internet: Language, Culture, and Communication Online.* Oxford University Press, New York.

Frederic Field. 2002. *Linguistic borrowing in bilingual contexts*. Amsterdam: Benjamins.

Penelope Gardner-Chloros. 2009. *Code-Switching*. Cambrudge University Press

J. Gumperz. 1964. Hindi-Punjabi code-switching in Delhi. In *Proceedings of the Ninth International Congress of Linguistics*, Mouton: The Hague.

J. Gumperz. 1982. *Discourse Strategies*. Oxford University Press.

S. Herring. 2003. *Media and Language Change: Special Issue*.

Jeff MacSwan. 2012." Code-Switching and Grammatical Theory." In *The Handbook of Bilingualism and Multilingualism* (2012). 323.

Carol Myers-Scotton. 1993. Duelling Languages: Grammatical Structure in Code-switching. Claredon. Oxford.

Carol Myers-Scotton. 2002. Contact linguistics: Bilingual encounters and grammatical outcomes. Oxford University Press.

Pieter Muysken. 2000. *Bilingual speech: A typology of code-mixing*. Cambridge University Press.

John C. Paolillo. 2011. “Conversational” codeswitching on Usenet and Internet Relay Chat. In *Language@Internet*, 8, article 3.

Slav Petrov, Dipanjan Das, and Ryan McDonald. 2011. A universal part-of-speech tagset. *arXiv preprint arXiv:1104.2086*

Shana Poplack, D. Sankoff, and C. Miller. 1988. The social correlates and linguistic processes of lexical borrowing and assimilation. *Linguistics* 26:47-104.

Shana Poplack and Nathalie Dion. 2012. "Myths and facts about loanword development." in *Language Variation and Change* 24, 3.

David Sankoff, Shana Poplack, and Swathi Vanniarajan. 1990. The case of the nonce loan in Tamil. *Language Variation and Change*, 2 (1990), 71-101. Cambridge University Press.

V.B. Sowmya, M. Choudhury, K. Bali, T. Dasgupta, and A. Basu. 2010. Resource creation for training and transliteration systems for Indian languages. In Proceedings of Language Resource and Evaluations Conference (LREC 2010).

Sarah G. Thomason. 2003. Contact as a Source of Language Change. In R.D. Janda & B. D. Joseph (eds), *A handbook of historical linguistics*, Oxford: Blackwell.

Paola Virga and Sanjeev Khudanpur. 2003. Transliteration of proper names in cross-lingual information retrieval. Proceedings of the ACL 2003 workshop on Multilingual and mixed-language named entity recognition-Volume 15. Association for Computational Linguistics.

Donald Winford. 2003. An Introduction to Contact Linguistics. Malden, MA: Blackwell.

DCU-UVT: Word-Level Language Classification with Code-Mixed Data

Utsab Barman, Joachim Wagner, Grzegorz Chrupała[†] and Jennifer Foster
CNGL Centre for Global Intelligent Content, National Centre for Language Technology
School of Computing, Dublin City University, Dublin, Ireland
[†]Tilburg School of Humanities, Department of Communication and Information Sciences
Tilburg University, Tilburg, The Netherlands
{ubarman, jwagner, jfoster}@computing.dcu.ie
G.A.Chrupala@uvt.nl

Abstract

This paper describes the DCU-UVT team's participation in the *Language Identification in Code-Switched Data* shared task in the *Workshop on Computational Approaches to Code Switching*. Word-level classification experiments were carried out using a simple dictionary-based method, linear kernel support vector machines (SVMs) with and without contextual clues, and a k-nearest neighbour approach. Based on these experiments, we select our SVM-based system with contextual clues as our final system and present results for the Nepali-English and Spanish-English datasets.

1 Introduction

This paper describes DCU-UVT's participation in the shared task *Language Identification in Code-Switched Data* (Solorio et al., 2014) at the *Workshop on Computational Approaches to Code Switching, EMNLP, 2014*. The task is to make word-level predictions (six labels: *lang1, lang2, ne, mixed, ambiguous* and *other*) for mixed-language user generated content. We submit predictions for *Nepali-English* and *Spanish-English* data and perform experiments using dictionaries, a k-nearest neighbour (k-NN) classifier and a linear-kernel SVM classifier.

In our dictionary-based approach, we investigate the use of different English dictionaries as well as the training data. In the k-NN based approach, we use string edit distance, character-n-gram overlap and context similarity to make predictions. For the SVM approach, we experiment with context-independent (word, character-n-grams, length of a word and capitalisation information) and context-sensitive (adding the previous and next word as bigrams) features in different combinations. We also experiment with adding features from the k-NN approach and another set of features from a neural network. Based on performance in cross-validation, we select the SVM classifier with basic features (word, character-n-grams, length of a word, capitalisation information and context) as our final system.

2 Background

While the problem of automatically identifying and analysing code-mixing has been identified over 30 years ago (Joshi, 1982), it has only recently drawn wider attention. Specific problems addressed include language identification in multilingual documents, identification of code-switching points and POS tagging (Solorio and Liu, 2008b) of code-mixing data. Approaches taken to the problem of identifying code-mixing include the use of dictionaries (Nguyen and Doğruöz, 2013; Barman et al., 2014; Elfardy et al., 2013; Solorio and Liu, 2008b), language models (Alex, 2008; Nguyen and Doğruöz, 2013; Elfardy et al., 2013), morphological and phonological analysis (Elfardy et al., 2013; Elfardy and Diab, 2012) and various machine learning algorithms such as sequence labelling with Hidden Markov Models (Farrugia, 2004; Rosner and Farrugia, 2007) and Conditional Random Fields (Nguyen and Doğruöz, 2013; King and Abney, 2013), as well as word-level classification using Naive Bayes (Solorio and Liu, 2008a), logistic regression (Nguyen and Doğruöz, 2013) and SVMs (Barman et al., 2014), using features such as word, POS, lemma and character-n-grams. Language pairs that have been explored include English-Maltese (Farrugia, 2004; Rosner and Farrugia, 2007), English-Spanish (Solorio and Liu, 2008b), Turkish-Dutch (Nguyen and Doğruöz,

Proceedings of The First Workshop on Computational Approaches to Code Switching, pages 127–132,
October 25, 2014, Doha, Qatar.

2013), modern standard Arabic-Egyptian dialect (Elfardy et al., 2013), Mandarin-English (Li et al., 2012; Lyu et al., 2010), and English-Hindi-Bengali (Barman et al., 2014).

3 Data Statistics

The training data provided for this task consists of tweets. Unfortunately, because of deleted tweets, the full training set could not be downloaded. Out of 9,993 Nepali-English training tweets, we were able to download 9,668 and out of 11,400 Spanish-English training tweets, we were able to download 11,353. Table 1 shows the token-level statistics of the two datasets.

Label	Nepali-English	Spanish-English
lang1 (en)	43,185	76,204
lang2 (ne/es)	59,579	32,477
ne	3,821	2,814
ambiguous	125	341
mixed	112	51
other	34,566	21,813

Table 1: Number of tokens in the Nepali-English and Spanish-English training data for each label

Nepali (*lang2*) is the dominant language in the Nepali-English training data but for Spanish-English, English (*lang1*) is dominant. The third largest group contains tokens with the label *other*. These are mentions (*@username*), punctuation symbols, emoticons, numbers (except numbers that represent words such as *2* for *to*), words in a language other than *lang1* and *lang2* and unintelligible words. Named entities (*ne*) are much less frequent and mixed language words (e.g. *ramriness*) and words for which there is not enough context to disambiguate them are rare. Hash tags are annotated as if the hash symbol was not there, e.g. *#truestory* is labelled *lang1*.

4 Experiments

All experiments are carried out for Nepali-English data. Later we apply the best approach to Spanish-English. We train our systems in a five-fold cross-validation and obtain best parameters based on average cross-validation results. Cross-validation splits are made based on users, i.e. we avoid the occurrence of a user's tweets both in training and test splits for each cross-validation run. We address the task with the following approaches:

1. a simple dictionary-based classifier,
2. classification using supervised machine learning with k-nearest neighbour, and
3. classification using supervised machine learning with SVMs.

Resource	Accuracy
BNC	43.61
LexNorm	54.60
TrainingData	89.53
TrainingData+BNC+LexNorm	90.71

Table 2: Average cross-validation accuracy of dictionary-based prediction for Nepali-English

4.1 Dictionary-Based Detection

We start with a simple dictionary-based approach using as dictionaries *(a)* the British National Corpus (BNC) (Aston and Burnard, 1998), *(b)* Han et al.'s lexical normalisation dictionary (LexNorm) (Han et al., 2012) and *(c)* the training data. The BNC and LexNorm dictionaries are built by recording all words occurring in the respective corpus or word list as English. For the BNC, we also collect word frequency information. For the training data, we obtain dictionaries for each of the six labels and each of the five cross-validation runs (using the relevant 4/5 of training data).

To make a prediction, we consult all dictionaries. If there are more than one candidate label, we choose the label for which the frequency for the query token is highest. To account for the fact that the BNC is much larger than the training data, we normalise all frequencies before comparison. LexNorm has no frequency information, hence it is added to our system as a simple word list (we consider the language of a word to be English if it appears in LexNorm). If a word appears in multiple dictionaries with the same frequency or if the word does not appear in any dictionary or list, the predicted language is chosen based on the dominant language(s)/label(s) of the corpus.

We experiment with the individual dictionaries and the combination of all three dictionaries, among which the combination achieves the highest cross-validation accuracy (90.71%). Table 2 shows the results of dictionary-based detection obtained in five-fold cross-validation.

4.2 Classification with k-NN

For Nepali-English, we also experiment with a simple k-nearest neighbour (k-NN) approach. For each test item, we select a subset of the training data using string edit distance and n-gram overlap and choose the majority label of the subset as our prediction. For efficiency, we first select k_1 items that share an n-gram with the token to be classified.[1] The set of k_1 items is then re-ranked according to string edit distance to the test item and the best k_2 matches are used to make a prediction.

Apart from varying k_1 and k_2, we experiment with *(a)* lowercasing strings, *(b)* including context by concatenating the previous, current and next token, and *(c)* weighting context by first calculating edit distances for the previous, current and next token separately and using a weighted average. The best configuration we found in cross-validation uses lowercasing with $k_1 = 800$ and $k_2 = 16$ but no context information. It achieves an accuracy of 94.97%.

4.3 SVM Classification

We experiment with linear kernel SVM classifiers using Liblinear (Fan et al., 2008). Parameter optimisation[2] is performed for each feature set combination to obtain best cross-validation accuracy.

4.3.1 Basic Features

Following Barman et al. (2014), our basic features are:

Char-N-Grams (G): We start with a character n-gram-based approach (Cavnar and Trenkle, 1994). Following King and Abney (2013), we select lowercased character n-grams (n=1 to 5) and the word as the features in our experiments.

Dictionary-Based Labels (D): We use presence in the dictionary of the 5,000 most frequent words in the BNC and presence in the LexNorm dictionary as binary features.[3]

Length of words (L): We create multiple features for token length using a decision tree (J48). We use length as the only feature to train a decision tree for each fold and use the nodes obtained from the tree to create boolean features (Rubino et al., 2013; Wagner et al., 2014).

Features	Accuracy	Features	Accuracy
G	96.02	GD	96.27
GL	96.11	GDL	96.32
GC	96.15	GDC	96.20
GLC	96.21	**GDLC**	**96.40**

Table 3: Average cross-validation accuracy of 6-way SVMs on the Nepali-English data set; G = char-n-gram, L = binary length features, D = dict.-based labels and C = capitalisation features

Context	Accuracy(%)
GDLC + P_1	96.41
GDLC + P_2	96.38
GDLC + N_1	96.41
GDLC + N_2	96.41
GDLC + P_1 + N_1	**96.42**
GDLC + P_2 + N_2	96.41

Table 4: Average cross-validation accuracy of 6-way SVMs using contextual features for Nepali-English

Capitalisation (C): We choose 3 boolean features to encode capitalisation information: whether any letter in the word is capitalised, whether all letters in the word are capitalised and whether the first letter is capitalised.

Context (P_i and N_j): We consider the previous i and next j token to be combined with the current token, forming an (i+1)-gram and a (j+1)-gram, which we add as features. Six settings are tested. Table 4 shows that using the bigrams formed with the previous and next word are the best combination for the task (among those tested).

Among the eight combinations of the first four feature sets that contain the first set (G), Table 3 shows that the 6-way SVM classifier[4]performs best with all features sets (GDLC), achieving 96.40% accuracy. Adding contextual information P_iN_j to GDLC, Table 4 shows best results for i=j=1, achieving 96.42% accuracy, only slightly ahead of the context-independent system.

4.3.2 Neural Network (Elman) and k-NN Features

We experiment with two additional features sets not covered by Barman et al. (2014):

Neural Network (Elman): We extract features from the hidden layer of a recurrent neural net-

[1] Starting with $n = 5$, we decrease n until there are at least k_1 items and then we randomly remove items added in the last augmentation step to arrive at exactly k_1 items. (For $n = 0$, we randomly sample from the full training data.)

[2] $C = 2^i$ with $i = -15, -14, ..., 10$

[3] We chose these parameters based on experiments with each dictionary, combinations of dictionaries and various frequency thresholds. We apply a frequency threshold to the BNC to increase precision. We rank the words according to frequency and used the rank as a threshold (e.g. top-5K, top-10K etc.). With the top 5,000 ranked words and $C = 0.25$, we obtained best accuracy (96.40%).

[4] We also test 3-way SVM classification (*lang1*, *lang2* and *other*) and heuristic post-processing, but it does not outperform our 6-way classification runs.

Systems	Accuracy
GDLC	96.40
k-NN	95.10
Elman	89.96
GDLC+k-NN	96.31
GDLC+Elman	96.46
GDLC+k-NN+Elman	96.40
GDLC+P_1N_1	96.42
k-NN+P_1N_1	95.11
Elman+P_1N_1	91.53
GDLC+P_1N_1+k-NN	96.33
GDLC+P_1N_1+Elman	96.45
GDLC+P_1N_1+k-NN+Elman	96.40

Table 5: Average cross-validation accuracy of 6-way SVMs of combinations of GDLC, k-NN, Elman and P_1N_1 features for Nepali-English

work that has been trained to predict the next character in a string (Chrupała, 2014). The 10 most active units of the hidden layer for each of the initial 4 bytes and final 4 bytes of each token are binarised by using a threshold of 0.5.

k-Nearest Neighbour (kNN): We obtain features from our basic k-NN approach (Section 4.2), encoding the prediction of the k-NN model with six binary features (one for each label) and a numeric feature for each label stating the relative number of votes for the label, e.g. if $k_2 = 16$ and 12 votes are for *lang1* the value of the feature *votes4lang1* will be 0.75. Furthermore, we add two features stating the minimum and maximum edit distance between the test token and the k_2 selected training tokens.

Table 5 shows cross-validation results for these new feature sets with and without the P_1N_1 context features. Excluding the GDLC features, we can see that best accuracy is with k-NN and P_1N_1 features (95.11%). For Elman features, the accuracy is lower (91.53% with context). In combination with the GDLC features, however, the Elman features can achieve a small improvement over the GDLC+P_1N_1 combination (+0.04 percentage points): 96.46% accuracy for the GDLC+Elman setting (without P_1N_1 features). Furthermore, the k-NN features do not combine well.[5]

4.3.3 Final System and Test Results

At the time of submission of predictions, we had an error in our GDLC+Elman feature combiner resulting in slightly lower performance. Therefore, we selected SVM-GDLC-P_1N_1 as our final approach and trained the final two systems using the full training data for Nepali-English and Spanish-English respectively. While we knew that $C = 0.125$ is best for Nepali-English from our experiments, we had to re-tune parameter C for Spanish-English using cross-validation on the training data. We found best accuracy of 94.16% for Spanish-English with $C = 128$. Final predictions for the test sets are made using these systems.

	Tweets	
	Token-Level	*Tweet-Level*
Nepali-English	96.3	95.8
Spanish-English	84.4	80.4
	Surprise Genre	
	Token-Level	*Post-Level*
Nepali-English	85.6	77.5
Spanish-English	94.4	80.0

Table 6: Test set results (overall accuracy) for Nepali-English and Spanish-English tweet data and surprise genre

Table 6 shows the test set results. The test set for this task is divided into tweets and a surprise genre. For the tweets, we achieve 96.3% and 84.4% accuracy (overall token-level accuracy) in Nepali-English and in Spanish-English respectively. For this surprise genre (a collection of posts from Facebook and blogs), we achieve 85.6% for Nepali-English and 94.4% for Spanish-English.

5 Conclusion

To summarise, we achieved reasonable accuracy with a 6-way SVM classifier by employing basic features only. We found that using dictionaries is helpful, as are contextual features. The performance of the k-NN classifier is also notable: it is only 1.45 percentage points behind the final SVM-based system (in terms of cross-validation accuracy). Adding neural network features can further increase the accuracy of systems.

Briefly opening the test files to check for formatting issues, we notice that the surprise genre data contains language-specific scripts that could easily be addressed in an English vs. non-English scenario.

Acknowledgments

This research is supported by the Science Foundation Ireland (Grant 12/CE/I2267) as part of CNGL (www.cngl.ie) at Dublin City University.

[5] A possible explanation may be that the k-NN features are based on only 3 of 5 folds for the training data (3 folds are used to make predictions for the 4th set) but 4 of 5 folds are used for test data predictions in each cross-validation run.

References

Beatrice Alex. 2008. *Automatic detection of English inclusions in mixed-lingual data with an application to parsing*. Ph.D. thesis, School of Informatics, The University of Edinburgh, Edinburgh, UK.

Guy Aston and Lou Burnard. 1998. *The BNC handbook: exploring the British National Corpus with SARA*. Capstone.

Utsab Barman, Amitava Das, Joachim Wagner, and Jennifer Foster. 2014. Code-mixing: A challenge for language identification in the language of social media. In *Proceedings of the First Workshop on Computational Approaches to Code-Switching. EMNLP 2014, Conference on Empirical Methods in Natural Language Processing*, Doha, Qatar, October. Association for Computational Linguistics.

William B. Cavnar and John M. Trenkle. 1994. N-gram-based text categorization. In Theo Pavlidis, editor, *Proceedings of SDAIR-94, Third Annual Symposium on Document Analysis and Information Retrieval*, pages 161–175.

Grzegorz Chrupała. 2014. Normalizing tweets with edit scripts and recurrent neural embeddings. In *Proceedings of the 52nd Annual Meeting of the Association for Computational Linguistics (Volume 2: Short Papers)*, pages 680–686, Baltimore, Maryland, June. Association for Computational Linguistics.

Heba Elfardy and Mona Diab. 2012. Token level identification of linguistic code switching. In *Proceedings of Proceedings of COLING 2012: Posters (the 24th International Conference on Computational Linguistics)*, pages 287–296, Mumbai, India.

Heba Elfardy, Mohamed Al-Badrashiny, and Mona Diab. 2013. Code switch point detection in Arabic. In *Natural Language Processing and Information Systems*, pages 412–416. Springer.

Rong-En Fan, Kai-Wei Chang, Cho-Jui Hsieh, Xiang-Rui Wang, and Chih-Jen Lin. 2008. LIBLINEAR: A library for large linear classification. *Journal of Machine Learning Research*, 9:1871–1874.

Paulseph-John Farrugia. 2004. TTS pre-processing issues for mixed language support. In *Proceedings of CSAW'04, the second Computer Science Annual Workshop*, pages 36–41. Department of Computer Science & A.I., University of Malta.

Bo Han, Paul Cook, and Timothy Baldwin. 2012. Automatically constructing a normalisation dictionary for microblogs. In *Proceedings of the 2012 Joint Conference on Empirical Methods in Natural Language Processing and Computational Natural Language Learning*, pages 421–432. Association for Computational Linguistics.

Aravind K. Joshi. 1982. Processing of sentences with intra-sentential code-switching. In J. Horecký, editor, *Proceedings of the 9th conference on Computational linguistics - Volume 1 (COLING'82)*, pages 145–150. Academia Praha, North-Holland Publishing Company.

Ben King and Steven Abney. 2013. Labeling the languages of words in mixed-language documents using weakly supervised methods. In *Proceedings of the 2013 Conference of the North American Chapter of the Association for Computational Linguistics: Human Language Technologies*, pages 1110–1119, Atlanta, Georgia, June. Association for Computational Linguistics.

Ying Li, Yue Yu, and Pascale Fung. 2012. A mandarin-english code-switching corpus. In Nicoletta Calzolari (Conference Chair), Khalid Choukri, Thierry Declerck, Mehmet Uur Doan, Bente Maegaard, Joseph Mariani, Asuncion Moreno, Jan Odijk, and Stelios Piperidis, editors, *Proceedings of the Eight International Conference on Language Resources and Evaluation (LREC'12)*, Istanbul, Turkey, may. European Language Resources Association (ELRA).

Dau-Cheng Lyu, Tien Ping Tan, Engsiong Chng, and Haizhou Li. 2010. SEAME: A Mandarin-English code-switching speech corpus in South-East Asia. In *INTERSPEECH 2010, 11th Annual Conference of the International Speech Communication Association*, volume 10, pages 1986–1989, Makuhari, Chiba, Japan. ISCA Archive.

Dong Nguyen and A. Seza Doğruöz. 2013. Word level language identification in online multilingual communication. In *Proceedings of the 2013 Conference on Empirical Methods in Natural Language Processing (EMNLP 2013)*, pages 857–862, Seattle, Washington, USA, October. Association for Computational Linguistics.

Mike Rosner and Paulseph-John Farrugia. 2007. A tagging algorithm for mixed language identification in a noisy domain. In *INTERSPEECH-2007, 8th Annual Conference of the International Speech Communication Association*, pages 190–193. ISCA Archive.

Raphael Rubino, Joachim Wagner, Jennifer Foster, Johann Roturier, Rasoul Samad Zadeh Kaljahi, and Fred Hollowood. 2013. DCU-Symantec at the WMT 2013 quality estimation shared task. In *Proceedings of the Eighth Workshop on Statistical Machine Translation*, pages 392–397, Sofia, Bulgaria. Association for Computational Linguistics.

Thamar Solorio and Yang Liu. 2008a. Learning to predict code-switching points. In *Proceedings of the Conference on Empirical Methods in Natural Language Processing*, pages 973–981. Association for Computational Linguistics.

Thamar Solorio and Yang Liu. 2008b. Part-of-speech tagging for English-Spanish code-switched text. In

Proceedings of the Conference on Empirical Methods in Natural Language Processing, pages 1051–1060. Association for Computational Linguistics.

Thamar Solorio, Elizabeth Blair, Suraj Maharjan, Steve Bethard, Mona Diab, Mahmoud Gonheim, Abdelati Hawwari, Fahad AlGhamdi, Julia Hirshberg, Alison Chang, and Pascale Fung. 2014. Overview for the first shared task on language identification in code-switched data. In *Proceedings of the First Workshop on Computational Approaches to Code-Switching. EMNLP 2014, Conference on Empirical Methods in Natural Language Processing*, Doha, Qatar, October. Association for Computational Linguistics.

Joachim Wagner, Piyush Arora, Santiago Cortes, Utsab Barman, Dasha Bogdanova, Jennifer Foster, and Lamia Tounsi. 2014. DCU: Aspect-based polarity classification for SemEval task 4. In *Proceedings of the International Workshop on Semantic Evaluation (SemEval-2014)*, pages 392–397, Dublin, Ireland, August. Association for Computational Linguistics.

Incremental N-gram Approach for Language Identification in Code-Switched Text

Prajwol Shrestha
Kathmandu University
Department of Computer Science and Engineering
Dhulikhel, Nepal
prajwol.shrestha18@gmail.com

Abstract

A multilingual person writing a sentence or a piece of text tends to switch between languages s/he is proficient in. This alteration between languages, commonly known as code-switching, presents us with the problem of determining the correct language of each word in the text. My method uses a variety of techniques based upon the observed differences in the formation of words in these languages. My system was able to obtain third position in both tweet and token level for the main test dataset as well as first position in the token level evaluation for the surprise dataset both consisting of Nepali-English code-switched texts.

1 Introduction

Nowadays, it is common for people to be able to speak in two or more languages. So, the propensity to use code-switching in spoken as well as in written text has increased. Code-switching occurs when a person uses two or more than two languages in a single piece of text. According to Elfardy and Diab (2012), the phenomenon where speakers switch between multiple languages between the same utterance or across utterances within the same conversation is referred to as Linguistic Code Switching. English, being an universal language is highly likely to be code-switched with some other language. This is specially true when English is studied or spoken in the community as the second language by a person. In a such case, the person is likely to use English words with his/her native language to form code-switched, yet, syntactically correct and meaningful sentences.

This paper deals with the code-switching that occurs when English is used with Spanish or Nepali. The problem of identifying code-switching is closely tied with figuring out how a language is acquired or learned. Auer (1988) identified the phenomenon of how Italians, who were raised in Germany developed fluctuation and variation in their native language as well as in German. They were also noticed to have a strong tendency to have a conversation dominated by the German words. This phenomenon was also observed by Dey and Fung (2014). The strong influence of Bollywood in the Indian culture and the high amount of code-switching with English in movie dialogues and song lyrics, led to Hindi-English code-switching, being common for the average Indian. Finding out the points in the text where people are most likely to code-switch, what word of a certain language is more likely to be used than a word with the same meaning of another language and which languages are more likely to be used in code-switching than others are all important research questions. Although my paper deals only with finding out the language a certain token in a code-switched text belongs to, this is a first step towards answering those other questions.

The main aim of this paper is to describe my system submission to the Computational Approaches to Code Switching task (Solorio et al., 2014). The training dataset provided for the classification task were tweets composed of Spanish and English words or Nepali and English words. The test dataset also consisted of similar tweets. In addition to this, there was also a surprise dataset consisting of Facebook posts and comments in the place of tweets. My system for this task performs language identification by using a number of techniques. The first one is based upon an assumption that words of different languages have varying sets of n-gram prefixes that occur predominantly throughout the language. There has been prior research on language identification through the use of n-grams. Cavnar et al. (1994) have ap-

Proceedings of The First Workshop on Computational Approaches to Code Switching, pages 133–138,
October 25, 2014, Doha, Qatar.

proached the task of identifying the language of an electronic mail taken from Usenet newsgroups with the use of n-grams. They obtained training sets for each language to be classified, which acted as language category samples. They computed n-gram frequency profiles on these training sets. They found that the top 300 n-grams of each language are used most frequently to form the words of the language. Nguyen and Dogruoz (2014) have used dictionary search and a n-gram based language model to identify the language on word-level of forum posts with Dutch and Turkish code-switching.

Lignos and Marcus (2013) found that data collected from social media to detect code-switching contained a lot of non-standard spellings of words and unnecessary capitalization. It was also true for this dataset. So, I made use of a lightweight spell checker in the event that the word was not spelled correctly and hence not categorised into any language. I have also used a rule based classification system that can also be used for named entities and non-alphanumeric language classes. With the system that I built based on these ideas, I achieved an accuracy of above 94% for English-Nepali and above 80% for English-Spanish in the token level evaluation. As the system works as a pipeline of smaller systems, it was time consuming. So, in order to improve speed, it is built to run on a multithreaded environment.

Language identification by using these techniques overcomes the drawback of other simpler methods like extracting a token's characters and then using its Unicode value to determine its language. But most of the time the words are not written in its own script by using Unicode, but rather, its Romanized form is used. Some languages like Spanish are almost fully written in roman letters, with exception being only a small subset of accented characters. Precisely these kinds of words require more robust classification techniques. Another alternative is manual classification but it has the downside of being time consuming and an uneconomical alternative. There is a need of an application that can overcome these drawbacks and create a system that can be used for similar sets of data.

2 Methodology

The classification of a token of a code-switched text into one of the six classes: lang1, lang2, ambiguous, named entity, mixed and other is performed by using four techniques described shortly. But before applying any of these techniques, the first step was the creation of a dictionary for each class by using the tokens from the training set. As a preprocessing step, for any token that starts with #, the # is removed. Also, any token that starts with @ is given the 'other' class label. The techniques used in my system are detailed below. They are applied in a pipeline, in the same order as they are mentioned.

2.1 Incremental N-Gram Occurrence Model with Dictionary Search

This model is used for test tokens whose length (L) is greater than three in the case of Nepali-English code-switching task and is greater than two in the case of Spanish-English code-switching task. Tokens that are shorter are classified by using a simple dictionary lookup. If the occurrence count of the token in the dictionary of class C is the highest, then the token is classified as belonging to class C.

In order to assign a class label to a particular token, this model uses only the first ngram of each size n ranging from 3 (for Spanish-English) or 4 (for Nepali-English) to L-1. The count of occurrence of this ngram in each class dictionary is taken as the score. The size n is increased iteratively and the score from each iteration is added at the end to obtain the final score. For named entity (NE) and ambiguous dictionary search, the whole token is used instead of just the ngram since the size of these dictionaries is small. Since a whole token lookup was performed, the occurrence count scores from these dictionaries are rated to be three times higher. After obtaining the final scores for each class, the one with the highest score gets assigned as the class label of the token.

This method is based on the hypothesis that tokens belonging to the same language will have more overlap of the preceding characters. If two tokens are from different languages, they might start the same way but will start deviating in the use of characters faster than two tokens of the same language. The Incremental N-Gram Model for Nepali-English Classification is shown in Algorithm 1.

Consider that we have to find the language of the Test token Parsin. The following assumptions are made:

Algorithm 1 Incremental N-gram Classification

```
if len(token) > 3 then
    n = 4
    while n < len(token) − 1 do
        if token ∈ dict[ambiguous, ne] then
            Increment Respective Language
            Occurrence Count by 3
        end if
        if FirstN-Gram ∈ Remaining Classes then
            Find the number of words in
            each class dictionary that starts
            with the First N-Gram.
            Add this number with the previous
            occurrence count for the
            particular class
        end if
    end while
end if
```

N-gram Size	First N-gram	English	Nepali	Ambiguous
4	PARS	2	6	3
5	PARSI	2	6	3
6	PARSIN	1	0	3
Total		7	12	9

Table 1: Incremental N-gram Classification Example

- The Word Parsing occurs twice and Parsimony once in the English Language Dictionary.
- Word Parsi occurs 6 times in the Nepalese Language Dictionary (Parsi means the day after Tomorrow).
- Test token Parsin occurs 0 times in Other Language and Named Entity Dictionary
- Test token Parsin occurs once each in Ambiguous words Dictionary

The algorithm works as shown in Table 1.

2.2 Rule Based Classification

A small fraction of test tokens are left unclassified by the above method. These tokens are further processed by using a rule based classification system. It consists of the following handwritten rules:

- Check if the token is an emoticon against an emoticon list. If the token is found in the list, it is of the class, 'other'.
- It was hard to find an off-the-shelf named entity recognizer for code-switched text. So, a simple named entity recognition rule was used. For a token consisting of only alphabetic characters, if there are more than one uppercase letters in the token or if the token starts with an uppercase letter, it is an NE.
- If the difference in the occurrence score of a token in lang1 dictionary vs lang2 dictionary is higher than three, the token is classified as belonging to the language with the higher score.
- If the token occurs in lang1 and lang2 dictionaries equally, the token is 'ambiguous'.

2.3 Lightweight Spell Checker

The test tokens that are still not classified are checked for spelling errors using a simple spelling checker, complementary to the idea of edit distance. If the above two classifiers were unable to classify a token, it might be because these tokens were misspelled. This method is based upon the idea that misspelled tokens are still similar to the language that they belong to. The spell checker checks the test token against every token in the dictionaries for similarity (defined below).

'Similarity' is defined as follows: First, a 'similar count' score (SC) is calculated as the number of characters that match between two tokens in order. A test token of length $L1$ is said to be similar to a dictionary token of length $L2$ if: SC>max($L1$,$L2$)-1 when $L1$<7 or SC>max($L1$,$L2$)-2 when $L1 \geq 7$

Here, when the test token is checked against a token in the Nepali dictionary, the characters 'x' and '6' in both tokens are replaced with the character sequence 'ch'. This normalization is performed because it is very common for the latter character sequence to be replaced by either of the former two characters, in the Nepali language. If a test token is found to be similar to a token in a dictionary of a certain class, the similarity score to the class is incremented. The class with the maximum similarity score is considered to be the class of the test token.

2.4 Special Characters Check

At this stage, only a minimal number of tokens are left to be labeled. These tokens are checked to see if they contain characters not belonging to English Unicode or modifiers. If one such character is found, the token is said to be from lang2, either Spanish or Nepalese. All the remaining tokens are categorized as 'other'.

3 Experimental Settings

For all my experiments, I divided the training data into a ratio of 70:30 for training and cross-validation. In order to tune the different parameters, I had to repeat the experiments multiple times. So, in order to improve the runtime performance, I made use of multithreading.

I tested the application by setting the first n-gram length in the Incremental N-Gram Model to 3 and 4. I varied the criteria of the least number of characters that should match between two tokens, in order for the two tokens to be similar. I observed the highest accuracy of above 94% in Nepali- English classification when the First n-gram length was 4. In the case of Spanish-English token classification, I observed the highest accuracy of 88% when the n-gram length was 3. The spellchecker gave the best results when it had the above mentioned similarity criteria.

The whole classifying task was sure to take a long time so I built it to scale with the increasing number of CPUs. I performed the experiments on a 1st Generation Core i7 (Eight Logical Cores) CPU and a Core 2 Duo CPU (2 logical Cores).

I observed the best performance when the application created the number of threads equal to the number of available CPU cores. The classification task completed in the i7 CPU with 8 active threads in 13 minutes compared to almost 35 minutes with 2 active threads on the Core 2 Duo CPU. The task completed in around 38 minutes in the i7 CPU with 2 active threads.

4 Results and Analysis

Language Pair	Recall	Precision	F1-Score	Accuracy
NE-EN	0.980	0.968	0.974	0.951
ES-EN	0.883	0.489	0.630	0.699

Table 2: Tweet level results on the test data.

My system obtained an accuracy of 95.1% in the tweet-level evaluation and 79.4% accuracy in the Facebook post-level evaluation of English-Nepali test tweets. Although, it was third in tweet-level evaluation, it was only 0.7% behind the best tweet-level system in terms of accuracy. My system was second in Facebook post-level evaluation by 6.9%. It had an accuracy of 94.6% and 86.5% in the token level evaluation of English-Nepali test tweets and Facebook posts respectively. The model was third in the tweet-token evaluation but stood first in the Facebook-post token evaluation. These results align with the hypothesis of the Incremental N-Gram Occurrence Model that token belonging to the same language will have more overlap of the preceding characters.

Category	Recall	Precision	F1-Score
lang1	0.944	0.949	0.947
lang2	0.965	0.964	0.965
mixed	0.000	1.000	0.000
ne	0.510	0.657	0.574
other	0.968	0.935	0.951

Table 3: Token level results on the test data for Nepali-English.

Category	Recall	Precision	F1-Score
lang1	0.866	0.761	0.810
lang2	0.750	0.861	0.802
mixed	0.000	1.000	0.000
ambiguous	0.000	0.000	0.000
ne	0.155	0.554	0.242
other	0.847	0.823	0.835

Table 4: Token level results on the test data for Spanish-English.

My system obtained an accuracy of 69.9% in the tweet-level evaluation and 70.0% accuracy in the Facebook post-level evaluation of the English-Spanish test data. It was the least effective in both the evaluation tasks. My system had an accuracy of 80.3% and 87.6% in the token level evaluation of English-Spanish test tweets and Facebook posts respectively. The model was again the least effective in both the token level evaluation task but by a smaller margin. The results do not exactly follow the hypothesis, but we can say it supports it because English and Spanish languages share a lot of common word prefixes. Hence my method is more likely to incorrectly predict some Spanish words as English and vice-versa.

It is evident from the results that this model is suitable when the languages being classified are

Language Pair	Recall	Precision	F1-Score	Accuracy
NE-EN	0.900	0.486	0.632	0.794
ES-EN	0.882	0.493	0.633	0.700

Table 5: Tweet level results on the surprise data.

Category	Recall	Precision	F1-Score
lang1	0.913	0.802	0.854
lang2	0.936	0.911	0.923
ne	0.394	0.833	0.535
other	0.886	0.696	0.780

Table 6: Token level results on the surprise data for Nepali-English.

Category	Recall	Precision	F1-Score
lang1	0.853	0.756	0.801
lang2	0.746	0.839	0.789
mixed	0.000	1.000	0.000
ambiguous	0.000	0.000	0.000
ne	0.145	0.550	0.230
other	0.826	0.808	0.817

Table 7: Token level results on the surprise data for Spanish-English.

highly dissimilar in syntax and structure. As English and Nepali language do not have the same ancestry they have very different syntax and structure. The word prefixes used frequently to form Nepali words and the syntax of forming various parts of speech in Nepali language is quite different than in the English language.

In both the training and test datasets, the ratio of code-switched to monolingual tweets is higher in Nepali than in Spanish, which probably led to my system performing worse on tweet level for Spanish. Although, this distribution can be anticipated because English is taught from primary schooling levels in Nepal. Almost all the literate population can communicate pretty well in English. Nepal is a country that relies heavily in the tourism industry, and English being a universal language is a second language in major cities and travel destinations of the country. All these factors have led to a lot of code switching in tweets Nepali tweets. On the other hand, Spanish is a widely spoken language itself. The people who know Spanish rarely need to learn a second language. This might be the reason that there are less code-switched tweets for Spanish.

My model also has a drawback, which is also demonstrated by my evaluation results. Spanish and English languages do share a lot of common prefixes. This maybe due to their shared Indo-European ancestry and the fact that English language has borrowed a significant number of words from the French language, which is very similar to the Spanish language. The word "precious" and "bilingual" in English is spelled "precioso" and "bilingue" in Spanish. This similarity of prefixes leads the Incremental N-gram model to classify tokens wrongly based upon the recurrence of the same prefixed words documented more frequently in one language than the other. It further results in a large number of English-Spanish tweets and Facebook posts to be verified as code switched because, just one token in a tweet that is wrongly classified as belonging to another language class, will validate the tweet as code-switched. To counter this drawback, when classifying words of the language that have the same ancestry and similar structure and syntax, only the prefixes should not be considered.

Another important thing to note is that the task of evaluation is very taxing on the CPU and takes a lot of time. Various evaluation techniques are applied to a token before its correct class is determined. This time consuming process can be accelerated significantly by designing a system that follows the data and task parallelism principles i.e. multithreading. The redesign of the system to support multithreading made the training process almost 3 times faster.

5 Conclusion and Future Work

The method described in this paper is useful in language identification of code-switched text. It works especially well when the two languages in question have different word formation syntax and structure. For the languages that are similar in ancestry and when one language contains many words derived from the other language, like Spanish and English, this method is not very reliable. For these types of languages, considering that they have similar syntax and structure, the use of all the possible n-grams of the tokens in the training set and their frequencies might be useful. Also considering the suffixes of the word rather than just the prefixes might provide greater accuracy for prediction of these types of languages. These tasks are left as future improvements.

Acknowledgment

I would like to thank the organizers of the Computational Approaches to Code Switching Workshop at EMNLP'14 who gave me an opportunity to participate in this task.

References

Peter Auer. 1988. A conversation analytic approach to code-switching and transfer. *Codeswitching: Anthropological and sociolinguistic perspectives*, 48:187–213.

William B Cavnar, John M Trenkle, et al. 1994. N-gram-based text categorization. *Ann Arbor MI*, 48113(2):161–175.

Anik Dey and Pascale Fung. 2014. A hindi-english code-switching corpus. In *The 9th International Conference on Language Resources and Evaluation (LREC)*, Reykjavik.

Heba Elfardy and Mona T Diab. 2012. Token level identification of linguistic code switching. In *COLING (Posters)*, pages 287–296, Mumbai, India.

Constantine Lignos and Mitch Marcus. 2013. Toward web-scale analysis of codeswitching. In *Annual Meeting of the Linguistic Society of America*.

Dong Nguyen and A Seza Dogruoz. 2014. Word level language identification in online multilingual communication. In *Proceedings of the 2013 Conference on Empirical Methods in Natural Language Processing*.

Thamar Solorio, Elizabeth Blair, Suraj Maharjan, Steve Bethard, Mona Diab, Mahmoud Gonheim, Abdelati Hawwari, Fahad AlGhamdi, Julia Hirshberg, Alison Chang, and Pascale Fung. 2014. Overview for the first shared task on language identification in code-switched data. In *Proceedings of the First Workshop on Computational Approaches to Code-Switching. EMNLP 2014, Conference on Empirical Methods in Natural Language Processing*, Doha, Qatar.

The Tel Aviv University System for the Code-Switching Workshop Shared Task

Kfir Bar
School of Computer Science
Tel Aviv University
Ramat Aviv, Israel
kfirbar@post.tau.ac.i

Nachum Dershowitz
School of Computer Science
Tel Aviv University
Ramat Aviv, Israel
nachumd@tau.ac.il

Abstract

We describe our entry in the EMNLP 2014 code-switching shared task. Our system is based on a sequential classifier, trained on the shared training set using various character- and word-level features, some calculated using a large monolingual corpora. We participated in the Twitter-genre Spanish-English track, obtaining an accuracy of 0.868 when measured on the tweet level and 0.858 on the word level.

1 Introduction

Code switching is the act of changing language while speaking or writing, as often done by bilinguals (Winford, 2003). Identifying the transition points is a necessary first step before applying other linguistic algorithms, which usually target a single language. A switching point may occur between sentences, phrases, words, or even between certain morphological components. Code switching happens frequently in informal ways of communication, such as verbal conversations, blogs and microblogs; however, there are many examples in which languages are switched in formal settings. For example, alternating between Colloquial Egyptian Arabic and Modern Standard Arabic in modern Egyptian prose is prevalent (Rosenbaum, 2000).

This shared task (Solorio et al., 2014),[1] the first of its kind, challenges participants with identifying those switching points in blogs as well as in microblog posts. Given posts with a mix of a specific pair of languages, each participating system is required to identify the language of every word. Four language-pair tracks were offered by the task organizers: Spanish-English, Nepali-English, Modern Standard Arabic and Colloquial Arabic, and Mandarin-English. For each language pair, a training set of Twitter[2] statuses was provided, which was manually annotated with a label for every word, indicating its language. In addition to the two language labels, a few additional labels were used. Altogether there were six labels: (1) lang1—the first language; (2) lang2—the second language; (3) ne—named entity; (4) ambiguous—for ambiguous words belonging to both languages; (5) mixed—for words composed of morphemes in each language; and (6) other—for cases where it is impossible to determine the language. For most of the language pairs, the organizers supplied three different evaluation sets. The first set was composed of a set of unseen Twitter statuses, provided with no manual annotation. The other two sets contained data from a "surprise genre", mainly composed of blog posts.

We took part only in the Spanish-English track. Both English and Spanish are written in Latin script. The Spanish alphabet contains some additional letters, such as those indicating stress (vowels with acute accents: á, é, í, ó, ú), a u adorned with a diaeresis (ü), the additional letter ñ (*eñe*), and inverted question and exclamation punctuation marks ¿ and ¡ (used at the beginning of questions and exclamatory phrases, respectively). Although social-media users are not generally consistent in their use of accents, their appearance in a word may disclose its language. By and large, algorithms for code switching have used the character-based k-mer feature, introduced by (Cavnar and Trenkle, 1994).[3]

Our system is an implementation of a multi-class classifier that works on the word level, considering features that we calculate using large Spanish as well as English monolingual corpora. Working with a sequential classifier, the predicted

[1] http://emnlp2014.org/workshops/CodeSwitch/call.html

[2] http://www.twitter.com

[3] We propose the term "k-mer" for character k-grams, in contradistinction to word n-grams.

Proceedings of The First Workshop on Computational Approaches to Code Switching, pages 139–143,
October 25, 2014, Doha, Qatar.

labels of the previous words are used as features in predicting the current word.

In Section 2, we describe our system and the features we use for classification. Section 3 contains the evaluation results, as published by the organizers of this shared task. We conclude with a brief discussion.

2 System Description

We use a supervised framework to train a classifier that predicts the label of every word in the order written. The words were originally tokenized by the organizers, preserving punctuation, emoticons, user mentions (e.g., @emnlp2014), and hashtags (e.g., #emnlp2014) as individual tokens. The informal language, as used in social media, introduces an additional challenge in predicting the language of every word. Spelling mistakes as well as grammatical errors are very common. Hence, we believe that predicting the language of a given word merely using dictionaries for the two languages is likely to be insufficient.

Our classifier is trained on a learning set, as provided by the organizers, enriched with some additional features. Every word in the order written is treated as a single instance for the classifier, each including features from a limited window of preceding and successive words, enriched with the predicted label of some of the preceding words. We ran a few experiments with different window sizes, based on 10-fold cross validation, and found that the best token-level accuracy is obtained using a window of size 2 for all features, that is, two words before the focus word and two words after.

The features that we use may be grouped in three main categories, as described next.

2.1 Features

We use three main groups of features:

Word level: The specific word in focus, as well as the two previous words and the two following ones are considered as features. To reduce the sparsity, we convert words into lowercase. In addition, we use a monolingual lexicon for English words that are typically used in Twitter. For this purpose, we employ a sample of the Twitter General English lexicon, released by Illocution, Inc.,[4] containing the top 10K words and bigrams from a relatively large corpus of public English tweets they collected over a period of time, along with frequency information. We bin the frequency rates into 5 integer values (with an additional value for words that do not exist in the lexicon), which are used as the feature value for every word in focus, and for the other four words in its window. This feature seems to be quite noisy, as some common Spanish words appear in the lexicon (e.g., *de*, *no*, *a*, *me*); on the other hand, it may capture typical English misspellings and acronyms (e.g., *oomf*, *noww*, *lmao*). We could not find a similar resource for Spanish, unfortunately.

To help identify named entities, we created a list of English as well Spanish names of various entity types (e.g., locations, family and given names) and used it to generate an additional boolean feature, indicating whether the word in focus is an entity name. The list was compiled out of all words beginning with a capital letter in relatively large monolingual corpora, one for English and another for Spanish. To avoid words that were capitalized because they occur at the beginning of a sentence, regardless of whether they are proper names, we first processed the text with a true-casing tool, provided as part of Moses (Koehn et al., 2007)—the open source implementation for phrase-based statistical machine translation. Our list contains about 146K entries.

Intra-word level: Spanish, as opposed to English, is a morphologically rich language, demonstrating a complicated suffix-based derivational morphology. Therefore, in order to capture repeating suffixes and prefixes that may characterize the languages, we consider as features substrings of 1–3 prefix and suffix characters of the word in focus and the other four words in its window. Although it is presumed that capitalization is not used consistently in social media, we consider a boolean feature indicating whether the first letter of each word in the window was capitalized in the original text or not. At this level, we use two additional features that capture the level of uncertainty of seeing the sequence of characters that form the specific word in each language. This is done by employing a 3-mer character-based language model, trained over a large corpus in each language. Then, the two language models, one for each language, are applied on the word in focus to calculate two log-probability values. These are binned into ten discrete values that are used as the features' values. We add a boolean feature, indi-

[4] `http://www.illocutioninc.com`

cating which of the two models returned a lower log probability.

Inter-word level: We capture the level of uncertainty of seeing specific sequences of words in each language. We used 3-gram word-level language models, trained over large corpora in each of the languages. We apply the models to the focus word, considering it to be the last in a sequence of three words (with the two previous words) and calculate log probabilities. Like before, we bin the values into ten discrete values, which are then used as the features' values. An additional boolean feature is used, indicating which of the two models returned a lower log probability.

2.2 Supervised Framework

We designed a sequential classifier running on top of the Weka platform (Frank et al., 2010) that is capable of processing instances sequentially, similar to YamCha (Kudo and Matsumoto, 2003). We use LibSVM (Chang and Lin, 2011), an implementation of Support Vector Machines (SVM) (Cortes and Vapnik, 1995), as the underlying technology, with a degree 2 polynomial kernel. Since we work on a multi-class classification problem, we take the one-versus-one approach. As mentioned above, we use features from a window of ± 2 words before and after the word of interest. In addition, for every word, we consider as features the predicted labels of the two prior words.

3 Evaluation Results

We report on the results obtained on the unseen task evaluation sets, which were provided by the workshop organizers.[5] There are three evaluation sets. The first is composed of a set of unseen Twitter statuses and the other two contain data from a "surprise genre". The results are available online at the time of writing only for the first and second sets. The results of the third set will be published during the upcoming workshop meeting.

The training set contains 11,400 statuses, comprising 140,706 words. Table 1 shows the distribution of labels.

The first evaluation set contains 3,060 tweets. However, we were asked to download the statuses directly from Twitter, and some of the statuses were missing. Therefore, we ended up with only 1,661 available statuses, corresponding to 17,723 words. According to the organizers, the evaluation was performed only on the 1,626 tweets that were available for all the participating groups. Out of the 1,626, there are 1,155 monolingual tweets and 471 code-switched tweets. Table 2 shows the evaluation results for the Tel Aviv University (TAU) system on the first set, reported on the tweet level.

In addition, the organizers provide evaluation results, calculated on the word level. Table 3 shows the label distribution among the words in the first evaluation set, and Table 4 shows the actual results. The overall accuracy on the word level is 0.858.

The second evaluation set contains 1,103 words of a "surprise" (unseen) genre, mainly blog posts. Out of the 49 posts, 27 are monolingual and 22 are code-switched posts. Table 5 shows the results for the surprise set, calculated on the post level.

As for the first set, Table 6 shows the distribution of the labels among the words in the surprise set, and in Table 7 we present the results as measured on the word level. The overall accuracy on the surprise set is 0.941.

Label	Number
lang1	77,101
lang2	33,099
ne	2,918
ambiguous	344
mixed	51
other	27,194

Table 1: Label distribution in the training set.

Accuracy	0.868
Recall	0.720
Precision	0.803
F1-Score	0.759

Table 2: Results for the first evaluation set, measured on tweet level.

4 Discussion

We believe that we have demonstrated the potential of using sequential classification for code-switching, enriched with three types of features, some calculated using large monolingual corpora. Compared to the other participating systems as published by the workshop organizers, our system obtained encouraging results. In particular, we observe relatively good results in relating words to

[5] http://emnlp2014.org/workshops/CodeSwitch/results.php

Label	Count
lang1 (English)	7,040
lang2 (Spanish)	5,549
ne	464
mixed	12
ambiguous	43
other	4,311

Table 3: Label distribution in the first evaluation set.

Label	Recall	Precision	F1-Score
lang1 (English)	0.900	0.830	0.864
lang2 (Spanish)	0.869	0.914	0.891
ne	0.313	0.541	0.396
mixed	0.000	1.000	0.000
ambiguous	0.023	0.200	0.042
other	0.845	0.860	0.853

Table 4: Results for the first evaluation set, measured on word level.

their language; however, identifying named entities did not work as well. We plan to further investigate this issue. The results on the surprise genre are similar to that for the genre the system was trained on. However, since the surprise set is relatively small in size, we refrain from drawing conclusions about this. Trying the same code-switching techniques on other pairs of languages is part of our planned future research.

Accuracy	0.864
Recall	0.708
Precision	0.803
F1-Score	0.753

Table 5: Results for the second, "surprise" evaluation set, measured on the post level.

Label	Count
lang1 (English)	636
lang2 (Spanish)	306
ne	38
mixed	1
ambiguous	1
other	120

Table 6: Label distribution in the "surprise" evaluation set.

Label	Recall	Precision	F1-Score
lang1 (English)	0.883	0.824	0.853
lang2 (Spanish)	0.864	0.887	0.876
ne	0.293	0.537	0.379
mixed	0.000	1.000	0.000
ambiguous	0.022	0.200	0.039
other	0.824	0.843	0.833

Table 7: Results for the "surprise" evaluation set, measured on the word level.

References

William B. Cavnar and John M. Trenkle. 1994. N-gram-based text categorization. In *Proceedings of the 3rd Annual Symposium on Document Analysis and Information Retrieval (SDAIR-94)*, pages 161–175.

Chih C. Chang and Chih J. Lin. 2011. LIBSVM: A Library for Support Vector Machines. *ACM Transactions on Intelligent Systems and Technology*, 2(27):1–27, May.

Corinna Cortes and Vladimir Vapnik. 1995. Support-vector networks. *Machine Learning*, 20:273–297.

Eibe Frank, Mark Hall, Geoffrey Holmes, Richard Kirkby, Bernhard Pfahringer, Ian H. Witten, and Len Trigg. 2010. Weka—A machine learning workbench for data mining. In Oded Maimon and Lior Rokach, editors, *Data Mining and Knowledge Discovery Handbook*, chapter 66, pages 1269–1277. Springer US, Boston, MA.

Philipp Koehn, Hieu Hoang, Alexandra Birch, Chris Callison-Burch, Marcello Federico, Nicola Bertoldi, Brooke Cowan, Wade Shen, Christine Moran, Richard Zens, Chris Dyer, Ondřej Bojar, Alexandra Constantin, and Evan Herbst. 2007. Moses: Open source toolkit for statistical machine translation. In *Proceedings of the Interactive Poster and Demonstration Sessions of the 45th Annual Meeting of the ACL (ACL '07)*, pages 177–180, Stroudsburg, PA, USA. Association for Computational Linguistics.

Taku Kudo and Yuji Matsumoto. 2003. Fast methods for kernel-based text analysis. In *Proceedings of the 41st Annual Meeting of the Association for Computational Linguistics (ACL)*, pages 24–31, Sapporo, Japan.

Gabriel M. Rosenbaum. 2000. Fushammiyya: Alternating style in Egyptian prose. *Journal of Arabic Linguistics (ZAL)*, 38:68–87.

Thamar Solorio, Elizabeth Blair, Suraj Maharjan, Steve Bethard, Mona Diab, Mahmoud Gonheim, Abdelati Hawwari, Fahad AlGhamdi, Julia Hirshberg, Alison Chang, and Pascale Fung. 2014. Overview for the first shared task on language identification in code-switched data. In *Proceedings of the First Workshop on Computational Approaches to Code-Switching. EMNLP 2014, Conference on Empirical Methods in Natural Language Processing*, Doha, Qatar.

Donald Winford, 2003. *Code Switching: Linguistic Aspects*, chapter 5, pages 126–167. Blackwell Publishing, Malden, MA.

Author Index